This book is *outs*  :t
page. This will b !
Mark helps us ti]
full of chaos, comusion, and consternation. It's compelling, profound, inspiring, and thought-provoking from beginning to end—a
modern-day classic.

CHRISTINE CAINE, founder, A21 and Propel Women

Mark is a voice I trust. Among the things I like most about him is that
he doesn't pull any punches but surrounds us with so much love that
he doesn't leave us bruised. He has written another terrific book, and
when you turn the final page, you will see more possibilities for your
life than you did before you started, more answers to your questions
than you have ever experienced, and if you are like me, more hope
than you have seen in a while.

BOB GOFF, *New York Times* bestselling author

If you believe that the unexamined life is not worth living, then this
is a must-read. These are the deep questions of life that not enough
of us are asking, and we're all paying a price for it. In a world where
too many of us—even Christians—settle for the shallows, this is a
beautiful, profound, and, at times, challenging look at the depths.
Mark tackles some of the hardest questions of existence and traces
out the meaning, purpose, and further questions that will make your
soul question, dream, and, ultimately, hope again.

CAREY NIEUWHOF, author, speaker, and podcaster

THE PROBLEM OF

THE PROBLEM OF
LIFE

HOW TO FIND IDENTITY, PURPOSE, AND JOY

IN A DISENCHANTED WORLD

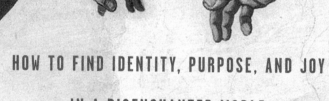

MARK CLARK

ZONDERVAN
REFLECTIVE

Library of Congress Cataloging-in-Publication Data

Names: Clark, Mark A., 1980- author.
Title: The problem of life : how to find identity, purpose, and joy in a disenchanted world / Mark Clark.
Description: Grand Rapids, Michigan : Zondervan, [2025]
Identifiers: LCCN 2024026883 (print) | LCCN 2024026884 (ebook) | ISBN 9780310108450 (softcover) | ISBN 9780310108467 (ebook) | ISBN 9780310108474 (audio)
Subjects: LCSH: Christian life. | Life. | Meaning (Philosophy) | Bible—Criticism, interpretation, etc.
Classification: LCC BV4501.3 .C5246 2025 (print) | LCC BV4501.3 (ebook) | DDC 248.4—dc23/eng/20240711
LC record available at https://lccn.loc.gov/2024026883
LC ebook record available at https://lccn.loc.gov/2024026884

For my mother, Carolyn. For giving me life, but also for birthing in me a desire not just to exist but to live.

I don't tell you enough, but you are my hero.

*My whole employment is to persuade the young
and old against too much love for the body,
for riches, and all other precarious things, of
whatsoever nature they be; and against too little
regard for the soul, which ought to be the object of
their affection.*

—SOCRATES

*Human history is the long terrible story of man
trying to find something other than God which will
make him happy.*

—C. S. LEWIS

*What does it profit a man to gain the whole world
and forfeit his soul?*

—JESUS

CONTENTS

Acknowledgments

My wife, Erin, without whom this book wouldn't have happened. She puts up with me, and without me, so I can write, and cheers me on more than anyone. More importantly, she shows me how to live out the things I explore in this book every day. She is the most *alive* person I know. Thank you.

My three daughters, Sienna, Hayden, Isabella, are also my biggest cheerleaders and models of being full of life. They show me how to live enchanted lives in a world trying to convince me that things are just as they seem. Every day they remind me that isn't true, that there is more to the universe, and to our lives within it, than meets the eye— and that we should live like it.

INTRODUCTION

Only He Who Sees, Takes Off His Shoes

> *The sweetest thing in all my life has been the longing . . . to find the place where all the beauty came from.*
>
> —C. S. Lewis, *Till We Have Faces*

> *It is only with the heart that one can see rightly; what is essential is invisible to the eye.*
>
> —Antoine de Saint-Exupéry, *The Little Prince*

Let me tell you about the worst day of my life: the day I told a woman that her husband of fifty years was dead—but he wasn't. I had the wrong guy.

It was late October; I was a pastor at a small church, and I went to visit David, a sweet decades-long member of the church whose health was failing. I arrived at the hospital, parked, and made my way to his room, where I'd shared a nice visit with him a few days prior. Upon entering, I saw that his body and face were turned toward the window, his skin ashen. As I went to walk around the bed, a nurse grabbed my arm from behind.

"Can I help you?" she said.

I turned around to face her. "Oh, yes, I'm a pastor. I'm just here for a visit—"

"I'm sorry," she said. "He passed away this morning, just a few minutes ago."

"Oh, I'm so sorry to hear that," I said. "Should I tell his family?"

"That won't be necessary," the nurse responded. "The doctor is on the phone with his wife as we speak."

Now, if you are taking notes on how to be a good pastor, here's lesson number one: When someone says a person is dead, ask a few very important follow-up questions: *Who is dead? What is their name? Spell it!* I didn't do any of these things. Instead, I simply drove back to the church, told the secretary that David was dead, and walked into my office to catch up on some work.

A few hours later, the secretary came to my door looking anxious. David's wife, Sarah, was in the lobby, a Subway sandwich in hand. *How could that be?* I rushed out and invited her into my office.

Sarah had a smile on her face as we walked through the hallway. "I'm just on my way to visit David," she said. "I was there with him this morning. We chatted, he told some jokes, and he said he was craving Subway, so I went home, took a shower, and grabbed him some lunch. I was just heading back there when I thought I would stop at church to pick up a couple of things. Oh, and thanks so much for visiting him last week. He said he really enjoyed his time with you."

I closed the door.

She stopped talking for a second and looked at me.

"What's up?" she asked.

"Well, I went to visit David this morning," I started, "likely a couple hours after you were there."

"Oh, nice," she said. "How was he?"

He was dead.

How do I say that?

"Well, I am so sorry, but . . . he passed away. He's gone."

The words hung in the air like smoke.

She stood still for a second, then her eyes tightened as if she were looking through me. "What?" she said.

"I am sorry."

At which point she fainted into my arms.

I slowly set her down on the couch in my office. When she came to, she was confused beyond belief. "How is that possible? I was with him this morning. We were— I don't get it."

"I am sorry. I don't know the details. He had already passed when I arrived," I said.

For the next hour, we talked about what he was diagnosed with, his life, how great a man he was and started planning his funeral. After a while I walked out to the office area to get her a glass of water and overheard the secretary mention the name of a particular old age home. For some reason it caught my ear, and I stopped mid-stride. "What were you talking about?" I asked.

"Where David was when he died," the secretary said.

"No," I said. "He died at the hospital. That's where I was when— Wait."

"You went to the *hospital*?" the secretary gasped. She went white as a ghost. "He got moved from there on Saturday."

The shock started to set in that I had gone to the wrong room, the wrong location altogether, and had the *wrong guy*. At this point, the room started to spin, and I did that thing you do with your eyes, squeezing them tight to wake up from a nightmare. It didn't work.

The secretary quickly picked up the phone to do something I hadn't done: confirm whether he was alive or not. The nurse at the retirement home David had been moved to said, "Yes, he is here, sitting up in his bed. He is waiting for his wife. He said she has his lunch."

I turned frantically toward the room where Sarah sat quietly waiting for me, sandwich in hand. I quickly gathered my thoughts and walked back into the room.

"I will miss him greatly," she started. "I knew he was getting older, but I guess the suddenness of it just struck me. I'm sorry, I—"

"No, please," I said, cutting her off. I couldn't wait another moment, nor could I listen to *her* apologize to *me*. I looked down at the ground, not able to bring myself to look at her, and then I had to. "I am so sorry; well, I guess I am not because it's good, but, well, I am just . . . um: your husband is not dead. I had the wrong . . . uh, I had the wrong, well, person. It was someone else. I'm sorry."

I will never forget the look in her eyes. It was a complicated one. Her head kind of kinked to the side. Her eyes searched me as if to ask one haunting question I didn't have the answer to: *How?* Or maybe, *Why? Why would you do this to me? Why would you cause me so much grief and pain? By your incompetency. By your stupidity. By your blatant disregard for all things good in this world.* I mean, she didn't say any of that, but I know she was thinking it. I explained to her the misunderstanding and how it happened. I'm not sure she heard a word. She stared at me as if waiting to be told she could go and see her husband, as if she needed permission. Her David was back from the dead, like Lazarus. He'd come back to fill her world again after she'd lost him.

She grabbed her belongings and quickly left my office, walked swiftly past the secretary and out to her car, and drove away—to her husband.

She had a lunch to deliver.

I am not certain how the rest of that day went for them. I imagine it sometimes, always in slow motion: She walks through the door of his room. His smile, even if weaker than before, is more glorious than ever. His touch more intense. Every breath and blink and move of the eyes more full and certainly more meaningful than the previous day.

At least in her eyes.

To him it is just another late lunch.

Why such a difference in their experiences of reality? Because from where he sat, *he had never lost his life.* He had never been erased from the ongoing story of the world. He hadn't yet stepped across to the other side of the great chasm we will all step across one day. But for her, he had. So the same words and events now unfolded for them very differently. Though they shared the same space, a rift had occurred in the universe; there was for her a vastly different appreciation. One person taking it all for granted, just doing what he had always done, the other breathing it all in, seeing *through* it almost. Her mind was now drawn to eternal things, deeper things—versus simply being preoccupied with things on the plane on which we tend to live our daily lives.

She was pondering the *meaning* of things: him, her, them, existence, significance. All of it suddenly rushed to the forefront of her mind in light of death—more than that even: in light of life and transcendence. The world behind the sun.

Soulish things.

She thought about things that can't be put through a test tube or examined by scientific processes. Things beyond, or above, all that. Things that give those things meaning, that fill them with their weight. Things that Tolstoy was talking about when he said, "Science is meaningless in that it gives no answer to our real question: 'What shall we do and how shall we live?'"[1] In other words, the existential journey of our lives is to find true happiness and fulfillment in the finding of ourselves. And that begins, as we will see, by seeing our ordinary lives not as ordinary at all but as shot through with the extraordinary. By seeing all the comings and goings of life not as asides, or just flesh and bone "dancing to DNA," as one scientist put it,[2] but as something more, putting us in touch with something deeper and broader than what our eyes can see. We long to connect to that thing behind the thing, to live in light of the challenge the Victorian poet Elizabeth Barrett Browning laid out:

> Earth's crammed with heaven,
> And every common bush is afire with God;
> But only he who sees, takes off his shoes,
> The rest sit round . . . and pluck blackberries.[3]

What if we could, from this day forth, be the first kind of people? The kind who really see, who live and walk in light of the sacred instead of ignoring it.

The problem is, we are surrounded by the second kind of people in almost every moment of our lives: people and places and systems and markets fighting for us just to sit round and pluck blackberries in the face of glorious things. They want us to see the physical, temporal world around us, with all its decadence and flavor and sparkle and pleasure, and just settle for all that—to believe this world is all there is. We do it every day. We go after money, or sex, or power, or beauty, or family, or security, or promotions. We search for contentment and joy and pleasure and a feeling of fulfillment in those things. But we find out that fulfillment is not *in* those things at all. They fail to deliver on what they promise. More than that, like a castaway drinking sea water to quench his thirst, we find that they make our situation worse every time we trust in them. We smell the scent of a flower, and we pick it up, take it home, set it by our bed, trying to retain the glory it birthed in us. But in our picking it, it dies. Because it was never the source of what it stirred up in us. C. S. Lewis explains our situation perfectly: our insatiable desire for joy, pleasure, and peace is the most powerful impulse we have, but, he says, "we are half-hearted creatures, fooling about with drink and sex and ambition when infinite joy is offered us, like an ignorant child who wants to go on making mud pies in a slum because he cannot imagine what is meant by the offer of a holiday at the sea." We settle for the drink or the sex or the ambition as if joy and happiness were in these things. Our problem, in other words, is not that we are too hard to please but the opposite.

> We are far too easily pleased. . . .
>
> . . . The books or the music in which we thought the beauty was located will betray us if we trust to them; it was not *in* them, it only came *through* them, and what came through them was longing. These things—the beauty, the memory of our own past—are good images of what we really desire; but if they are mistaken for the thing itself they turn into dumb idols, break-ing the hearts of their worshipers. For they are not the thing itself; they are only the scent of a flower we have not found, the echo of a tune we have not heard, news from a country we have never yet visited.[4]

This deep longing or desire within us is a common theme in Lewis's writings, and I think in life itself. It is a yearning within us for our true home and it drives our whole life. The mistake we make, he says, is that we think the echo we hear (an experience of happiness, peace, pleasure that happens and then disappears), however faint, *is* that home—that the news from a distant land *is* the country itself. But we are wrong every time. These are just signposts, small pointers to the real thing. And though these echoes never give us lasting joy and happiness, we keep going back and trying them again and again.

And we aren't the first. We learned it from our parents. And they learned it from theirs. It goes all the way back.

Remember the biblical story: Adam and Eve traded God for blackberries in the garden a long time ago: "When you *eat* from [the tree] your eyes will be opened, and you will be like God," the serpent said. So Adam and Eve "saw that the tree was good for food, and that it was a delight to the eyes, and that the tree was to be desired to make one wise," and so they ate (Gen. 3:4–6 ESV, emphasis added). They traded God and all his goodness for the world they could see and taste. And we are just like them, aren't we? "Sons of Adam" and "Daughters of Eve," as Lewis called us. We repeat the same mistake over and over every day. We see a nice house, the newer and more exciting woman or man, the new product that sparkles a little bit more than last year's version, and we wonder, "What if?" What if this or that person, or experience, or whatever, could give me what I really want faster than God can? I wonder what the effect would be if I just tried a different route—just this once (or this hundredth time). Maybe then I would feel truly alive.

Part of our journey in this book will be to realize that all of that is good stuff; it just isn't the way we find the joy and fulfillment we are looking for. Those things can't deliver on the promise of getting life to the full, which is what we all are hunting for, because only God can do that. Only he can provide a *way of being* in the world where you go through life different from everyone around you—unaware of all the things behind the things. This way of being means the world is *alive to you* in ways it used to be dull; as Sarah experienced, a smile is no longer just a smile but comes to have meaning and purpose; a sunset isn't just a mathematical movement of the planets and stars but is something beautiful—a feeling you can't really explain but that makes it seem like those things are *from somewhere*.

I want to suggest the opposite of what the world suggests, with its billions of dollars in marketing trying as hard as it can to keep you from the truth, or at least to distract you from what is best for you. I want to suggest that you aren't silly or off course when you sense that there is a world bigger and more profound than you first may think. Rather, you are exactly right. There *is* more to this universe than meets the eye. More than you could ever dream. That reality is far vaster and more interesting than you are made to believe. While your constant temptation may be to settle for the world as it is, with the idea that humanity is the pinnacle and center of all things, the part of you that from time to time suggests otherwise is actually right. In the film *Amadeus*, when the composer Antonio Salieri, Mozart's jealous competitor, explains what it was like for him to look at Mozart's music sheets, he attests to this truth: "These were his original scores. First and only drafts of the music. Yet they looked like fair copies. They showed no corrections of any kind. It was puzzling—then suddenly alarming. What was evident was that Mozart was *simply transcribing music*." It was, as Salieri says, "like staring through the cage of those meticulous ink strokes at—Absolute Beauty."

Many of us, if we are honest, are a little asleep at the wheel of life, going through each day as if our lives are small and insignificant, as if this is all there is, while a whole world awaits us—a world of absolutes, and beauty, and joy forevermore. The only decision to make is whether we want to settle for this world as it is, wherein nature is all there is. Where we are all just products of chance, living, making money, maybe raising a family, having a few good friendships, all unto nothing more than living our seventy-seven years on this planet and then ceasing to exist, with this happening over and over again to billions of us until the sun burns out one day—in other words, a disenchanted world. Or we don't settle for that story and we look to a kind of existence where there really is music to transcribe, and it's beautiful, being the kinds of people who are tapped into something bigger and deeper and more profound and true and fundamental than anything else. The kind of people who can really see and, in seeing, live in such a way that the world takes note and, like Salieri, is baffled by it. Those around us become almost jealous because they want this deeper life themselves.

As David's wife, Sarah, discovered when she brought him lunch that day, and in the flood of meaning that came from every day after that, there is a *deeper way* of living. When you take a walk, or look at the stars, or get caught up in something that feels *more than*, and you feel—you don't know how to explain it—*connected*, that isn't a mistake but a true index of your situation. As you stroll through the streets on a winter evening and pass by all those houses—filled as they are with the cries of newborn babies, the coughing of a life at its end, the lovemaking, the homework, the medication, the divorce papers—you know these are much more than just bodies and brains, cells and synapses: these are *soulish things*.

When you understand that there is something *behind* laughter and lovemaking, *behind* music and math, *behind* beauty, then you are on the brink of understanding what true life really is and your role as a voyager in this universe. As an explorer, not a settler. Someone whose heart is restless until it finds rest in God, as Saint Augustine said. Someone whose desires are for greater things, which are there to lead you not away from God but toward him. Someone who comes to see that every moment of passion you have, every time you go after pleasure and delight or feel the "other world" *breaking through* and bringing you a joy that nothing common in this world gives you, it's fine to chase that feeling and try to answer the question, Where does it come from? Because it's more than just your emotions connecting to some quick hit of nostalgia or a chemical reaction firing in your cerebral cortex. It is more than just your imagination. Love really is more than romance. Pleasure and joy and our longings and aspirations and glimpses of pure delight are the great *tell* that God, in all his hiding, doesn't keep secret.

The songwriter Josh Garrels, reflecting on Ulysses's journey back to his beloved Penelope in Homer's *Odyssey*, says words that are true of us all as we find ourselves on this journey of life:

> I'm sailing home to you, I won't be long.
> . . . I will press on . . .
>
> So tie me to the mast of this old ship and point me home
> . . . before my chance is gone.

That is what I want to do in these pages: Tie you to the mast of what I think are the answers to your longings. Point you home to the place where all your passions are trying to take you. And to do so by answering life's biggest and most important questions—those of our purpose and origins, of pain and suffering, of love and joy and pleasure, of peace and beauty and eternity. And to do so, as Garrels says, *before your chance is gone.*

The Two Kinds of Knowledge That Matter

Our journey in this book is based on a foundational idea that the theologian John Calvin (1509–1564) laid out many years ago in the opening words of his *Institutes of the Christian Religion*, said to be one of the greatest presentations of philosophy and theology ever written: "Our wisdom, insofar as it ought to be deemed true and solid wisdom," he says, "consists almost entirely of two parts: the *knowledge of God* and the *knowledge of ourselves*."[5] If my first two books—*The Problem of God* (2017) and *The Problem of Jesus* (2021)—were about the first kind of knowledge (God), this book is about the second kind, the knowledge of *ourselves*. In other words, this book is about *you*. It's about *us*. And it's about who we are in relationship to one another, to God, to ourselves. It's about how to finally find joy, purpose, and meaning in our lives by discovering our identity—in other words, it's about how to solve the problem of life.

Some say that the preoccupation with answering questions about ourselves is somehow selfish or wrong, but nothing could be further from the truth. The two searches are bound together. We can't do one without the other.

Often the first mistake we make while trying to find ourselves is to forget not about God but about *ourselves*. Theologians, pastors, and Christians write and preach and talk about God and his ways endlessly. Our lives are full of books and essays and paintings and songs—volume upon volume—about God, the Bible, theology, etc. These are scrutinized and explained within an inch of their lives and have been for literally thousands of years. But we in the religious world seem reluctant to do the same deep dive about *us*, to explore the knowledge and revelation of ourselves. But we must.

And the Bible tells us to. In Revelation 4–5 the apostle John weeps when he sees heaven filled with singing angels and a scroll (the story of the whole history of the world) rolled up because no one has the authority to take hold of it and open it—to take control over the world and give it meaning and direction. But then the Lamb who was slain, Jesus, appears and takes it. John's crying stops, and then something interesting happens: *he begins to sing*. Why?

Because, as Eugene Peterson says, "it is not enough to see the glorious throne of God and hear the wondrous songs if I do not discover that they include me. I will not praise but weep. It does little good to know that God is holy if I am excluded from his holiness."⁶ In other words, it is not enough to know certain truths; we must feel a part of them. And here is the wonderful news: we *are* a part of them!

Yes, the main character of the story of the world is God and his plan. But one of the many reasons God does what he does is *us*. This is why so much of the New Testament is about what *we* are supposed to do in light of what Jesus has done. And even when the New Testament writers talk about what God has done in Christ—accomplishing our salvation through his life, death, and resurrection—they constantly speak about us as one of the main motives: "For Christ also suffered once for sins . . . *to bring you to God*," Peter says (1 Peter 3:18, emphasis added); and of course, the most famous verse in the Bible, John 3:16, confirms it: "For God so *loved the world* that he gave his one and only Son . . ." (emphasis added).

Isn't it amazing that something God felt for us motivated him to do something as important as the cross? And one further, what does the application of the cross to our lives create? Well, something that may surprise you. It creates what God wants for us more than anything: a life of pure, unadulterated joy and pleasure forever. This is why Jesus said, "I have told you this so that my joy may be in you and that your joy may be complete" (John 15:11). It is astounding, when you think of it, that Jesus came and taught and suffered and died and rose so that the joy he has enjoyed from eternity past would be ours—would be *yours*. He doesn't want to just have joy and pleasure himself; he wants to share them with us at a level we can only dream of.

Which means Jesus solved and removed our sin not only

because it was standing in the way of our relationship with God but also because it was standing in the way of the thing we want more than anything: our own happiness. Sin is our enemy because it is the enemy of our joy. John Piper is right in saying, "The gospel is not a way to get people to heaven. . . . It's a way of overcoming every obstacle to everlasting joy in God."[7] So, contrary to secular or atheistic thinking, you are the opposite of a mistake or a product of chance or whatever you have come to believe about yourself. You are a treasure, worth so much that God went through pain and suffering to connect you back to himself.

His desire to connect you back to himself was shown in Jesus's work on the cross and is demonstrated in the message of every book of the Bible and in every experience of his grace. In every rising and setting of the sun. In every shooting star that makes you yell out to the people around you and point up almost instinctively, though always too late. In every birth of a new child. In every moment of joy and bliss and pleasure. In every prayer answered. In the small things. In the big things. In the nature of things.

God tells us in every way he can that we were made not only *by* him but also *for* him, which means you are of infinite worth.

So, we have neglected ourselves in the search for ourselves. But something else has happened. We have neglected *God* in the search for ourselves as well, which is just as misguided. The modern emphasis on individualism, personal psychology, etc., while good and helpful, has displaced God's role from our lives, which is to miss the forest for the trees.

When we pursue "self-actualization" or "self-discovery" or "self-expression" disconnected from the question of God and our spiritual lives, we miss all the beauty and wonder of a life where both are found and explored *together*, like different sides of the same coin. This is a big reason why missing this point is so dangerous: we are *designed* to run best when God and the transcendent are a central part of our lives, not an aside or an afterthought. When we refuse this connection, we are like a car designed to run on gas but that has dirt and sand in the motor instead; we seize up and stop working as intended. As designed.

Though we may be tempted to neglect God in the search for ourselves, there is another way. Theologian Paul Tillich says it clearly: "Man discovers himself when he discovers God . . . something from which he was estranged, but from which he never has been and never can be separated."[8]

This new way is what we need because we've tried what we've tried. We are still trying. And yet, if you are anything like me, you haven't been able to settle into this world. You are still searching. Like a moth trying its best to fly to the moon, we know there is something bigger and better, but despite all our efforts we can't get there in our own strength.[9] One of the challenges of life is seeing and recognizing this. In not looking *upward*, we sentence ourselves to a cycle that fails us in this life and the next. The Irish poet Micheal O'Siadhail asks the question, Why are you here on earth? His answer? *"To behold . . . To saunter and gaze. To own the world."*[10] We are here to stand in awe. To gaze, not just to see. To go one level deeper than how the world presents itself to us.

Some of us lack this sense of awe. As Lewis says, we are "half-hearted creatures" who don't push far enough into that *something* we felt speaking to us from the other side of the veil that time. Or we misdiagnose where the awe comes from and, more importantly, where it is supposed to lead us. "We are haunted by doubt," the philosopher Ron Dart said, "cross-pressured, caught between modern versions of the world and the *haunting of transcendence*, and so we find ourselves in perpetual unease. This is the unique discomfort of our lives as modern people."[11]

We *are* haunted by transcendence, aren't we? By the itching feeling that this isn't all there is. Maybe there is a world inside the wardrobe after all. Maybe that's what makes the most sense: a world we know is there based not on what we see or taste or touch but on how we *feel*, or rather, what we *behold*. We sense that beauty is *from* somewhere. We hear the voice across the water, however faint it may seem sometimes.

If it's true that there is something more than just flesh and blood and bone, maybe we need to listen to the voice pulling us toward our real purpose and destiny and destination, back to the country we hear that news from, however dimly we hear it. If we listen, we'll suspect what God repeatedly tells us in Scripture: that things are not as they seem, that our lives aren't just made up of nature but supernature. That they are spiritual, moral, epic, enchanted.

For now, all I ask is that you remain open to the idea that there is more to the universe than meets the eye. In the chapters that follow, we'll look at what it means to acknowledge this and then follow the hints to discover where they are pointing us: toward the God who created the scent and wrote the tune and who is sending the news, hoping we will hear it and respond.

"My sheep hear my voice," Jesus said (John 10:27 ESV).

Oh, that we would not forget his voice in the search for ourselves, among all the voices, the loudest of course being our own. For like sheep, we can never really be and do all we were made to without the guidance of one who sees and knows more than us.

————

So, we face two problems in life, two sides of the same coin that shape our identity and purpose as human beings: coming to know not just God but also ourselves, not just ourselves but also God. These are connected in ways we may never have realized but will explore in depth.

We'll look at eleven simple challenges—approaches to life, ways of being, some would call them principles (I don't think that is too strong a word)—that, if followed, can and will change and transform your life for the better, now and for the next billion years or so. These aren't random principles; they've been mined from the biblical story as it addresses what it means to be human and framed up for us according to the exact questions we all need answered to truly flourish in life—those of our origins, our identity, the place of pain in our lives, our purpose, and even our death. In other words, our beginnings, endings, and the mess in between. We'll look at what the Bible says about all of this, as well as explore what modern thinkers in the realms of philosophy, psychology, theology, and the arts say, all in an effort to understand ourselves better so we can flourish and not flounder in this amazing thing called life.

Problem: A question raised for inquiry, consideration, or solution; an intricate unsettled question.

PART I

The Problem of ORIGINS

*In the darkness something was happening
at last. A voice had begun to sing. . . . It was
beyond comparison, the most beautiful sound
he had ever heard. It was so beautiful he could
hardly bear it. . . . The Voice rose and rose, till all
the air was shaking with it. And just as it swelled
to the mightiest and most glorious sound it
had yet produced, the sun arose. . . . You could
imagine that it laughed for joy as it came up. . . .
The earth was of many colors: they were fresh,
hot, and vivid.*

*They made you feel excited; until you
saw the Singer himself, and then you forgot
everything else.*

—C. S. Lewis, The Magician's Nephew

I have the most amazing mother. She worked the same job from the time she was out of high school until she retired. When my dad wasn't working (which was most of the time), she worked for both of them, sacrificed a ton, sold beloved possessions of hers so she could put food on the table, and day in and day out put up with my dad's incompetence, narcissism, and general unkindness as she tried to build and sustain a home—all while raising two busy sons by herself. I owe her everything.

I have only a few memories of my father. Flashes of a big smile and playing catch, and a few Christmases together, but mostly of him and my mother fighting, or of him yelling at football games with a pipe or cigarette in his mouth and a drink in his hand. And then there was the day he and my mother sat me down and told me they were getting a divorce. I was seven years old. That day is burned into my memory. How could it not be? It was the end of the world and the beginning of another.

And that's when the nightmares began.

For my brother, they were literal dreams that were so vivid he would wake up screaming at all hours of the night. My mom would rush in and calm him down. I would sit up in my bed, seeing their shadows on the wall as he would calm and go back to sleep. In time, his nightmares went away. Mine didn't. They were just getting started—and I live with them to this day. They aren't literal nightmares. They are mental and physical ones. They don't visit me in my sleep; in fact, sleeping is the only time they cease.

My nightmare is that the trauma of my parents' divorce broke something in me, and I developed what the doctor called Tourette syndrome (the way he said it didn't sound good) and obsessive-compulsive disorder (that didn't either). If you don't know what these are, I can assure you they are not ways to be cool in high school. I developed odd habits and tics. My body would twitch and flinch. I would make weird noises. I would randomly swear under my breath and then out loud. The F-word, the S-word—all the words. I'd be standing at a bus stop and randomly swear or make noises that made people look at me, then look away. I remember sitting in a quiet room full of hundreds of high school students writing a math exam in the school gym, and I was doing my best to hold in my noises, but I just couldn't. Every few minutes they would echo through the room.

I wanted to hide, to be invisible, to be *normal*. But that didn't happen. It still hasn't.

The obsessive-compulsive stuff started when I hit my mid-teens. A deep fear of dying or getting sick or whatever would come over me, and it could only be appeased if I did certain habits: smacking my hands together, clearing my throat obsessively, slapping a tabletop five times, walking over cracks in the street with only my left foot. There was a season when I would constantly drop down on my knees and bang them on the ground two or three times while tossing my hat in the air. This would happen anywhere: walking down the road in the summer, on the sidewalk outside my school as I had a smoke, in the ice, the snow, the rain. I walked around my school with soaked pants half the time. To put it mildly, life was tough.

And then it got a little tougher.

After my parents divorced, I would see my dad every few months; then it became once or twice a year. He would take my brother and me out for lunch for an hour and then drop us back at home. It went on like that for a while, and then it became even less frequent. Then a year went by without hearing from him. And then *the phone call.*

I was at the table for dinner when the phone on the wall rang. The voice on the other end said they were calling from the hospital. My father was sick, and we should come visit him before he passed away. *Sick?* This was the first we had heard of it. We later found out he kept it from everyone, even his own father. He had lung cancer; it was aggressive, and he was in his last days, the doctor said. The plan was to visit him the next morning, but we would never get the chance. They called that night. He was gone. He was forty-seven years old. I was fifteen.

I tell you all this because you will better understand me, and all that we will explore in the chapters ahead, by understanding *where I came from.* My background. My origins. They shape and inform everything about me: who I am, how I carry myself in the world, what causes me stress, how I respond to criticism, and a hundred other things about me. In the same way, we only understand ourselves and our lives as human beings (which is what this book is about) if we go back, if we look hard at our beginnings, where we came from, and how we got here. Without this knowledge, we never catch the nuances of or fully grasp who we are and what we're doing here on this planet. With it, however, there is no telling how fulfilling and beautiful our lives can be.

And so, let's begin at, well, the beginning.

CHAPTER 1

Listen to the
OLD ACHE
INSIDE YOU

*"Orual," she said, her eyes shining, "I am going,
you see, to the Mountain. You remember how
we used to look and long? . . . The sweetest
thing in all my life has been the longing—to
reach the Mountain, to find the place where all
the beauty came from . . . my country. . . . Do
you think it all meant nothing, all the longing?
The longing for home? For indeed it now feels
not like going, but like going back. Oh, look up
once at least before the end and wish me joy. I
am going to my lover."*

—C. S. Lewis, *Till We Have Faces*

Human beings are unique among the creatures of the world. We
are "wise" and became this way when God breathed his Spirit
into us. "The Man came alive—a living soul!" (Gen. 2:7 MSG), the
Bible says. But alive and wise to what?

Sociologists tell us we became so in several ways. We became self-
conscious, self-aware, romantic and not just instinctual. We became
conscious of the universe and began wondering what our place within

it is. We organized ourselves socially, creatively, behaviorally and began pondering deeper, more profound existential questions than any of the animals could ever hope to ask.

We also came alive *religiously*, drawing on walls or sketching the stars out of a desire to connect to the gods, always reaching out for something, or someone, beyond us. We became awake to the idea that there was a person, or persons, behind or above or beyond this world. This phenomenon is so common around the world that Yuval Harari, in his book *Sapiens*, calls it "The Law of Religion."[1] He says this has been the third great unifier of humankind—alongside money and empires—throughout history. Every people group on every continent in every era has been religious: the Egyptians, the Polynesians, the Mayans, the Greeks; from Mesopotamia to Persia, from China to South America, you will find similarities. There are temples, drawings, stories, sacred writings, sacrifices, priestly systems, prayers, and songs. Every culture in history has had these, long before they ever interacted with one another. One of the distinct things about human beings as a species is that we *worship*.

We know at some level that we are more than just meat and synapses. Deep inside we know we are more than what we see, taste, or touch. We have something else written into us, telling us there is meaning and emotion and love and beauty, what C. S. Lewis called our "lifelong nostalgia": "our longing to be reunited with something in the universe from which we now feel cut off, to be on the inside of some door which we have always seen from the outside. And to be at last summoned inside would be both glory and honor beyond all our merits and the healing of that old ache."[2]

Sometime after God made us in his image, we began doing something that nothing else in the world does. We began *longing*. We sensed something missing and felt a desire to connect to the one who made us and the kind of world he created for us—a world with no more crying, or pain, or death. No more terrorism, or depression, or heart attacks that steal those we love. No more single moms trying their best, or dads so lost they take their own lives, like a man from our church recently did. No more earthquakes, or child abuse, or divorce, or poverty. No more racism, or hatred, or disease, or pandemics. Then and only then, when we find this world, or the One who can take us there, does the heart settle.

This is why while there are several secular theories about how to find happiness and fulfillment and meaning as human beings, but none of them adequately answer the problem of our longings. A century after testing out the secular answers to those longings, and adding to our lives the technology to connect us, the medicine that can heal us, and the psychology that can explain us, the Western world is worse off. We are *more* depressed, more suicidal, more anxious, and more lost than ever:

- 60% of college students meet the criteria for a mental health condition.
- 84% of Gen Z report burnout.
- Suicide rates are at an all-time high—more than tripling among fifteen- to twenty-four-year-olds in the past two decades (the United States alone has an average of 49,000 per year, which is twice the number of homicides, making suicide one of the top ten causes of death for nearly every age group).
- Up to 90% of doctor's office visits are for stress-related symptoms.
- The pandemic tripled the rate of depression in adults in all demographic groups.
- Anxiety disorders are the most common mental health challenge, affecting forty million adults in the United States alone (10% of the population).[3]

All of this is what secular culture is producing in us. Because the problem with trying to live without God is that we ignore the way we were made, and we do so to our own demise.

The search for "home," as Saint Augustine called it, the state of being at peace with God, is what our whole life is about, and nothing causes us more pain than our disconnection from and denial of that journey. It is the worst kind of homesickness. "In my experience," the Christian thinker and pastor Dietrich Bonhoeffer wrote from a Nazi prison camp before he was killed, "nothing tortures us like longing. . . . When we are forcibly separated from those we love, we simply cannot, like so many other things, contrive for ourselves some cheap substitute. . . . There have been a few occasions in my life when I have had to learn what homesickness means. There is no agony worse than this."[4]

So it is true, what the theologian Donald Bloesch contends, that "our greatest affliction is not anxiety, or even guilt, but rather home-sickness—a nostalgia, a yearning to be at home with God."[5]

This is what "the fall" story is in the biblical narrative—how we ended up separated from the One we love most, the One who loves us most, and all the dysfunction that came from it. The fall explains why we are homesick and why the longing to return home is such a powerful image of redemption. Jesus himself uses this longing for home in his famous parable about the prodigal son, who returns home to his village and his father after a life of immorality and self-ishness that would have been punishable by death in that culture. Instead, he is met with grace. "The image of coming home is a pow-erful, archetypal symbol of returning to one's deepest self, to the soul. To come home is to return to the place of inner origin, that original imprint within."[6] To spend our lives not settling but journey-ing, moving, searching, and never resting until we find our rest in God is *what life is.*

Despite the lies our culture throws at us about who we are and who we aren't, the biblical story says *we belong to God*. Jesus affirms this when he holds up the coin with Caesar's image on it and says to the crowd, "Whose *image* is this?" The crowd says Caesar's, and Jesus replies, "Give back to Caesar what is Caesar's and to God what is God's" (Mark 12:16–17, emphasis added). It begs the question, though nobody in the crowd asks it: *What is God's?* The answer is obvious. Every person in the crowd is God's, for they *bear the image* of God. When you look in the mirror, you should hear that question of Jesus: "Whose image do you see?" Because whatever bears the image of God is God's. You, me, your neighbor, your ex, your boss, *those* people you have come to hate, the others you love so dearly—we all bear God's image. Our human duty, according to Jesus, then, is to *give ourselves to God*. We bear his image, and we belong to him, so we are to give ourselves to him. No matter how gentle or soft or cultured or smart or nice or righteous a person may be, no one experiences their full potential as a human being unless they do this. This is the human design, the reason we were created.

Never shy away from the longings of your heart and soul. Secularism has taught us to, calling them illusions, cognitive misfirings, or hopeful thinking of the weak. Rather, realize they are there as guides to lead you to finding the One your heart beats for, and then in finding him, *live a life worthy of him*.

These are the things that connect to us on a soul level. These are just as central as anything else in our search for both God and ourselves. "We don't read and write poetry because it's cute," Robin Williams's character John Keating says to the boys in his English class in *Dead Poets Society*:

> We read and write poetry because we are members of the human race. And the human race is filled with passion. And medicine, law, business, engineering, these are noble pursuits

and necessary to sustain life. But poetry, beauty, romance, love, these are what we stay alive for. To quote from Whitman, "O me! O life! . . . of the questions of these recurring; of the endless trains of the faithless . . . of cities filled with the foolish; what good amid these, O me, O life? Answer. That you are here—that life exists and identity; that the powerful play goes on, and you may contribute a verse."

What will your verse be?

God made beauty for a reason, or, better said, for reasons. Among them, I think, to *arrest us by our senses*. To awaken us from the slumber of the mundane and the practical. To hint to us of the bigger world. The bigger things to come. Bigger and more profound feelings and experiences than this world can ever give. And so, we must give these things much-needed attention and see where they lead us.

Enchanted Lives

If we do this—follow the impulse for joy and pleasure and give ourselves to the One who gave us those longings—then we are called to live with the magic of someone who has discovered him. To show the world that there really is One who all the beauty comes from. The philosopher Charles Taylor once said our job on the other side of the modern experiment is not merely to prove Christianity's *truth* but "to undercut our neighbor's confidence in the secular take on the world, encouraging them to be *open to transcendence*."[7] Why? Because the secular story turns out to be an "inadequate source for meaning and morality, leaving our neighbors starving for transcendence." Our task as God-followers, Taylor says, is to "re-enchant the world."[8] To make the world take notice. To invite it to see that there is a spiritual reality beyond anything they might imagine. And that that is a good thing, maybe the best of things. And to let that draw their hearts upward.

The best way to do that is to *live enchanted lives*. This is precisely what Jesus told us to do when he said we are the light of the world and to shine our lives before others. The goal of that kind of life, he said, is "that they may see your good deeds and glorify your Father in heaven" (Matt. 5:16).

We must learn to see people and enter into their stories, as my wife, Erin, did the other day while sitting outside a coffee shop with a homeless man she befriended. She sat with him for an hour and heard his story and called him by name and touched him, and he wept because, as he told her, right in that moment he needed all those things. And all because in a flash she heard God tell her to do these things. She isn't one to claim to hear from God directly, but she is learning how to listen. And why not? If God exists, those who are attuned to him will hear him. As Jesus said, "My sheep hear my voice" (John 10:27 ESV). Why wouldn't that include Erin? Why wouldn't that include you?

All to what end? To re-enchant the world! In the face of loneliness, addiction, fear, sickness, poverty, pain, only we, on fire with the fire of God in us, can stand against it all and show the world that things are not as they seem. That there really is a God above and over it all who is in control and who will not let evil have the last word. As Eugene Peterson says, "Nothing evil has the staying power of goodness."[9] We do this by reminding the world of order and love and sane things in the face of disorder, hatred, and insane things.

And there is much evil and insanity to stand in contrast to. In the book of Revelation, for instance, conquest, war, famine, and death are ravishing the world, and in the midst of half the population of the earth dying of starvation, a voice cries out with these haunting words: "Do not damage the oil and the wine!" (Rev. 6:6). So Peterson, in his reflections on this passage, says, "What is necessary for minimal lives is unavailable while the luxuries of life, oil and wine, are abundant," and then he offers this prophetic warning about our lives and the times we live in:

> We put millions of people to work at idiot jobs to make machines that pollute the air we breathe, so that we can move rapidly from one place to another in projectiles at lethal speeds (killing and maiming other millions—more than have died in all the wars ever fought on the earth) so that we have more time to sit before outrageously priced electronic devices that flicker with forms of flesh fantasies that attempt to convince us (usually successfully) that we must have oil and wine, luxuries for which we must go back to the idiot jobs to make the lethal machines.[10]

Amazingly, Peterson wrote these words long before the invention of smartphones and the internet. But oh how those flickering devices and flesh fantasies have only become more and more a part of our lives since then. Our situation is dire: "We have most of what we don't need and almost nothing of what we do need."[11] Our task in re-enchanting the world is to show that in God the opposite is true: that even if we don't have what the world says we need, we have enough, precisely because we have him. As the psalmist says,

> Whom have I in heaven but you?
> And earth has nothing I desire besides you.
> My flesh and my heart may fail,
> But God is the strength of my heart
> and my portion forever. (Ps. 73:25–26)

Living like this makes the world wonder, "Is there a way to live that is better than all the flash and sparkle?" Our answer, in word and deed, is yes. It is possible to live content in this world. And so it is true, as John Piper said, that "God is most glorified in me when I am most *satisfied in him.*"[12]

This divine satisfaction is how we stir up our culture's innate desire for something bigger and beyond the natural world.

Pinocchio and the Revolution of the Soul

This reality about us raises us above the plane of the animal. We belong to the sensuous world because we are earthly, but by virtue of our spiritual nature, we transcend this earth. We are *forever creatures*— spiritual to our core; eternal, not temporal. We are built for a world that isn't limited by the effects of sin and death. This spiritual center explains why we can never quite settle for the pleasures we experience with food and sex and just surviving. That's why nothing in this world can fully satisfy us. We are wired for another kind of world. Saint Augustine, in *Confessions*, said it this way: "Because you have made us for Yourself . . . our heart is restless until it rests in you."[13]

I agree with the philosopher Peter Kreeft that this is one of the greatest sentences ever written.[14] The "restless heart" is every human heart, and it settles only when it finds the One who made it.

This is the plot of many of the stories we tell. Think, for instance, of Geppetto and his puppet, Pinocchio. Geppetto, grieving the loss of his only son and wanting to love and be loved again, looks upon his creation and knows there is no hope for human life in it. Unless, of course, he wishes upon a star, raises his eyes above the horizon, and puts his hope in something that transcends this world. And so, as in the story, "it is necessary in our lives to do the same. To lift your eyes above the horizon, to establish a transcendent goal; if you wish to cease being a puppet, under the control of things you do not understand and perhaps do not want to understand."[15]

This failure to look up beyond the horizon for meaning and purpose affects both our private and social worlds in hundreds of ways, and we see that play out every day. Our private worlds are in crisis, anxiety is at an all-time high, mental health problems are on the rise, IQ levels are *lower* than they were a generation ago, and we suffer from addictions and obesity at a scale we haven't seen before. A few years ago, it was even reported that life expectancy in parts of the Western world had fallen for three years in a row![16] For the first time in decades, people are living shorter lives. While these changes aren't directly tied to atheism per se, belief in a transcendent reality works as a shock absorber in our lives when we experience crisis and pain. It also brings a sense of hope to our lives: centering us in a loving community, a way of viewing the world that says our suffering isn't the final word. Rodney Stark, the celebrated sociologist of religion, has pointed out that for this reason, religious people live longer than nonreligious people, on average up to seven years![17]

And then there are all the social implications. Justice for minorities and women, the spread of education, better healthcare, the fight against trafficking and poverty—all of these are motivated by ethical and religious convictions that are the fruit of Christianity. On the flip side, many of the challenges we face as a culture are connected to denial of God's role in our lives. The collapse of marriage, the fracturing of the family, partisanship in politics, loss of public trust in institutions, debt, a lack of shared morality, consumerism. We know these exist, but what we are coming to see is that without God we are powerless to move beyond them.

And while all of this is tied to the question of God, it is also tied to how we as a culture are answering the question of *our own souls.* Even secular theorists contend that a sense of the transcendent—a higher meaning and purpose—is necessary for human flourishing and that without it we struggle to live. Without God, we live baseless, disoriented lives.

Years ago, the prime minister of Bulgaria, who had watched his country descend into chaos, came to Washington, DC, to give a speech to the US Congress. He spoke about why communism had collapsed in Europe and in his own country. The world had interpreted this collapse through a *political* and *economic* lens, declaring that socialism doesn't work. But he contended that there was more to the story and that the real lesson was that *secularism* doesn't work. "Around 1917 was the first time we tried to build a society without God," he said, "and to say it didn't flourish is an understatement." He continued:

> Moral confusion under communism was accompanied by an utter confusion of values. . . . People thought nothing of cheating and stealing. There was no faith to lean on since religion and belief in God were considered outdated and unscientific. This state of mind became "If God does not exist everything is permitted." The whole history of mankind has proven that without God or a higher moral authority the things most precious to us are often denied us. There is a new and intense striving of my people, especially the younger generations, to find the *moral foundations of their existence* and to rediscover age-old values and ideals. There is a renewed interest in religion, the church, and spirituality in general. There is now among my people *a revolt of the soul against soullessness.*[18]

The same is true about our lives personally. We are searching for ourselves but will never find ourselves if we rule out the possibility of God. All of us, at some point, need a revolt of the soul against soullessness.

Making ourselves the highest authority means there is no bigger story for us to be a part of. There is no ultimate point or place or destination, so this moment in time is directionless and meaningless.

Against the prevailing view of our day (that you are what you make of yourself), union with God tells us you can discover your real self *only in relation to the one who made you*. You are not and cannot be self-made, and thus you cannot be self-satisfying.[19] There really is a version of things that is a *more* solid reality than the world we see, hear, taste, and touch. While the world looks like a madhouse, with evil, pain, and unguided randomness in charge, we open our Bibles and see that nothing could be further from the truth.

The last book of the Bible tells us that Jesus Christ, raised from the dead, holds in his right hand seven stars or planets, which in that culture were seen as the things that define what happens in the world (Rev. 1:16). Again, Eugene Peterson explains: "What is in my right hand is what I am capable of doing and what, in fact, I am ready to do. What does Christ do? He runs the cosmos. . . . [So] the planets do not control us; Christ controls the planets."[20] Failure to have this conviction—that God not only exists but is in control of all things—at the center of our lives makes life a mess, for it "consigns us to a life of spasms and jerks, at the mercy of every advertisement, every seduction, every siren. Without it we live manipulated and manipulating lives."[21] We move between panic and laziness, fear and indifference, swept into a vast restlessness with no direction and no purpose.

Halloween, Horror, and the Ethics of Elfland

I was recently surprised while reading a book by Russell Moore. Moore is a conservative, Bible-believing Christian, and he opens his book on family by saying that if you were to ask him as a kid what his favorite holiday was, he would have said Easter or Christmas. But he would have been lying, because his favorite was always Halloween. In his religious circles, that holiday was frowned upon, but to his thinking, if it really was the devil's night, where the veil between the evil spirit world and our own thinned a little, why wouldn't we pay close attention to it rather than ignoring it? At least Halloween "took seriously what I intuitively knew to be true," he says, "that the world outside was terrifying." It also reinforced what he read in his Bible: "that the universe around me was alive with invisible forces, some of which meant to hurt me."[22] In other words, Halloween was the one time of year when people who normally don't think about it too much might consider that the universe may be more than material.

It is the same reason Chad and Carey Hayes, the Christian brothers behind such films as *The Conjuring*, say they make horror movies for a living. What other movies would we want to make? they say. Plots that *don't* raise the question of evil and spirituality? Stories that don't elicit an awareness of the spiritual realm, that of both evil and good? If we are honest, we almost want to believe in this version of reality, even if it scares us.

I can't tell you how many people I meet who have read my book *The Problem of Jesus*, and among all the stories and theology in that book, they jump right to a question about the opening story—about demons in my house and what I did about it. They don't ask with skepticism but with interest and intrigue, as if they *know* it's true and is part of the story of our world—but just don't know what to think about it. The world today seems divided between those willing to believe in the spiritual nature of things and those who reject it.

So why do we deny the spiritual? Some say it's because they are too smart for it all. They have followed the evidence and come to *scientific* and materialist conclusions rather than believing in fantasy and stories. But that isn't the whole picture. There are always reasons behind the reasons. We are each an ecosystem of ideas and motivations, and none of those are as pure or innocent as we like to think. College students often admit that contrary to what they tell their friends and families, they didn't stop believing in God and *then* begin thinking about their sexuality and saying, "I can start sleeping around now," but rather the opposite: they chose to do something with their bodies, liked it, and moved backward from that to decide that they didn't believe in God anymore. Our rejection of the life of the soul and the spiritual is not always based on our experience or any kind of evidence. And it certainly isn't as simplistic as "smart people" versus everyone else. In fact, G. K. Chesterton, who was himself one of the smart people, says it may be the opposite. In his famous chapter "The Ethics of Elfland" from his classic book *Orthodoxy*, he contends that the atheist view is the simplistic version because it lacks the imagination to see beyond what we see in the physical world. It forsakes "wonder" for "law," and those who choose that way, Chesterton says, have forgotten who they really are.

> One may understand the cosmos but never the ego; the self is more distant than any star. Thou shalt love the Lord thy God; but thou shalt not know thyself. We are all under the same mental calamity; we have all forgotten our names. We have forgotten what we really are. . . . That I think is our curse—and the truest clue to solving our deepest search in this life. Our remembering. Those glimpses of pleasure and joy that prove, or at least point to, something beyond ourselves.[23]

Pleasure and joy as the way to find ourselves and to find God? As we have seen, this is not a detour in the knowledge of self but a central part of it, because it speaks to the part of ourselves that nature can't explain.

All this to say, as a first principle, life must begin with God. The recognition of the transcendent, that there is a spiritual component to reality, is the beginning of wisdom. We take our hint from the opening words of the story of the universe: "In the beginning, God . . ." The story begins with him, but then it moves on to what this God has to do with us. Yes, "God is spirit," as Jesus says (John 4:24), but he did not remain the only spiritual being in the universe. He decided to share his nature, imparting that privilege to us. And that changes everything about both our present and our future.

So listen to that old ache inside. It's the most important thing about you. It might be trying to guide you home.

CHAPTER 2

Find Out Where
YOU CAME FROM

*This twofold nature of man is so clear that some
have thought that we had two souls.*

—BLAISE PASCAL

"Where are you from?"

It is one of the first questions we ask people we are meeting for the first time. Sometimes it is a question we ask just for the sake of conversation. "Oh, I have a friend from there," we say, or "You know, I have never been there. What's it like?" But often something else is going on too.

We ask this question because we are in some way trying to *locate* or *place* that person. If we know where they are from, we know (or are at least closer to knowing) them. We might be able to take a guess at their politics or the sports teams they cheer for. If they are from San Diego, they likely think or live a little more like this or that (*sandalsy* maybe, if that's a word) than someone from, say, Manhattan. Or if they are from Europe versus Alabama, we can probably predict what kind of "football" they'd rather watch. We can know a lot about a person just by knowing where they're from. That's why knowing where *we're* from—humanity's origins as a whole—will help us understand ourselves, which is why it's an essential starting point for our journey as we explore this thing called life.

In the first verse of the Bible, we are confronted with an affirmation of something scientists since Herbert Spencer, writing in the mid-1800s, have been saying about reality itself—namely, that all natural phenomena in the universe can ultimately be divided into interactions among five basic, fundamental "manifestations": time, force, motion, space, and matter.[1] What took us thousands of years to figure out was right there in Genesis 1:1 all along: "In the beginning [time] God [force] created [motion] the heavens [space] and the earth [matter]."

Most agree that the universe came into existence in a single moment wherein all space, time, energy, and matter *began* to exist. There is debate about when exactly this was, but the instantaneous beginning of the universe has always "smelled of religion," as one atheist said, because since the beginning of science and philosophy, we have always known that if something *begins* to exist, it must have a *cause*—something outside of it that made it come into existence. Throughout the centuries, those who didn't believe in God concluded that the universe was an uncaused, eternal reality. It just *always was*. But then scientists, led by people like Edwin Hubble and several others in the mid-twentieth century, discovered that the universe did have a beginning. Only some kind of explanation that included a cause outside the universe (i.e., God, whatever or whomever that was) would do.

> Whatever begins to exist has a cause.
> The universe began to exist.
> Therefore, the universe has a cause.

This universe has the additional problem that mathematicians and scientists acknowledge as the greatest evidence for the existence of God, what they call the "anthropic principle." This refers to the odd and hard-to-explain reality that our world has many highly unlikely variables that permit life: earth's perfect distance from the sun, the rate of the universe's expansion, the average distance between stars, how precisely perfect the makeup of oxygen is for our species. All of this is perfectly tuned to the million millionth degree so that we can exist, and the astronomical odds of that being the case make academics of all disciplines blush and even admit that it looks like the universe has been monkeyed with in some way.

Into such a universe come . . . us. Human beings. Unique beings amid everything else—very creaturely (sharing many attributes with animals) but very different as well. So what are we? Some worldviews throughout history have answered that question by saying we are part of a cosmic consciousness of some sort, others by saying we are part of an ecosystem of energy that gives and takes away from all that lives, and still others by saying we were made by the gods for entertainment. There are as many answers as there are cultures. In the modern scientific era, roughly three proposals are popular, whether or not people would articulate it exactly in these words:

1. We are *animals* improbably appearing for a moment in a cosmos without purpose or significance.
2. We are *sensualists* who have nothing higher to aspire to than gratification, using possessions and physical sensations to consume.
3. We are *bodies* only, with the capacity to define ourselves by the exercise of will and self-definition.[2]

The biblical answer to the question of our origins is unique in the marketplace of ideas because it corrects two pitfalls characterizing most anthropologies: the tendency to *downplay* our humanity, as if we are merely animals working off instinct, and the tendency to *up-play* it, as if we are somewhat divine ourselves. The biblical presentation instead says that we are, on the one hand, *creatures*—part of creation, not over it—and yet, at the same time, made *in the image of God*. You don't need to accept it at this point, but I hope you agree that it is a unique and profoundly different proposal.

In short, we're not gods—but we're also not animals. This is where we must begin our journey of finding ourselves and what we were made for—namely, where we came from. And the answer is more exciting than we may realize.

More than Animals

First, then, *we are more than animals.* In Genesis 1, everything that gets made—the sea creatures, the land animals—comes into existence "according to its kind" (Gen. 1:21, 24). But when God creates humans, there is none of that. Instead, God creates Adam "from the dust of the ground" (Gen. 2:7). Human beings are unique, different from the rest of creation. But how?

Are we wholly separate from the natural world? No, we were created on the sixth day just like the other animals, so there is kinship. We humans have a great deal in common with many of our fellow animals: we breathe like them, eat like them, and reproduce like them. We are creatures. God alone is on the creator side of the creator-creature relationship.[3]

At the same time, God made us—and not the animals—in his "likeness" and "image" (Gen. 1:26), and we became human when God breathed the "breath of life" into us (Gen. 2:7). The Hebrew word for "breath of life" here is variously translated as "soul," "living being," or "self." It is at this moment, the Bible says, that "the man became a living being" (Gen. 2:7). Distinct and more than just an animal or a physical creature, humankind has a spiritual existence as well. Beyond that, in the biblical view, a person does not just *have* a soul, as we say, but *is* a soul. There is still much room for debate about what all this means for us as human beings, but it at least means we are different from the other creatures of creation, having been breathed on by the God of the universe. The life of God himself was in some way gifted to us, and as a species we have been especially animated by it. We have a spiritual, eternal, transcendent aspect that animals don't have. In the New Testament, Jesus, referring to an aspect of our created nature, says, "Do not be afraid of those who kill the body but cannot kill the soul. Rather, be afraid of the One who can destroy both soul and body" (Matt. 10:28). Jesus affirms that we are both body *and* soul. The Greek word for "soul" here is *psychē* (where we get our English word *psychology*), and it denotes our whole self: our identity and our personality.[4]

If you're a skeptic, you may be thinking this is all just religious nonsense, but even modern science and psychology now admit there are good reasons to believe we have something resembling a soul. The respected social scientist Dr. Marilyn Schlitz, in her book *Death Makes Life Possible: Revolutionary Insights on Living, Dying, and the Continuation of Consciousness*, says, "There are ways in which people's experience refutes the position that the mind is the brain and nothing more. There are solid, concrete data that suggests that our consciousness, may surpass the boundaries of the brain."[5]

The existence of a soulish reality certainly does not play into the atheist framework of the universe very well, which is why philosopher Alvin Plantinga concludes that on the question of human consciousness "things don't look good for Darwinian naturalists" and why Steven Weinberg, an atheist scientist, says it is best to "bypass the problem of human consciousness" altogether in the debate between atheism and theism, because "it may just be too hard for us [atheists]" to explain.[6] As we know, something can't come from nothing. A soul, consciousness, a sense of the transcendent, can't come from pure matter alone. This is a problem atheists in debates admit they can't answer, but claim that it is only a problem because we don't have the technology yet to understand it and at some point in the future computers will be able to tell us why and how we became soulish beings versus just animalistic (a faith position if I have ever heard one!). The ancient answer of the Bible is that God took the creature he made and then made it a living soul. We are conscious, eternal, moral, and beautiful in ways that matter evolving by itself could never be. Human beings became *more than creatures.* We became spiritual beings—rational, thinking, feeling, self-aware, conscious, soulish beings connected in our very nature to something over and above our experience of this world. This explains why you long for a world different from this one. It explains why you see and sense the divine in great works of art or in other experiences that lift you up out of this "worldly" plane, even if you catch only short glimpses.

Darwin, DNA, and the Origin of Our Species

This is as good a time as any to deal with the question of our origin as a species. The biblical story is clear: God was the *first cause* that gave life to us and to all things.

Something difficult for naturalistic evolutionary theory to explain is the problem of a first cause. Even if human beings are the product of millions of years of unguided evolution in which one species became another and then another, on and on, advocates of that view still must explain when and *how* that process started. How did the first living organism "become alive" and start multiplying? Several suggestions have been proposed. Scientists have attempted to re-create the first cause that started the process of natural evolution, but they are still not close to an explanation.

This has led most scientists to agree that "more than sixty years of experimentation on the origin of life in the fields of chemical and molecular evolution have led to a better perception of the immensity of the problem of the origin of life on Earth rather than its solution. At present all discussion on principal theories and experiments in the field either end in stalemate or in a confession of ignorance."[7]

Even Francis Crick, the Nobel Prize–winning scientist who discovered and identified the structure of DNA in 1953, one of the most important discoveries in the history of ideas, admitted something similar about our origins when he confessed, "An honest man, armed with all the knowledge available to us now, could only state that in some sense, the origin of life appears at the moment to be almost a miracle, so many are the conditions which would have had to have been satisfied to get it going."[8]

Of course, Charles Darwin was working on his theories of our origins before we knew anything about DNA or biochemistry or had the ability to look at life at a *molecular* level. When we consider all we are as a species and what we now know—that every cell in the human body (of which there are 37 trillion) contains three *billion* base pairs that make up our DNA, which is basically to say, billions of lines of code and information that define everything about us, right down to our hair and eye color—we must admit the unlikelihood of just matter over time, without influence, as an explanation. At minimum, we must consider the possibility of a "mind" existing and guiding the information to an intended goal. This is one reason the Oxford philosopher Antony Flew, who spent his life as an atheist debating people who believed in God and destroying them in front of large audiences with his mind and quick wit, went back on his years of skepticism before he died in 2010 and said he was open to belief in God. The one factor that changed his mind? The enormous complexity of even the simplest self-producing cell, he said, and the fact that unguided evolutionary explanations in the face of that complexity aren't *better* explanations than those that factor in a mind or guided-ness to it all. To get life going would have required some form of biological information. So Flew, in his book *There Is a God: How the World's Most Notorious Atheist Changed His Mind*, wrote:

> People overlook the fact that Darwin himself in chapter fourteen of *On the Origin of Species* pointed out that his whole argument began with a being which already possessed reproductive powers, a creature that evolution must give some account for. Darwin knew he hadn't given an account and now it seems to me that the findings of years of DNA research have provided materials for a new and enormously powerful argument to design.[9]

Why? Because while patterns occur everywhere in nature, *codes* do not occur in the natural world. They are the invention of a mind and intelligent consciousness.[10] This is why in the modern era, many scientists conclude that "God is now a more respectable hypothesis than at any time in the last one hundred years."[11]

———

My point here is not to settle these debates, which will rage on, but simply to point out that we now have enough information to reasonably admit the possibility that we're not just creatures that came into existence out of nothing for no reason whatsoever, but creatures that seem *designed* in some way, for some purpose (which we will explore in depth later). And further, that we are distinct from the animals in that we are self-conscious and, dare we say, spiritual beings, capable of things beyond surviving and reproducing according to our instincts— things like love, art, and music. We are a fusion of this world and another of sorts: "The centaur, half-man, half-animal . . . is probably more realistic in picturing the human condition."[12]

This distinction also gives us a better sense of what God thinks of us. We are his most precious creation. We are special, the most beloved of all things he has made. The fact that when he created us, he did so by breathing on us and making us alive is one of the hints at how special we are. He did that only to us we are told. Not the animals or the angels. "Breathing on someone implies wordless intimacy. If you are close enough to feel someone's breath on your face, chances are you're married to them, or about to be!"[13] Such is the relationship between God and his humans. You're not just an animal to be discarded, or even "one with creation" as New Age thinking says, but both a *part* of creation and also *over* it, representing God and his ways in it.

You and everyone you have ever met have worth and value on a scale you could never imagine. When you look in the mirror in those moments when you feel worthless and as though no one loves you because you aren't good-looking enough, or don't have nice enough clothes, or don't have any friends, or don't feel like you have anything to offer the world, you can know that's a lie, because you are God's. You have worth from the top of your head to the bottom of your feet. Human life, from the womb to the tomb, is sacred. This truth, if you accept it, means that a thousand things that have plagued humankind die welcome deaths— racism, prejudice, sexism—all because God's image is imprinted on every person of every color, tribe, gender who makes up the world. And it means a hundred other things as well that we have sadly lost sight of but which we must recapture as we journey through life.

Homo Divinus

Skeptics push back at the idea of us being more than just animals, questioning the biblical story and saying instead that we should believe scientific conclusions about humankind, not biblical ones. What they usually mean is that we should acknowledge that we came from a lower life form and *evolved* into what we are today rather than believing in fairy tales about being made by someone. To which I say, too much time and energy has been wasted arguing about this, for even if humankind did progress from a lower life form within our own species, this is not in contradiction with the biblical picture. The pastor and theologian John Stott helpfully argued exactly this:

> I myself believe in the historicity of Adam and Eve as the original couple from whom the human race is descended, but my acceptance of Adam and Eve as historical is not incompatible with my belief that several forms of pre-Adamic "hominid" seem to have existed for thousands of years previously. These hominids began to advance culturally. They made their cave drawings and buried their dead. It is conceivable that God created Adam out of one of them. You may call them *homo erectus*. I think you may even call some of them *homo sapiens*, for these are arbitrary scientific names. But Adam was the first *homo divinus*, if I may coin the phrase, the first man to whom may be given the specific biblical designation "made in the image of God." Precisely what the divine likeness was, which was stamped upon him, we do not know, for Scripture nowhere tells us. But it seems to have included those rational, moral, social, and spiritual faculties which make creatures like God.[14]

In other words, there is room for compatibility between scientific and biblical data on the subject, more than is often recognized. This is why Oxford professor Alister McGrath has rightly said that the "sun has begun to set" on the empire of atheism that has ruled the Western world for the last one hundred years and considers the idea that science and religion are in any kind of conflict to be the most "mistaken of mistaken ideas . . . and no longer taken seriously by any major historian of science despite its popularity."[15]

This moving away from a purely atheistic view of humankind is partly because of our inability to continue to live with the contradictions of it. As G. K. Chesterton famously pointed out, we will "denounce a policeman for killing a peasant, and then prove by the highest philosophical principles that the peasant ought to have [just] killed himself. . . . The man of this school [of thinking] goes first to a *political* meeting, where he complains that [people] are treated as if they were beasts; then he takes his hat and umbrella and goes on to a *scientific* meeting, where he proves that they practically are beasts."[16]

The contradictory nature of this view of humankind, held out by secularism today, is losing its hold on popular thinking, and rightfully so.

Slaves, Women, and Favored Races

The nature of humankind, as we have seen, isn't merely a personal issue, though it has been relegated there in the modern era. It is also a scientific one—i.e., were we created as a distinct species, or did we simply evolve from animals? Furthermore, the question of our origins and identity turns out to be a political question as well. Stott contended that it is *the* political issue of the twentieth century.[17] After all, who is it that governments are leading? It is one of the key conflicts between Marxism and capitalism, or a more traditional vision of a democratic republic, for instance: Do human beings have an absolute value in and of themselves, at the level of *essence*, or is their worth only relative to the community? Are we servants of institutions, or are institutions servants to us?[18]

What one believes about *what we are* affects everything. And every culture has a slightly different way of answering this. Certainly, the ancient world had its answers. The poor existed to serve the rich and lacked any inherent value in and of themselves. Women existed as bearers of children and were less valuable than men. A worldview founded on Genesis 1 and 2 challenges these ingrained values, instead saying that everyone has equal, inherent value and worth, regardless of whether they are rich or poor, a woman or a man, a child or an adult, slave or free.

We naively think the modern world invented the beliefs that underlie liberal democracy, and in our arrogance, we hold them to be true while at the same time laughing and criticizing the Bible as ancient, prudish, irrelevant, and oppressive, not realizing it is that same Bible that gave us the notion of a person's inherent worth. Luc Ferry, an atheist, in his book *A Brief History of Thought*, points out that Christianity was the first worldview to contend that humans were all equal (Gen. 1:26–28; Gal. 3:28). "The Greek world was fundamentally an aristocratic world," he says, "organized as a hierarchy in which the most endowed by nature should in principle be 'at the top.' . . . It was founded on slavery."[19] Christianity, he says, introduced the idea that humanity was equal in dignity—an unprecedented concept at the time and one to which our world today owes its entire democratic inheritance.

The same is true about the value of women or the poor. While many criticize Christianity for being oppressive to these groups, Ferry points out that from a historical perspective, Christianity is by far the best thing that ever happened to them. Everywhere it has gone, Christianity has lifted women and children out of poverty, educated them, and set them up as equals—not merely subservient to men as was the norm in oppressive patriarchal cultures. And it continues to do so today.[20] This is because the Christian view of the nature of humankind holds that we aren't just bodies living out animalistic instincts but are something more. We have spirits and souls, and immortality is part of who we are. That truth makes all the difference. Think of it this way: "If Darwin had announced his theory of evolution in India, China, Japan, it would have hardly made a stir. If—along with hundreds of millions of Hindus and Buddhists—you have never believed that humans differ from everything else in the natural world in having an immortal soul, you will find it hard to get worked up by a theory that shows how much we have in common with other animals."[21]

It was the Christian conviction with its high view of human beings that made the theory of naturalistic evolution so controversial. Beyond its glaring scientific weaknesses, one could easily see how it takes us backward regarding the equality of people (races, genders, etc.) and rewrites the biblical conviction that we all have inherent worth by virtue of being human. According to natural selection, there are races within the human species that are more advanced than others and therefore are "favored" to survive and reproduce, passing on their genetic material. This is illustrated by the full (and less commonly referenced) title of Darwin's most popular work, *On the Origin of Species by Means of Natural Selection, or the Preservation of Favoured Races in the Struggle for Life*. Darwin's explanation of origins contains within it a racial prejudice against "unfavored" races, or unfavored subcategories like the cognitively delayed, who, he contends, should not be allowed to marry or reproduce because they will hinder our progress as a species: "Man scans with scrupulous care the character and pedigree of his horses, cattle, and dogs before he matches them," he says, "but when he comes to his own marriage he rarely, or never, takes any such care. . . . Both sexes ought to refrain from marriage if they are in any marked degree inferior in body or mind."[22] As horrific as this dangerous idea sounds, it flows naturally from a Darwinian, naturalistic view of our origins and beginnings.

There Are No Ordinary People

The Bible alone, in the marketplace of ideas, says that God shaped us from the matter of this world and "breathed into" us so we became living beings (Gen. 2:7) made "in the image of God" (Gen. 1:27), distinct from animals and angels. The Old Testament scholar Bruce Waltke in his commentary on Genesis tells us that an *image* in the ancient Near East was understood to possess the life of the being it represented and that it functioned as a ruler in the place of a deity: "It was believed that a god's spirit lived in any statue or image of that god" so that the image could function as "a representative or substitute for the god, ruling on its behalf."[23] When we add to this the fact that only a king or queen was ever considered to be made in a god's image, representing and ruling on their behalf, we see that the Hebrew perspective is quite radical. Being created in the god's image is now democratized to *all humanity*, not just the ruling elite.

This is why Christianity has always had a different perspective on where to live and be on mission, for instance. Many have found comfort away from the progressive ideas of big cities and moved out to the suburbs or the country, believing them to be godlier and less tainted by sin. Others, like Timothy Keller, have pointed out that this is a misguided route because "cities, quite literally, have *more of the image of God per square inch* than any other place on earth."[24]

The implication that we carry what the ancients called the *imago Dei*, the image of God, in us means every person you meet, whether rich or poor, employed or homeless, ugly or beautiful, smart or dumb (according to you!), is made in this image too. In their very *essence* and at an infinite level, they are important, of worth and value. This is why it matters more to take a human life than the life of a fly or a deer. If we were consistent in our beliefs and believed that humans were just another animal, we wouldn't get all that upset about death or murder or rape or genocide, as these (or something akin to them) are natural in the animal kingdom. But we do get upset because we know—even if we don't know why we know—that human beings are unique.

So we are *part* of creation, but we also *transcend* it. This duality prevents us from thinking too little of ourselves or too highly. It counters views of humankind wherein we are *gods*—spirits without bodies—empowered to create our own reality, or wherein we are mere *animals*—bodies without spirits—roaming the earth, eating, and procreating our way into the next generation with the sole goal of surviving. The biblical view subverts these extremes and gives us a vision of a holistic being whose soul and body both matter and are intertwined at every level. This understanding of ourselves enables us to flourish, both as individuals and as a culture, because it acknowledges that we are people, not things.

One of the great challenges of being human today is that we don't live like this anymore. Long before the smartphone existed, philosopher John Kavanaugh argued that we have depersonalized human beings and personalized things, such that people now relate to things as if they were people and relate to people as if they were things.[25] The biblical story resists this way of life, calling us to fight the temptation to depersonalize anyone at any time. If we lose this battle, we lose ourselves. But we might also lose the person next to us, for if the biblical picture is true, "there are no ordinary people. You have never talked to a mere mortal. Nations, cultures, arts, civilizations—these are mortal, and their life is to ours as the life of a gnat. But it is immortals whom we joke with, work with, marry, snub, and exploit—immortal horrors or everlasting splendors."[26]

In other words, all of us will live forever *because* we are more than bodies. Our lives will go on, as everlasting horrors in an existence where the grace of God no longer extends—a place of darkness and fear, without doors—or as everlasting splendors in a place where the radiance of God envelops us with an intensity nothing in this life comes close to matching. Where, as Tolkien imagined it, "the sound of singing comes over the water," and "the grey rain-curtain of this world is pulled back and all turns to silver glass: white shores and beyond a far green country under a swift sunrise."[27] When you think of such a wonderful place and state of being, don't you long for it to be true? That kind of transcendent reality? I think most of us do. When we think of our origins in the way we are seeing here, we begin to understand why. It's the *way we were made*.

The book of Ecclesiastes says it this way: God "set eternity in the human heart," adding that "the dust returns to the earth as it was, [but] the spirit returns to God who gave it" (Eccl. 3:11; 12:7 ESV). That is why you have a sense that there is a joy and pleasure and fulfillment that is beyond this world and why you are constantly reaching, and glimpsing, and then fighting to hold on to a world that is *more* than this one.

The flash of happiness you felt that time as you laughed with friends around a dinner table, or when you were listening to that piece of music, or staring at that sunset, and it all, as my kids would say, "hit different" even for a moment or two. It's not an illusion; it's real. It's part of what it means to be not only made by God, for all things were, but made in his image and for him. You are not only a creature but a treasure. That transcendent joy and beauty in you is what you wake up chasing every morning. In every cup of coffee, in every conversation, in every "I love you" and hug and kiss and smile, in every novel that transports you to another world. It's all a longing for another level of existence, for a true and everlasting *something*.

C. S. Lewis called it a kind of euphoria, that recurring sensation he felt when he was a kid and his brother handed him a miniature garden in the top of a tin cookie box with twigs and moss. When he looked back as an adult, he called that experience Joy (always capitalizing the term)—and he spent the rest of his life searching for it and *where it came from*. When we understand who we are and how we were made, we begin to see these longings as guides. The deep awe explains something about us that a purely naturalist view of things cannot.

So what is our origin? Where are we from? God took the dust of the earth, formed it, and breathed into it. Nature became supernature. The machine was given a ghost. That is our history. The fusion of body and soul. Physical and spiritual. That's why we love this world and yet know it is not quite what it should be.

Even the secular story says a similar thing. In his award-winning book *Sapiens*, Yuval Noah Harari explains that at some point in the development of our species, we moved from one stage using basic tools and procreating because of pure instinct to officially becoming *Homo sapiens, Homo* meaning "man" and *sapien* meaning "wise, discerning, or, thinking,"[28] a mutation that allowed cognitive powers of speech and imagination, what he calls the Cognitive Revolution, some seventy thousand years ago. Now, whatever the timeline or the exact details, the point is human beings at some point in our development became "wise" and "conscious" and "moral" and "spiritual."

How did this happen? Atheism has no good answer. Scripture says it's because God breathed on us. We went from whatever we were to the "wise man." And with that, the forever man, eternal man, living not just seventy years but seventy million and seventy million after that—on and on forever.

PART II

The Problem of
IDENTITY

The first gulp from the beaker of knowledge
estranges us from God, but at the bottom of
the glass God is waiting for him who seeks.

—Carl Friedrich von Weizsäcker

If you look closely at Leonardo da Vinci's painting *The Last Supper,* you will notice a series of bread rolls running across the table. Several years ago, a musician discovered that if the five lines of a musical staff are drawn across the painting, the bread rolls on the table can be combined with the apostles' hands, and when lined up together they can be read as musical notes. If read from right to left, which was da Vinci's common writing style, the notes can be played to produce a forty-second song. Even those who don't fully buy the theory have admitted that the composition's perfect harmony is too good to be just a coincidence. Da Vinci, after all, was an expert musician as well as a world-class painter.

A song, *hidden in plain sight.*

What if I were to tell you that something similar is true of human existence and our identity? At the core of our humanity lies something most of us haven't seen or understood yet, even if we've been staring right at it for years. It's a secret that is not so secret if you know what you're looking for, like a key that opens another world that is already there, just waiting to be discovered.

This is where we turn next, to those things at the center of the human painting, to questions of existence, of what it means to be human, and how to use this knowledge to flourish instead of flounder in life. In many ways the world is divided up between people who have come to see the answer to this question and those who haven't. Those who have unearthed what has been waiting for them their whole lives, like a secret hidden in a painting, and those who haven't yet, who still look from time to time but only see hands and bread rolls.

CHAPTER 3

Don't Try to
BE GOD

The pursuit of knowledge can lead to
enlightenment or to destruction. It depends on
the heart of the seeker.

—MARY SHELLEY, *FRANKENSTEIN*

This product will become more important than the internet." So said the legendary investor John Doerr (who had bet successfully on Google and a dozen other startups) about the invention in front of him, investing $80 million. He told others this company would be the fastest ever to reach $1 billion in net worth. No less than Steve Jobs declared it the most amazing piece of technology since the personal computer and offered $63 million for just a 10 percent stake in the company. The inventor himself, an accomplished technology whiz named Dean Kamen, was described by many as the next Thomas Edison. The company projected it would be producing ten thousand units a week within one year of going public.

The product in question was the Segway, the personal transporter. As we now know, all these predictions were very, very wrong. Six years after it formed, the company had sold only thirty thousand units, and the idea itself was labeled one of the ten biggest technology flops of the decade. "I made some pretty bold predictions," Doerr later said, "that were dead wrong."[1]

Have you ever thought too highly of yourself? Have you ever overreached and suffered the consequences? This is one of the great errors we make as a species, creating a world of problems for us collectively. There is good news, however. If we can understand the problem, a solution is available so that this mistake doesn't ruin us on a personal level.

The problem of our overreaching, and the pride that follows, is one of the sources of our decay, both personal and cultural. The Greek myth of Prometheus (reinterpreted to us through names like Freud, Darwin, Nietzsche, and perhaps even Jobs and Musk) is all about the god that gave humankind fire (which represented technology and knowledge), which of course gave us life but also fooled us into thinking we had the power of the gods ourselves.

And we continue to do so. We believe we can work our way out of our predicament. Science, philosophy, psychology, medicine, and technology are all looked at as ways we are collectively saving ourselves. At the very least, we believe they give us the potential for salvation, allowing us to rise above our fellow creatures. Now we have no need of God.

This folly, of our pride and the destruction that follows, is the warning of God in the garden of Eden to us. The "tree of the knowledge of good and evil" in Genesis has been interpreted to mean many things throughout history (e.g., a symbol of sexual awakening, moral discernment, etc.), but at least one thing is clear from the story itself: the choice of whether to eat from the tree is "presented as the alternative to discipleship under God himself: to be self-made, wrestling one's knowledge, satisfactions and values from the created world in defiance of the Creator."[2] In other words, eating of the forbidden fruit is a declaration that we're not satisfied and content being made by God and instead want to *be* God. We want to know all things and control all things and have all things. Which, the biblical story is telling us, is where all our problems began.

And our problems still begin this way, each day of our lives.

There are a hundred ways we try to be gods. We think we need to be in control all the time, which is where much of our anxiety comes from. We think we know what is best for ourselves, our families, our work. And we take these things in our own hands and mold them, hold them tight, and direct them within an inch of their lives as if we are in fact sovereign, not realizing that this god complex is crushing both us and the objects and people we are seeking to control under our will. We don't realize that true freedom comes when we *stop* trying to build a tower to heaven and instead lean into our place as God's image bearers.

We don't try to be gods because we wake up each morning trying to be evil. We try to be gods for one reason, which is almost the opposite of what feels evil: we believe that it is somehow the *right* thing to do. As John Mark Comer says, "We sin because we believe a lie about what will make us happy."[3] We believe that by seizing autonomy from God and doing things our own way, we will be better off. But the fall story tells us this is the lie beneath all the other lies. As the story also points out, we aren't very good listeners. We keep making the same mistakes Adam (which means "human") and Eve (which means "life") made. We don't accept the boundaries God has placed on us. We've read the story about how *humans* and *life* got into their present state—but haven't learned a thing. We keep falling for the same deceptions.[4] Especially in an age where the self has become the most important entity in the universe. We are told a thousand times a day to emphasize and publicize and post the self, as that is where significance comes from and is the only route to wholeness—a lie the enemy has brought into our lives now at a mass scale through social media and all the pressures of constantly posting photos of ourselves and our lives. This is a subtle but powerful deception when you realize how recent the concept of a "selfie" or even constant access to mirrors is in the scope of history. In this world, the words of Fernando Pessoa about our reflection are humbling: "Nature gave him the gift of not being able to see it and of not being able to stare into his own eyes. Only in the water of rivers and ponds could he look at his face. And the very posture he had to assume was symbolic. He had to bend over, stoop down, to commit the [shame] of beholding himself. The inventor of the mirror poisoned the human heart."[5]

There are countless examples of this in our own lives as well as several on a broader, cultural level. Let's look at two that are particularly relevant in our modern world that fall under the banners of science and sex.

AI and the World's Most Dangerous Idea

The first example from the world of science is infiltrating our everyday lives more and more each day, and that is the reality of AI—artificial intelligence. With every year that passes, AI gains influence over us in ways we don't even realize. Algorithms monitor and influence our shopping habits, our time on social media, our healthcare, and the world of education. AI is changing our world in a million ways. It is the future whether we like it or not. Vladimir Putin has said it as clear as it can be said: "Artificial Intelligence is the future not only for Russia but for all humankind. Whoever becomes the leader in this sphere will become the ruler of the world."[6] In 2016 a team from the Future of Humanity Institute at the University of Oxford worked with over three hundred academics and industry experts in machine learning and concluded that in the next ten years AI would do better than any of us at translating languages, writing high school–level essays, writing top-40 songs, and driving trucks. Much of this is true already—and it all arrived ahead of schedule. They went on to say, "By 2049, A.I. should be writing *New York Times* bestsellers and performing surgeries by 2053. Overall, A.I. should be better than humans at pretty much everything in about 45 years."[7]

In the church world, pastors use AI each week to translate sermons and church services into a variety of languages. I preach on a weekend in California, and AI takes my words and translates them into whatever language we want, even matching my mouth to that language in my own voice and with all my inflections! And the more we use it, the more it learns how I use words and phrases so it can more clearly communicate to those watching online. What an amazing tool, we say—and it is—but of course all this comes with grave risks, which are making themselves clearer every day.

Over time, as AI becomes ever smarter and more helpful by eliminating sickness and disease (some even say death!) and providing us with unprecedented knowledge and advancement, it will be impossible to resist merging with it to create a new kind of human being. And that is where the future of AI is especially relevant to our exploration of life and being human in this world. This making of a new kind of being is called *transhumanism*, or what some describe as post-humanism—a chilling title for sure. But what is it?

Well, in some ways it is what movies have been showing us for decades—a kind of cyborg that fuses an organic human being with a computer. The idea is that what we now know as human beings will be replaced over time by the next (and some say *final*) stage of our species's evolution wherein AI is fused together with human beings to create a being that is made of both. This is seen as *upgrading* humanity, giving us superhuman intelligence. You might call it *homo deus*, humankind being upgraded to a godlike state (though think of it more like the Greek gods). And while a decade ago this still seemed to be just science fiction, that's no longer true. Companies like Elon Musk's Neuralink and others are already working on making this come true, and the first human being has already fused his mind with the system.

His name is Noland Arbaugh, and he is paralyzed from the shoulders down. After joining his mind to the Neuralink system, he can now play chess and explore the internet using only neural signals—simply what he thinks about. After seeing its real-time effects on Arbaugh, Elon Musk called this development "a species level game changer."[8]

In his exploration of our species, Yuval Harari said that transhumanism is an attempt at "human self-deification."[9] We aren't happy with our limitations, and so we grasp at knowing and being able to do all things in an attempt to evolve beyond our intended limitations. Others, however, might see this as just another replaying of what the serpent tempted us with in the garden. Several academic researchers are sounding warning bells, like Jonathan Haidt in his work *The Anxious Generation*. After exploring the psychological effects social media has had on us as a society, especially our children, Haidt predicts that we are headed for disaster if we don't change course. One of the solutions he proposes is that we "heed the warnings of the ancients, of religious authorities, who warn us, we are leaving our humanity and we are stepping into an unknown zone, where so far the initial verdict is horrible."[10]

In the same vein, some are rightly afraid as they imagine the kinds of creatures we might make ourselves. If Mary Shelley's *Frankenstein* has taught us anything since it was written in 1818, it's that we don't know what we don't know when we cross the line into being creators—remaking ourselves into something new—versus creatures living as designed. The warnings of our history tell us we don't make very good gods. But that hasn't stopped us from trying.

All of these warnings and unknowns feed into an ever-growing uncertainty. Will we make something that will become the very source of our own extinction? Musk himself, though at the forefront of much of this research, has testified multiple times at Senate hearings that we need worldwide restrictions on AI. Many academics who study AI deem it the greatest threat facing humanity. Political scientist and author of *The End of History*, Francis Fukuyama, claims it is "the world's most dangerous idea."[11] One cannot help but think of the words of Dr. Ian Malcolm in *Jurassic Park*, speaking of the re-creation of extinct dinosaurs: "We were so preoccupied with whether we *could* do it, we never stopped to think whether we *should*."

All of which brings us back to the biblical account. As Paula Boddington writes, "If we see the Genesis account of the Fall of man as a foreshadowing of fears about robots, then Genesis gets the problem exactly right. . . . What might robots do if we can't control them fully? Will they decide to obey us? What will our relationship with our creations be? . . . We can thank Genesis for pre-warning us."[12] And it does warn us. It says to us, as philosopher J. Budziszewski has written, "What God has been to man is his absolute superior, and man cannot be his own superior. A thing cannot be greater than itself. You say you want to change the human design. But in that case, there must be two groups. Those who caused the change, and those who result from it. And the former hold all the power. What do we do if these new species of humans turn on us?"[13]

But even more pressing are questions of how these developments, while created to make us better and freer, will bite back. We now see countries using AI to track and control their citizens. C. S. Lewis warned of this as far back as 1943: "There cannot be any simple increase of power on Man's side. Each new power won *by* man is a power *over* man as well. Each advance leaves man weaker as well as stronger. In every victory, besides being the general who triumphs, he is also the prisoner who follows the triumphal car. . . . Man's final conquest has proved to be the abolition of Man."[14]

Love Thy Body: Sex, Gender, and Self-Creation

A second area where the question of our identity as human beings and our grasping at being gods comes together is the controversial question of our sexuality—more specifically that of *gender*. The last few decades have seen the Western world embrace theories of person-hood that have fundamentally challenged our understanding of these matters. For example, we now routinely make distinctions between one's sex and one's gender.

- *Sex*, we say, is what you were *born* as, meaning the classic categories wherein a doctor could look at your external sex organs and write down "male" or "female."
- *Gender* is what a person *identifies* as, or socially expresses their identity as, which of course can be different from the sex they were assigned at birth.[15]

The traditional arguments between those on the right and left politically have been about whether sex is determined by which external organs you were born with. But this is somewhat misguided because, according to science, one's sex isn't technically defined by organs but by *gametes*, which are *reproductive cells*. This means that aside from whatever external sex organs a person has, they are a parti-cular sex at the cellular level. This also means that the sex of a person is stable and technically unchangeable. Someone who identifies as transgender—which some studies indicate represents up to six in every one thousand Americans—can change their external organs, but their sex technically remains male or female. Transitioning doesn't address a person's sex. It only addresses their *gender*—how one feels in relation to their sex and how they choose to express that socially.[16]

Still, whatever the case may be scientifically, the words *male* and *female* are now routinely interchangeable as if they have no fixed meaning. At worst, the use of these binary categories is seen as judg-mental and oppressive, while at best it is seen as archaic and outdated. Many see it as part of an older system that controls people through their identity and limits what they can do with their bodies (whom they sleep with, marry, love, etc.). One's gender is now viewed on a spectrum and is no longer binary (male *or* female). It is an *internal* distinction—how one feels about themselves. And this, we say, is who they *really are* versus how they were born or how society views them. In this movement of thought, the body is no longer a true indicator of one's identity. It gives no hint of reality. It is merely a physical thing. And so a person can be "trapped in the wrong body," we say, which must thus be manipulated and changed to fit the internal, psychological world of the individual so they can be free. How one *feels* about oneself is the deciding factor, and the body must adapt. One's gender should remain undetermined until the individual *decides* who or what they are, which could later change at any time based on their feelings. While there are certainly nuances, this is the current cultural thinking on the issue of sex and gender.

But what are the implications of this way of thinking for us more broadly as human beings? To be honest, we don't know yet. At the bare minimum there is a level of cultural confusion. "If the inner psychological life of the individual is now sovereign, then identity becomes as potentially unlimited as the human imagination."[17] This has caused great confusion for the individual and affected every sphere of society: the healthcare industry, sports, education, science, religion, psychology, and politics. Each sector has had to adjust in light of this cultural shift. It is no exaggeration to suggest that how one thinks about gender and sex is the defining issue of our time. Dr. Debra Soh, a neuroscientist whose work argues against the cultural tide of numerous genders and contends for a more traditional model, has been criticized and threatened for her research because, as she says, "scientific research is no longer about exploring new ground" or explaining what is true, but is now about "promoting ideas that make people happy."[18] She explains that in the modern academic world, it is next to impossible to distinguish *politically* motivated ideas from *scientific* truth because science is threatened constantly by the sway of politics.[19] She, along with many other scientists, concludes that

> biological sex is either male or female. . . . Sex is defined by gametes, which are mature reproductive cells. There are only two types: small ones called sperm that are produced by males, and large ones called eggs produced by females. . . . Biology, not society, dictates whether we are gender-typical or atypical. . . . At about seven weeks, if the embryo is male, the testes will begin to secrete testosterone, masculinizing the brain. If the embryo is female, this process does not occur.[20]

Again, science tells us that we are male or female at the cellular level. At the chromosomal level it is indisputable that women have XX chromosomes and men have XY chromosomes.

It is also true that men and women are different at the *brain level*. Dr. Louann Brizendine, a neuropsychiatrist at the University of California, San Francisco, and previously on the faculty of Harvard Medical School, explores the differences between male and female brains in her *New York Times* bestselling book, *The Female Brain*. In utero, she says, the male brain floods with testosterone, which increases sexual urges and aggression, and the female brain floods with estrogen, which increases information laneways across the left and right hemispheres. The male brain is also 9 percent larger than the female brain, on average, though men and women have the same number of brain cells. Women's brain cells are simply packed more densely into a smaller skull. The female brain fully develops two years earlier than the male brain and is far more attuned to reading faces and hearing emotional tones in voices and responding to unspoken cues in others. It is a machine built for connection.[21] These differences aren't a matter of right or wrong or which is better; they are just different. And this is a key point for us to hold to: men and women have clear differences biologically, physically, emotionally, spiritually, and even chemically, and those differences matter. They aren't arbitrary; nor are they meant to be set aside, ignored, or overhauled as if they are secondary to what it means to "find ourselves," as if our feelings are the only true indicator of who we really are. Yet this is the modern position; "with its stress on how we ourselves have a godlike power to create truth, it lends itself to the repudiation of stable categories such as male and female."[22]

Richard Dawkins, J. K. Rowling, and Serena Williams Walk into a Bar

The basic science behind the biology of sex and gender is clear, but, Soh says, these conclusions have now been *canceled*. Science has been overruled by activists, philosophers, and psychologists, which is ironic, as we have just emerged from an intellectual age wherein Christians were told to listen to the science and stop fighting against it. "Science deals with truth," we were told, "so get in line and don't base your conclusions on subjective experiences of feelings, or prayer, or whatever; believe what the cold scientific lab tells us. About ourselves, God, the world, etc." Now, just a few decades later, our culture is telling people to do the opposite.

One of the most well-known opponents of Christianity for the past three decades has been a scientist named Richard Dawkins. Years ago he wrote a bestselling book debunking the concept of God called *The God Delusion*. Yet on the issue of sex and gender, he agrees with the traditional view of gender, not because he wants to or has some religious reason to (he doesn't!) but *because of the science*. "As a biologist, there are two sexes, and that's all there is to it. . . . Sex really is binary. You're either male or female, and it's absolutely clear you can do it on gamete size. You can do it on chromosomes. To me, as a biologist, it's distinctly weird that people can simply declare 'I am a woman though I have a penis.'"[23] He says that any challenge to these conclusions is a "distortion of reality," and while he would be willing to refer to people by their preferred pronouns, he refuses to refer to biological men as women. "To say 'I am a woman' is a debauchery of language and that's where I draw the line," he says.

Another unforeseen ramification of this ideological shift is that it may end up being oppressive and dismissive of the social justice work of past generations. Take the fight for women's equality. Because women lacked the cultural power and influence of men, they have worked for hundreds of years to be respected as equals in society. Yet today, these gains are now being relativized because to protect women's rights we must first be able to say *what a woman is*. For women to be treated equally in the workplace, they must be distinguishable from men. There are many examples of where biological women have lost the gains they've made in recent years. Perhaps the most obvious are the many trans women who have won women's sporting events by wide margins (swimming, track, running, boxing, etc.) because by nature males have a biological advantage and are generally larger, faster, and stronger than women. When men transition, they carry that unfair advantage into competition. Today even saying *this* will get you canceled. Recently, a 2013 interview with Serena Williams, one of the greatest women tennis players of all time, resurfaced, wherein talking to David Letterman she said, "For me, men's tennis and women's tennis are completely, almost, two separate sports. If I were to play Andy Murray, I would lose 6–0, 6–0 in five to six minutes, maybe 10 minutes. No, it's true. It's a completely different sport. The men are a lot faster, and they serve harder, they hit harder, it's just a different game. I love to play women's tennis. I only want to play girls because I don't want to be embarrassed."[24]

People criticized Williams at a fever pitch and called for her to be canceled because of this interview, but she is not saying anything unusual or radical. She is simply interacting with the givenness of things, how nature has ascribed certain traits to men and others to women. Cardiologist Paula Johnson points out this reality from a scientific angle versus a social or political one, saying, "Every cell has a sex—and what that means is that men and women are different down to the cellular and molecular level. It means that we're different across all our organs, from our brains to our hearts, our lungs, our joints."[25] In other words, no matter what your gender philosophy is, when you are ill and the doctors put you on the operating table, they still need to know your original biological sex to give you the best possible care. What is inside and outside *really* counts. Science, not just psychology or philosophy or politics, really matters. And it impacts the real world in every way.[26]

These questions about sex and gender apply to many related aspects of our identity. Consider the question of race. I'll never forget the day during the pandemic when my friend called a walk-in clinic in Canada, where we lived at the time, because he wanted to receive the COVID vaccine. He was told the wait would be weeks. But then the person on the other end of the phone asked, "Are you First Nations?" (This refers to the people group in Canada who were the original settlers in the land and who have special tax status, etc. and who at the time were able to get the vaccine earlier than the general population). As a white German man, he quickly said no and was about to hang up, but the person on the other end quickly added a follow-up question that took him by surprise: "Are you identifying as one today?" He paused for a moment to let that question sink in. Was that really an option? Could he identify as a race he didn't belong to *in reality*? I can think of nothing more offensive to First Nations people than for anyone at any time having the option of choosing just to "identify" as one of them. After all, this is a people group that has been oppressed, tortured, killed, and marginalized for hundreds of years. How could this be?

Where does it all end? Who decides when this reality-denying relativism goes too far? Is it not the case that men being able to be identified and celebrated as women in ways that biological women haven't been yet turns out to be a way that the patriarchy so many of them have been fighting actually continues? After hundreds of years of women fighting feminist battles to be treated as equal to men in the workplace, culture, family, etc., is it not the case that that work is now being threatened?

In June 2020 the author of the Harry Potter series, J. K. Rowling, spoke into this debate, creating a firestorm with a single tweet. She was reacting to an article about creating equality and the hygiene practices of poorer communities globally. The article cited the hygiene needs of girls, women, "and all people who menstruate."[27] Rowling reposted the article with this comment: "People who menstruate? I'm sure there used to be a word for those people. Someone help me out. Wumben? Wimpund? Woomud?" And so began Rowling's challenge of trans ideology, which, as a feminist, she views as dangerous for the future of women. She also believes it is working *against* the advances the gay community has made over the last three decades: "If sex isn't real, there's no same-sex attraction," she says. Her point in relation to homosexuality is a pressing one worth considering. For most of the past thirty years, our culture was forcibly told to embrace the idea that a person is "born this way" (as Lady Gaga sang it). But now, in a retreat from that, declaring you are born a certain way (whether that is physical or emotional) is supposedly *not* a sign of who you really are at all. Instead, you're not born any particular way and should be open to adapting to whatever you want to be. Rowling, with her feminist filter on, makes the point clear that sex matters: "If sex isn't real, the lived reality of women globally is erased. I know and love trans people, but erasing the concept of sex removes the ability of many to meaningfully discuss their lives. It isn't hate to speak the truth."[28]

The debate will continue, with one side contending that love means we accept what anyone feels they are, without question or challenge, and the other side contending that love means there are limits to all this. It is difficult to deny there must be limits of some kind; the question is who decides what those are. For example, can people choose to identify as Black when according to biology they aren't? Or what about age, wherein people choose to identify as younger than they are to get certain benefits with dating? A new category to this conversation is those who are sexually attracted to children. This type of person is being called a MAP, which stands for minor-attracted person. And some believe they are or should have been disabled or handicapped and then choose to make themselves that way through amputation or forced paralysis. I recently read of one person who believed they were supposed to be blind and so made themselves blind. This is a very rare and extreme condition, but it is common enough that it has a name. It is referred to as body integrity dysphoria (BID) because these individuals felt internally that being disabled or blind was who they were *supposed* to be.[29]

These are serious issues, of course, but they also raise questions about who controls what we say and the words and language we utilize to communicate. As Ron Dart notes, "Western society is not simply built on free speech, but *true* speech because that forms the structure of any justly created order."[30] This means there is a shared assumption that we use words (pronouns in this case) truthfully (to represent reality) rather than in accordance with social or political pressure. Communicating in ways that are true and real is essential to having a working, functioning social order.

As a pastor, I see people walking through these issues every day, whether they are wrestling with gender dysphoria or simply grappling with this worldview and trying to think clearly about the issue. I stress that it is important for us to deal with this delicately. It is easy to forget that this isn't simply a political or psychological issue and that in fact these are real people and real feelings. Jesus was clear that in our interactions with others we should be full of not only truth but grace as well.

I remember in the early days of our church I met with a young man for several months. He had no church background and a lot of questions. I would meet him for coffee, read the Bible with him, and do my best to answer his questions about Jesus and how salvation works. He was sincere, humble, and excited about his new faith. In particular, I remember the day we talked about human sexuality, and he had a lot of questions about how it all worked from a biblical perspective. We read Genesis 1 and 2 together, and I explained, to the best of my knowledge, how the binary realities of male and female seem to be part of how human beings carry and reflect the image of God into the world. I remember him sitting back in his chair and thinking deeply, as if he had never heard or thought of it before. We continued studying God's Word together with vigor and excitement, and a few months later he came to know Christ and was baptized. He met a girl at the church, started serving, and began attending a small group.

One day I was talking to someone in the church lobby who had grown up with this young man, and they said to me, "You know he used to be a girl, right?" That stopped me in my tracks. "What do you mean?" I asked. They shared how they knew this person when he was a she and how a few years ago she had decided to transition to male. She started taking testosterone pills and over time became the person I had been hanging out with all this time, just another young man in the community (I was mentoring several at the time) with a beard, chest hair, and baggy jeans. This was my first experience with someone in this scenario, but it wasn't my last. And each and every time, I remind myself that in front of me is a person with hopes and dreams and convictions and a past and a soul connected to a body. They are a person God loves and made in his image.

This is not an exhaustive commentary or a comprehensive theology on the topic of transgenderism (that would be outside the scope of this book) but some preliminary thoughts on the topic. We can't think about being human in our time without addressing the question of sexuality and gender at some level, and it is an interesting case study of what we are talking about here: the tendency of our species to at times *break out of our limitations* of not being in control, and even to apply control to areas of our lives where we are not meant to. Instead of accepting that we are creatures, we attempt to be creators, believing in ways akin to ancient Gnosticism that the physical world has nothing to do with our identity and that who we really are is up to us. We treat the reality we've been dealt as an illusion and declare that the truth is not external but internal and private and spiritual as opposed to anything physical or biological. The Bible, however, pushes against our temptation to think this way, affirming the inherent goodness of physical creation. Further, it tells us that the physical world is a pointer to a deeper reality, that our bodies are a central and important part of who we are in every way. What if it really is the case that God stitched us together in our mother's womb and our frame was not hidden from him (Ps. 139:13, 15)? If this is true and we were created by design, this has much to say about who we are and why we were placed on this planet. And even more, it tells us God knew what he was doing when he made us in love.

In our journey to find ourselves as we wrestle with our identity, we have to come to terms with the fact that we're not animals (against naturalistic evolution) and we're not gods (against modern ideology). We are something more than the first and less than the second, and any other view falls off the narrow ledge of truth on one side or the other. We can *underestimate* ourselves and see ourselves as nothing more than creatures who should do whatever we want with our bodies and our lives, or we can *overestimate* ourselves, believing we can heal all things through our efforts, achieving our own salvation through psychology, technology, or even things like politics, art, business, and education. Both of these errors miss the truth of who God says we really are, leading us down a wrong path as we seek to discover our unique place in the world.

So it is the case that to truly live, we must reject outright the constant temptation to be God.

CHAPTER 4

Look Up,
NOT IN

*To realize one's destiny is a person's only
obligation.*

—PAULO COELHO, *THE ALCHEMIST*

A few years ago, my wife, Erin, and I were invited to a Christmas Eve party with some friends. I had been preaching all day at several Christmas Eve services and was looking forward to unwinding. My wife had planned the party with her friend via text and decided that instead of being a more formal dress-up type of party, it would have a more laid-back, old-school, like-we-were-kids vibe. The key component for this story: everyone had to wear Christmas onesie pajamas.

I was not particularly excited about that. The only Christmas onesie pajamas I had were a little small on me and looked ridiculous. I know I asked Erin four times whether we *really* needed to wear these silly outfits. She was certain we did. It was all in the text invitation.

And so, after finishing up my preaching, I swapped my nice suit for the onesie, and our family piled into the car laden with food and games. The house was already alive with buzz and energy when we stepped up to the porch and knocked on the door. As we waited for our hosts to greet us, I peered through the window—and to my horror I saw that everyone in the house was dressed in suits and gowns, eating classy appetizers from trays and sipping champagne. And there we were: five morons in green-and-red onesies holding chip dip. "Let's get out of here!" I exclaimed to my wife. But it was too late. Our hosts had already opened the door.

To make a long story short, we were stuck and spent the entire evening at the most formal party of the year looking like we'd just come off the set of the movie *Elf.*

Later, Erin carefully reread her text invitation: it invited everyone to bring along onesie pajamas to change into *after* the party while we opened some gifts with the kids. It was all there in black and white—we had just breezed over the details.

Here is the lesson I learned very painfully that day: Pay close attention to the details. This is especially true when God himself is giving us details about *the most important* things. This is exactly what he does in one of the central moments of Jesus's life and ministry. Picture it: A crowd has gathered around Jesus, and a brave soul steps out and asks him this question: What is the most important thing we can do in our lives? Which, of all the six hundred commands in the Bible, is the most important to follow? (Mark 12:28). In other words, what should we center our lives on, above and beyond anything else?

Jesus answers him clearly, which is great if we *pay attention* to his answer. Will we read the details and heed them, or just know them in theory? If we ignore his words, the stakes are higher than looking dumb at a party. They are everything—in this life and the next. His answer gets to the heart of what it means to exist and flourish as a human being, and it does so in ways we often don't notice or appreciate.

Jesus's answer to the man's question was this: "'Love the Lord your God with all your heart and with all your soul and with all your mind and with all your strength,'" and "'Love your neighbor *as yourself.*' There is no other commandment greater than these" (Mark 12:30–31, emphasis added). Jesus was as clear as can be.

But have you ever stopped to ask: What does Jesus mean by "yourself"? What even is that? What makes up a person's self? What dynamics are at play when this "self" journeys through the world interacting with others just like it?

Sacred Order

One of the primary challenges we face is what Mark Sayers describes as "the enthroning of the self as the greatest authority."[1] Regarding the topic explored earlier, who could have predicted a generation ago that one of the most offensive, scandalous verses in the Bible would be "[God] created them male and female" (Gen. 1:27 GNT)? We have failed to see this proclamation over us for what it is—not a statement of control by a traditional, religious patriarchy but the climax of a great and sacred story. N. T. Wright points out exactly this when he contends that the way the creation account is told is: God creates light and dark, day and night, sea and sky, water and land, sun and moon. All these binary realities are meant to complement one another and to set up the final and most glorious of all: male and female. Opposites in many ways, not just externally but internally too. Yet *together* in the beautiful vision of creation, they reflect God into the world in a way that one alone by itself or several on a spectrum just don't.

When we say we have no limits and can determine our nature for ourselves, we are grasping for self-determination, for a role that was previously God's alone, ascribing it to human beings. We think we are now gods with the right to say, "I AM WHO I AM" (Ex. 3:14). Yet this is a lie: "Human beings are not self-explanatory. They derive their meaning from outside themselves, from God. . . . We are not autonomous individuals, creating ourselves constantly by the decisions and choices we make. No, we are images, we are reflections. The dignity of our humanity is derivative. . . . We are dependent beings."[2] In other words, we don't *own* ourselves, and we have no authority to remake ourselves at will.

Fifty years before our current controversies, the Jewish philosopher Martin Buber looked into the future and predicted our situation: a world where we elevate "personal development and the preference of spirituality over religion."³ Of course, we have arrived at that place, saying that God's opinions on something have ceased to have relevance, whether that be family, money, beauty, forgiveness, war—anything that matters deeply to us.

We keep forgetting, or not caring, that there is built into the fabric of creation *a* way and the more we push against it the more we go out of tune. Our culture encourages us to push back against any givenness or authority—even if it comes from God—and to see it as limiting and oppressive: "It takes sacred order and not only casts doubt on it but makes it *repulsive*."⁴ It believes the order of things is somehow *wrong*, misguided, and even immoral: "Religion is not rendered untrue. It is made distasteful and disgusting."⁵

At the very least, we should question whether this might be a dangerous direction for us to go, especially if the warning of the philosopher Philip Rieff turns out to be even half true: "Culture and sacred order are inseparable. . . . And no culture has ever preserved itself where it is not a registration of sacred order. . . . The notion of a culture that persists independent of all sacred orders is unprecedented in human history."⁶ This is a haunting warning, and the solution to this cultural arrogance, the pushing back against the sacred order, is humility. The humility to admit that we are not gods, or God, but creatures who need to come under a way of things and, in the end, need saving. This is hard to admit; maybe that's why pride has been called the "great sin." It was a lesson I learned at the Christmas party that night: that for all my efforts to be the cool guy who has it all together, I'm just a man in a onesie standing somewhat naked before the world. And yet, by embracing that realization, I find my way into the kingdom (Matt. 18:1–3). In humility, the door opens for us to come in, not over or as God, but under him.

When my second daughter was born, I spent several hours walking around the hospital with her as my wife recovered from surgery. Nurses and doctors would ask me her name, and I, being a J. R. R. Tolkien fan, would excitedly say, "Arwen"—one of the elven princesses from *The Lord of the Rings*. For two hours, my daughter's name was Arwen. And then my wife came to. When the nurse asked her what our daughter's name was, she said, "Hayden." My dream was shattered.

Parents get to name their children. And part of that is because they have authority over that child. They are saying, This child comes under my care and guidance. In the creation story, Adam names the animals because he now has authority over them, but let's not forget that God names Adam. Have you ever noticed that in the Christmas story Joseph and Mary don't get to name Jesus? Instead, the angel—speaking on behalf of God—commands them to name him Jesus. Even Mary and Joseph don't get to rule over Jesus; they must come under his authority if they want to truly live.[7] It's the same with us. We must come to the end of ourselves and place our whole self into his hands. For all our human ingenuity, all our education and technology and art and accomplishment, we are still vulnerable, insecure, and unsure of ourselves. We are groping in the dark and subject to the ultimate offense against our self-determination: sickness and death. We haven't solved these, nor have we solved the problem of ourselves, the problem of life. We need to come under the authority of the One who can. That is the order of things—the only order that sets us truly free.

We tend to have a form of amnesia about our true situation and history. As Andrew Wilson points out in his *Remaking the World*, there are progressive and conservative versions of this amnesia. The progressive version is that our current morals are correct, which means anyone who thought differently a hundred years ago or even ten years ago must have been (and still is) stupid or evil or both. The conservative version is that the only reason for a person's success is their own ability and effort, which means anyone who points out any historical advantages, privileges, or oppressions must be either jealous or lazy. In contrast to either version, Wilson says that our memory of reality "should generate humility" on both sides.[8] Both sides should recognize that their version of things is not 100 percent right or fair in its assessment of the situation. But this kind of humility is hard to come by today.

To admit we aren't always right and may need some help or guidance from God because we're not gods ourselves is hard—but it is the first step toward truly human life.

Our modern world is driven by the question "Who am I?" A menu of choices drives the market, dividing us into camps and groups so we know where we belong and where we don't. But Christianity says this is not the real question we must answer, or at least not the *first* question. That question is one Jesus posed to his disciples: "Who do you say I am?" (Matt. 16:15). In other words, the question is not just "Who am I?" but "*Whose* am I?"[9] Who do I belong to in this universe?

Saint Augustine takes us deeper on this point, saying we must depend on God in our identity quest because while we are looking inward to understand who we are, in the end it turns out that "God is more inward than my most inward part and higher than the highest element within me."[10] There is someone who is closer to me than I am to myself, who knows me better than I can know myself. This challenges our ideology of a closed, self-sufficient person: the pure individual who finds themselves by looking inside *in isolation from God or their own soul.* So American sociologist Christian Smith's conclusions about who or what we are as a species ring true:

Human beings are free, ensouled creatures of a particular kind, with the kind of nature about which we must get over our mental and emotional difficulties. . . . They are material, embodied animals, nurtured and sustained in a physical world governed by causal powers and laws and their natural effects that we cannot simply deconstruct away. . . . Reductionistic moves toward either the physical or the spiritual, the material or the ideal are unacceptable and self-defeating. Humans are embodied souls who can only be well understood and explained in light of that complexity.[11]

Sea World and Why We Are So Anxious

When I was in college, many of my non-Christian friends made fun of my belief in God and yet at the same time were staunch environmentalists. "God doesn't exist," they said, "but we are morally obligated to protect the earth from the capitalist power structures that rape and pillage it for profit!" They held a purely naturalist view of the world wherein there is no spiritual component, no enchantment, no absolute moral standard given by God. I understood why they felt so strongly about protecting the earth, but their logic was contradictory. As the writer Kirsten Birkett points out, it is not "only humanity that fails to matter if there is nothing more than the natural world. Ironically, the natural world ceases to matter as well."[12] If everything in the world is nothing but a collection of atoms and molecules, it is simply the case that "some of us like our collections of atoms in the form of trees and meadows. Others prefer cars and fuel. But who is to say which is better?"[13]

Without an organizing principle behind the universe, there is no authority to say one way is better and nobler than another. If the individual is the authority, then individual opinions rule. If one person wants to shut down Sea World and save the trees and another wants to empty the oceans of sharks or whales for soup, who is to say which is nobler? If there is no God and no transcendent reality that enchants the world beyond our senses, then no one can or should decide these things.

But we do just that. We elevate the self above anything outside the self, without any obligation to anything outside of us, whether that is God or even society. We have moved away from the class struggles of the 1950s and '60s and the science/theology/philosophy emphasis of the previous fifteen hundred years and have moved to an emphasis on the self. Politics, science, and theology have been replaced by psychology. Where past generations found their identity in revolutions aimed at changing external forces (the abolition of slavery, the civil rights movement, feminism, etc.), we've exchanged those for therapeutic quests to discover individual fulfillment. *Social* revolution has been replaced by *personal* revolution.[14]

At one time in Western culture, the Bible and other religious texts (the Talmud, the Qur'an, etc.) carried authority that guided our ethics and moral standards. People believed these ethical norms were good, true, and beautiful, able to take us beyond ourselves into the will of God. People looked to these texts for answers to their questions of how to think and behave, what to value, what was right and wrong, and even what humankind was. In our time, religious texts have been replaced by personal experiences and individual desires, preferences, and feelings. The new religion of the West is personal development, and we prefer spirituality over religion.

But the elevation of self in the attempt to heal ourselves is a failed experiment. The prioritizing of ourselves, however, is starting to bite back, which is why the West is facing a level of private crisis on a scale we have never seen before, with rising rates of anxiety, suicide, isolation, and depression.[15] Our attempts to take control of the world are revealed to be based on a "hugely inflated estimation of human potential."[16] We feel the need to be in control, to be the final sovereigns over it all, but we aren't up to the task. "The vast expansion of human responsibility in and for the world, while liberating us from the supposed suffocating weight of such things as tradition and religion, has turned out to be a heavy burden"[17]—one, I think, we cannot bear.

How to Be Free

Today, we believe freedom is the highest good—that being free is the heroic story we are all living out. Giving individuals that freedom is now the primary task of institutions, science, art, and even the church. One of the doctrines of this new religion is that, if I am free, I may do whatever gives me pleasure, because that is my "true self." But if freedom is the ability to do whatever one *wants*, what happens when one's wants conflict with each other or with those of others?

Timothy Keller suggested we imagine a man in his sixties who likes to eat whatever he wants but also loves to spend time with his grandchildren. Both activities are important to him. At his annual checkup, his doctor says, "Unless you seriously change up your eating habits, you are going to die soon of a heart attack. You must stop eating your favorite foods." If he doesn't change what he eats (a restriction), he will lose the freedom to be with his grandchildren. "It is impossible that he will have freedom in both areas. There is, then, not just one thing called 'freedom' that we either have or do not have. At the level of life lived there are *numerous freedoms*, and no one can have all of them. . . . The question is not, then: how can this man live in complete freedom? The proper question is: which freedom is the more important, the more truly liberating?"[18]

Freedom turns out to be more complicated than we think, even at the individual level. But it makes more sense when lined up with the true nature of things, the God-given shape to life wherein we accept our limitations. Like a fish in water, we find our flourishing in how we were designed and made, submitting to the limitations of water rather than seeing it as a form of oppression. Pushing back against this design not only suffocates us but can leave us shriveled and dead. We work against our ultimate joy rather than seeking to accomplish it.

Contrary to our culture's narrative of the human being having godlike power and control, the vision of God is that we find ourselves by "*giving up the right to self-determination*," and instead dying to self and following Christ.[19] I love how this is expressed in the closing words of my favorite book, *Mere Christianity*:

> The principle runs through all life from top to bottom. Give up yourself, and you will find your real self. Lose your life and you will save it. Submit to death, death of your ambitions and favorite wishes every day and death of your whole body in the end: submit with every fiber of your being, and you will find eternal life. Nothing that you have not given away will ever be really yours. Nothing in you that has not died will ever be raised from the dead. Look for yourself, and you will find in the long run only hatred, loneliness, despair, rage, ruin, and decay. But look for Christ and you will find Him, and with Him everything else thrown in.[20]

False Gods and Trying to Gain from Life

When we take matters into our own hands and do our best to be creators versus creatures, what was previously seen as fate in regard to our identity (being this or that personality, or race, or whatever) now becomes "an arena of choices" wherein we find "salvation" in remaking ourselves any way we want.[21] We assume we are the ones doing the making, investing the world with meaning we have created as if there were no givenness to things. We argue about things like "justice" and "dignity" and "freedom" as if these things belong to us or to the *political arena* and can be offered to us by one party or the other by their policies. But could it be the case that we have this wrong? That these things are part of *a created moral order* and that our social and political organizations end up posing a threat to them because the tendency of power is to corrupt and the tendency of political aspirations is to eclipse all other human purposes (i.e., serving God)?[22] I think so. As it has been said, when you mix religion and politics, you get politics.

It is in our nature to "transcendentalize" things, to make gods out of things, to see a good and then say it is an *ultimate* good. The Bible calls this idolatry, and it is arguably the sin behind all the sins. We don't just remove God from our way of life; we *replace* him. We take the normal everyday things that are part of the created order, and we *deify* them. Money, sex, power, family, relationships, status, beauty— these define our lives, and we look to them to give us happiness and joy and peace. We shape our souls around them as if having them is the most important thing, and then they take and take and take.

- We become workaholics because we never have enough money.
- We live life in anxiety, terrified something will happen to our relationships or our family or our looks.
- We find ourselves lying to get ahead or insecure because we've defined ourselves by the people around us and how good they are doing at their jobs or their finances or their marriages.
- We go through the day fantasizing about others because our sexual urges, originally a good and beautiful thing put there by God to play out in the context of marriage, have been warped by distorted images and are now impossible to satisfy. But it doesn't stop us from trying—over and over again.

One writer has said the way to figure out what your idols are is to ask yourself, "What, if I lost it, would make me not want to go on living anymore? What would suck all the joy out of my life?"[23] Maybe it's a spouse, or a family member, or money, or your house, or your beauty. There are endless options, of course. One of the things we all must do is put our finger on what our idols are. If we don't know what enslaves us, we will never be free.

So what *good* thing in your life has become a *god* thing? What are you chasing after at the cost of everything else? As a pastor friend of mine often says, what if our lives are a mess partly because we are catching what we are chasing? Many of us are chasing things that aren't God, and this is playing out in our lives. The daily choices we make shape us throughout life. As my friend says, "When we are born, we look like our parents, and when we die, we look like our choices."

We now begin to see Jesus's answer to the problem of life, why Jesus said the most important thing we can do is love God with our whole heart, soul, mind, and strength (Luke 10:27). This isn't another pithy religious saying. Rather, it is the great strategy to defeat the dehumanizing, soul-turning habits of idolatry. Jesus knows the human heart can't *remove* an idol; it must *replace* the idol with something it loves more, exchanging an old love for a new one.[24]

Searching inwardly for our true self or looking outwardly to this political group or that social one won't fill the void. Loving God with our whole heart and soul and mind and strength is the *only* balm for the wounds that run deep in our souls.

Psychologizing ourselves and looking inward isn't all bad. No doubt it has given us some helpful insights as we've delved deeper into the human psyche. We have a better understanding of what helps and hurts us, but it has also had what sociologists call "a boomerang effect." All our inward searching has taken the weight of life and placed it upon *us* rather than pointing us to something bigger than ourselves. It has left us struggling to carry the weight and burden—and that is breaking us. The solution to this problem is *living in light of the way things are* instead of trying to create our own order. And this is where the ancient wisdom may be more helpful than the latest psychological study. As Old Testament scholar Iain Provan points out in his commentary on the book of Ecclesiastes,

> The message of the Bible is that to all those trying to "gain" from life: the universe is not designed to enable "gain" to happen, and those who attempt to fly in the face of reality can only ever know grief and frustration in the end. The universe is not designed to contain gods and heroes, but mortal beings who accept the limitations that have been set upon their lives and get on with them in humility. This life on earth is intended to have as its center the God who created everything and who holds everything in his hand.[25]

In contrast to the repeated modern failures to fix our problems, Christianity offers a beautiful solution. It invites us to a way of life in which we find our personal identity rooted in a reality *beyond* us (the one true God) but also *before* us (the one true world). Unlike myths of the ancient past, which present us with distorted versions of both, Christianity says we were *created* and *designed* in a particular way and for a particular purpose, and when we conform our lives around that, even with all its limitations, we become all we could ever be.

Contrary to New Age and Eastern religious philosophy, life and pain are not just an illusion. Tragedy and suffering really exist, and yet we aren't the ones who can ultimately change that. The reason for the brokenness and pain is relational disconnection from our Creator, what the Bible calls sin; and God, not us, has solved it all. He made a way to put the world to rights that we can either reject or align ourselves with, and for those who embrace his way, a future is coming that will not *erase* all brokenness but *restore* it; and that reality changes everything about how we live now.

There is a story taking place on a higher plane than the observable world. Sometimes we catch glimpses of it. But most of us go through life unaware of the reality behind the reality we see—the true story being told. This is the story that shoots life full of meaning. It has been revealed and must be accepted, and if we believe, it tells us we are made for something. Something is happening, even when we are asleep or awake and bored and contributing nothing to it, because it isn't ultimately up to us to write this story. It's his story and he is over every part of it. We're not in a romantic comedy but an epic and cosmic adventure that is going somewhere.

That being said, it is also true that we matter in the telling; we have a part to play. We are needed to hold back the evil, as *servants* of the One who will defeat it, but not as the heroes. Our identity is found in embracing our God-given task to turn the wild and waste into beauty and awe, all pointing to him, the one there in the midst of thorns and thistles and cancer and all things "unnatural."

Some of you don't believe you are needed for this fight. I often speak to people who feel unneeded, and I believe it is one of the epidemics of our species—a lie that, once believed, shrivels us and sends us to dark and isolated places. I remember a scene from an old movie where the father is trying to explain to his family why he worked so much. He begins by appealing to the idea that men had to provide for their families. And then he stops himself and says, "You know what? That wasn't why. It was because at work I knew who I was, and I was needed, but at home . . . I felt *useless*." As a husband to a very competent wife and also a father of three girls, I can relate. At work I feel important and needed; at home sometimes, though, I am just in the way. "Dad, why did you put that there!" "Dad, why did you do this!"

"Honey, did you forget to take out the garbage again?" (*Send me back to work!*) This feeling is common among both men and women: at work they are contributing, problem-solving, leading, making a difference, while homelife feels slow and monotonous. The world is moving and shaking and evolving and changing, and they feel like they are standing still. Exciting things are happening outside their window, but they are left to watch. Depression, anxiety, fear, and frustration follow. They have a million things to offer but feel stifled and alone.

If this describes you, can I encourage you?

The biblical story says that *whatever* we are doing, however small and insignificant it may feel, matters. Our work, over time, accumulates and becomes a contribution to the world as it fits together with the contributions of others into the greater reality Jesus declared: *God's kingdom come, and his will be done, on earth.* Small things can lead to big things: the daily work of raising a child, the "quiet life" (1 Thess. 4:11–12) that impacts the world one person at a time, the small acts and gifts and blessings that feel like a mustard seed today but grow into a great tree that makes the world a brighter place. These efforts become part of God's work in staving off the darkness in your corner of the world. This is no small thing. C. S. Lewis, reflecting on his own domestic life, said:

> Before I became a Christian I do not think I fully realized that one's life, after conversion, would inevitably consist in doing most of the same things one had been doing before: one hopes, in a new spirit, but still the same things. . . . Christianity does not exclude any of the ordinary activities. . . . All of our merely natural activities will be accepted, if they are offered to God, even the humblest will be sinful if they are not. [As you pray to be conformed more and more to the likeness of Christ], you may realize that instead of saying your prayers, you ought to

be downstairs writing a letter, or helping wash-up after dinner. Well, go and do it.[26]

In other words, you are needed! And not because you will achieve big and flashy results or will be loved because of the work you do. No, first and foremost, we bring our contributions to the table as an offering to be used because we serve a God who loves us no matter how big or small we think our impact will be.

Believe me, it is far more than we can ever dream, even if we never know it in this life. All of this we come to live into when we do what we must: look up, not in, to find the meaning of life.

CHAPTER 5

Live as a Victor,
NOT A VICTIM

But in the end one needs more courage to live than to kill himself.

—ERNEST HEMINGWAY, A FAREWELL TO ARMS

Some of us look in the mirror and see a pale reflection of who we once were. Discouraged and wondering what went wrong, we catch a glimpse of an old picture, maybe of us as a kid, when our eyes were full of wonder and a future where the world was ours for the taking. Where we could become anything, but now all of that feels lost. We have made too many mistakes. We've failed at life, and the world seems set against us. The gods, it turns out, *are* angry, and they seem especially angry with us. Life feels chaotic.

Yet the Bible is hopeful. It contends that the universe is *not* chaotic. We don't live under the rule of a karmic system of a mindless universe that gives good things to good people and bad things to bad ones. Reality isn't driven by the selfish, lust-driven gods of myth and ancient religion. We live under the rule of a God *of order* who created order in this world. And if we follow, listen to, and obey that rule, things tend to work out more often than not.

This is where self-help books have a fundamental flaw. They

assume the universe is set up for you to succeed. The "force is with you" if you want it to be. But the biblical picture is more nuanced. While there is good, we live in a world that is contested; it's a world in conflict, a world bent on making sure that our flourishing *doesn't* happen. We must push back against a life that pushes back—and does so constantly. We catch glimpses of beauty and joy, but there is also pain, brokenness, disappointment, and discouragement at almost every turn, as if these realities are inescapable. We face pushback, inside us and around us. Childbirth brings pain, not pleasure. Work brings agonizing sweat on our brows. The ground has thorns and thistles that bite and sting. We will all experience pain and frustration and agony in our lives. I read somewhere recently that the fact we have scars simply means we have lived. Pointing this out is the easy part. The goal is to figure out *what to do about it*. How do we avoid the pitfalls and navigate a world where what we want is contested?

The Nature of Things

Let's start by embracing a basic conviction, one that is routinely ignored and directly challenged in modern Western culture in almost every sphere of society—education, media, psychology, politics, the arts, and even some in the scientific community—namely, that there is *an order to things*. The universe is set up to work better in some ways than in other ways. By careful observation we learn that a *givenness* to things is built into the fabric of creation—physically, socially, morally, spiritually. Either we conform to it and flourish, or we don't. For instance, we know we can't treat our bodies any way we want without consequence. Similarly, we can't treat people any way we want and expect to have good friends and a strong family. If we eat right and exercise, we will be more fit than if we don't. And loving our neighbor as we love ourselves generally leads to strong relationships and good community. The universe has a *mechanical* ordering. There are ways things were designed to function, ways of fueling ourselves so we grow, but also boundaries and limits we need to submit to.

Today we see this ordered design conflicting with the idea that each person's truth or way of being in the world is their own. Most people believe their life is private and to be lived out the way they want and not scrutinized by others. But we must be careful because as Christian Smith, professor of sociology at the University of Notre Dame, warns us,

> Many people today think that what is good for people is whatever they *think* is good for themselves. Everybody must decide what is good for his or her own life. I suggest that this view is wrong. . . . Human goods are not simply up to each individual to decide. There actually *are* real, true human goods. The implications of this are immense. . . . Human flourishing, well-being, and the resulting happiness are in some important sense *given by the facts of reality*, specified and guided by the *nature of things*.[1]

If this is so, Timothy Keller is right: "The only wisdom by which you can handle everyday things is in conformity with their nature and how they were divinely made and ordered."[2] Try fighting the law of gravity by jumping out of an airplane without a parachute. Or ignore your own design and attempt to breathe water like a fish. Sooner or later, you will realize that order can't be rearranged around your desires.

In the same way, there is also *a spiritual order* to things. The disordered life is out of tune, in disarray, not only with what we want or desire for ourselves but also with what actually is. Centering our lives on anything but God leads to a fragile identity. We become out of sync with reality. When things seem "off" in our lives—those times when our job isn't satisfying, our marriage seems out of whack, our temptations are getting the best of us—we must stop and ask, *In which areas of life might I be pushing against the fabric of ordered creation?*[3] *How might I be living in a way that doesn't recognize the order of things in this world?* This disorder is what drives our discontentment and dysfunction, not the other way around. It's not that we are unhappy because we don't have what we want. It's that what we want is sometimes wrong and misguided; our desires are shaped by a less-than-ideal reality, a kind of nonreality, that is not as solid as that which makes us flourish and find peace.

The truth, as theologian J. I. Packer says—and we all must hear this—is that "we are cruel to ourselves if we try to live in this world without knowing about the God whose world it is and who runs it. The world becomes a strange, painful place, and life in it a disappointing and unpleasant business, for those who do not know God."[4] Disregard him and we are bound to stumble and blunder our way through life blindfolded, with no sense of direction. The theologian Richard Lovelace points out that people who aren't sure "God loves and accepts them in Jesus apart from their achievements, are subconsciously radically *insecure persons*," he says. "Their insecurity shows itself in pride, a fierce defensive assertion of their own righteousness and defensive criticism of others."[5]

This is what I love about Christianity. Not only is it true; it is *wonderful.* It works to solve your real problems. It makes your life and the lives of those around you better in every way. We can all agree that a way of being in the world that is not driven by pride or envy or insecurity or guilt or fear is better than one that is. Objectively, it is just true. Insecure people filled with pride and defensiveness hurt the world. The solution to which isn't inside of them but in their experience and knowledge of something outside of them—something or rather someone who loves them deeply despite themselves and secures them in a kind of salvation that changes not only what they do but what they *want* to do. And what they want to live for! This is not just a different way but a better way to live this life.

This is why the biblical account begins with a choice: You can eat from this tree, and that one and that one, God says. In fact, you can eat from all of them, except this one—and if you listen to me, it will result in your flourishing (Gen. 2:16–17). But the first humans didn't listen, and they broke the world. They didn't heed G. K. Chesterton's warning that if you are taking down a fence, you may want to ask why it was built in the first place. The result: We inverted the gift of life in exchange for death, rejecting God's ordered way. This doesn't mean the order in the world was completely lost and all order dissolved, only that it has been poisoned. In other words, we die now and suffer, but we still have a soul.

The Coddling of the Modern Mind

This reconnection to God as a way to flourish isn't just about going to heaven when we die, as is often emphasized in modern Christianity. It has more immediate impact on our daily lives. It impacts our emotional life; the way we handle criticism, failure, mistakes; the way we make decisions; how we face our insecurities, our fears. To put it simply, knowing we are God's children, beloved and empowered and having received all things in him, can move us from feeling like victims to seeing ourselves as victors—"more than conquerors" as the apostle Paul says (Rom. 8:37).

We should be able to admit that we are broken people full of insecurity, pain, fears, and ego. Who hasn't faced trials? Who hasn't dealt with the challenges of life in an unhealthy way to some degree and then handed down that hurt and dysfunction to others? Who hasn't been the recipient of the dysfunction and failings of others? I certainly have.

My dad, aside from being an atheist, was also a deadbeat dad. He couldn't keep a job to save his life. He drank too much. He smoked too much (it killed him in the end). He left us when I was just seven years old. And when I was fifteen and he was dying of lung cancer, he never even called me or my brother to tell us he was sick so we could say goodbye. A few years before all that, the trauma of my parents' divorce broke my mind, and as I mentioned earlier, I developed Tourette syndrome. By the time I was age nine or ten, my symptoms were out of control. I would make weird noises, hit things a certain number of times, smack my hands together, swear, bang my nose. I had a hundred tics. Needless to say, none of this made life easy as a teenager—and it's still not great as a man in my forties, especially as a pastor and a preacher. My dad's dysfunction became my dysfunction. As they say, hurt people hurt people.

It would be easy for me to blame my father for all his flaws and how they impacted me. And he does play a part. We are not only the sum of the choices we make but also the product of choices others make. Our decisions, for good or ill, impact those around us to various degrees. My dad made his choices, and they negatively impacted me in ways a therapist would have a field day with. But life must always be framed in context. My dad himself grew up with an absentee father who was a rageaholic. He also had a schizophrenic sister who tried to kill herself on several occasions as they were growing up. He was the first to find her after those attempts. She would slit her wrists, take pills, or try to jump out of their moving car onto the highway. One day, in her early twenties, she finally succeeded by jumping off the roof of an apartment building. What choices would any of us make in my father's shoes? We can't know. Pain gives birth to pain, and we pass down that pain and the scars it creates to those closest to us. Not because we *want* to or intend to but because those we love most are in our orbit. The pain we cause is unintended collateral damage.

As I have understood more and more the work that God did in Christ, I have come to see the beauty of it as it relates to all of this. Most religion says, Yes, there is sin and brokenness, we are both violators and victims, but in the end we can't do much about it. Maybe work harder, try harder, do a few more good deeds to make the world a better place. That's about it. Christianity, however, has within it something theologians call "expiation," and while it is sometimes a neglected part of Christian teaching, it is helpful here because it tells us that Jesus's sacrifice on the cross cleanses us from not only our *own* sins but also the sins committed *against* us. The cross of Christ not only forgives our sins but also washes our lives clean from the ways the world has messed us up (1 John 1:9; Heb. 9:22). What better hope is there than that?

To put it practically, if you have experienced abuse, that wound may never fully heal (Jesus still had scars after he rose), but you can know that God washes you clean and you don't need to feel dirty anymore. The shame and guilt others have projected on you no longer need to define you. The voice of a parent or spouse who yelled at you doesn't need to echo in your heart any longer. The boss or stranger or family friend who went too far but then laughed it off doesn't get to ruin your life anymore. Why? Because Christianity offers a new identity; you're a new creation. In Christ, you are no longer defined by things others have done to you.

Pathways of Hope

This identity, given to us by God, transcends anything you or I may have done, as well as whatever has been done to you. If you are in Christ—no matter who you are, how hard your life has been, what others have said about you, to you, at you—God says you are no longer a victim but a victor. "To the one who is victorious," Jesus says, "I will give the right to sit with me on my throne, just as I was victorious and sat down with my Father on his throne" (Rev. 3:21). No matter who you are and what your life has been like, when your identity shifts from you-living-as-you-want to you-in-Christ, something cataclysmic happens. It is a fundamental shift from being whatever you were and however the world sees you to being so much more than you ever thought, dreamed, or imagined. God declares to you what he declared to Jesus in his baptism: You are "my beloved . . . with whom I am well pleased" (Matt. 3:17 ESV). You are now a new creation: "The old has gone, the new is here!" (2 Cor. 5:17).

So why is this so difficult for us to live out? One reason is that our culture feeds us the opposite message, that we aren't victors but victims. We are told that our pain and suffering will forever define us, that we will never rise up and out of our mistakes, that we will never escape our environment or the way we were raised or the failings of our past. For many, this identity has a profound negative effect on how their lives turn out.

The modern university is a great example of this. In their book *The Coddling of the American Mind*, Greg Lukianoff and Jonathan Haidt explore the landscape of university life in the Western world. What they expose is that students and parents alike now protest certain books as being "triggering" and get them removed from assignments and even libraries. Recently at Columbia University in New York City, a number of books were eliminated from the curriculum. These weren't weird books filled with perverse sexuality or violence. They were the writings of Ovid, Homer, Dante, and Augustine—all banned from a course titled Masterpieces of Western Literature![6] The problem was that these books, which have been read and discussed for over a thousand years, now made students feel unsafe.

Recently, Brown University hosted a debate between Wendy McElroy and Jessica Valenti, two feminist thinkers, on the concept of whether America is a rape culture. Valenti argued that it is, citing the misogyny that is endemic to American culture. McElroy, who was brutally raped and beaten as a teenager, leaving her blind in one eye, contended that the statistical data indicated that the framing of America as a rape culture was an overstatement. She felt it was not helpful to public discourse and took away from real examples of rape culture that exist in other places around the world.

Certainly, wherever you land on the issue, it seems like a worthy topic of debate at the highest levels of learning. But some students at Brown who strongly believed that America is a rape culture thought that even debating the question, as they said, "invalidated people's experiences" and would be damaging to them if the debate took place. Students rallied to get McElroy disinvited on the premise that the university should be a "safe space." But of course, these students weren't in any real danger. This was an exchange of ideas, and no one was forced to attend. The discussion then became more a question about whether safety for students at a university should include their emotional comfort.[7]

If institutions simply affirm our already-decided-upon ideas and biases about things (including ourselves), that will always just reinforce those narratives—and possibly us as victims in them—instead of equipping us to rise above what the world may say about us. As Adam Grant says, from a psychology perspective we don't just hesitate to rethink our answers to questions; we hesitate at the very idea of rethinking. "We favor the comfort of conviction over the discomfort of doubt. . . . We favor feeling right over being right."[8]

There are hundreds of examples of this across modern Western culture. My point in raising this is not to suggest we overlook or minimize pain and suffering. We must look honestly at the injustice in the world, the real inequities that exist, and the histories and systems wherein people groups are held back by powers and policies that won't let them get ahead. Certainly, these have existed for many in the black community throughout American history and in the First Nations communities in Canada. We see these issues in every culture, and they're very real. We must approach them carefully and honestly.

But the question still remains: What is our identity? Should we allow the pain and hate and evil of the world to define who we are? The beauty of the gospel whispers pathways of hope and a new future for all who have suffered. Prophetic visions upend the way things are. "Dreams," as Dr. Martin Luther King Jr. called them, give us a vision of life *different* from what we have experienced and what we have been handed. Not as idealistic and naive hopes but real visions of healing and freedom on both a corporate and, more to our point, an individual level. This vision tells us that the power of our mistakes and failings and those of others no longer has the final say or sway over us. Generational sin can be overthrown. Victims can become victors.

I know this because it has been true for me. Everything about my life says that I should be in jail or a gutter somewhere—anywhere but where I am. I grew up in a broken home, we didn't have much money to our family name, and the first time I did drugs I was no more than ten years old. By grade nine I was a smoker and partier, had mental illness, and rolled with the gang kids. I stole money from cars and houses to buy drugs. My life could have ended up very different—and if it had, I could have blamed it all on generational influence, my environment, or my deadbeat father.

But instead, I met Christ.

He told me I was a "new creation." He gave me a new identity, a new direction, and a new power to overcome the difficulties I faced. I took responsibility for my own life, worked hard, and by the grace of God escaped that certain future. I refused to be another cliché, just the product of the people around me. Instead, I decided that what God said was true and trusted he would make something of my life.

Not many believed me. They laughed when I said I wanted to be a pastor. Everyone in my world saw me as a dreamer. But as Tolkien reminds us, "At last, comes their answer, through cold and through frost. That not all who wonder, or wander, are lost."[9]

And that certainly ended up being true for me. I was a wonderer and a wanderer, lost for a time, but then, like the younger brother in Jesus's parable, I was found. I gained a Father who would never leave me, who would never drink too much or not hold down a job. The minute he saw me coming his way, he ran out to me, hugged me, wrapped his robe around me, and threw me a party. That kind of love changes a person.

That's the power of a new identity. Defining who you are in connection to the transcendent reality of God is one of the most important steps in the journey of life. It addresses one of the key problems of life, helping us realize that we can be more than the product of our past, that the stories everyone says or believes about us do not have to be true. Notice how the apostle Paul responded to criticism and approval: "Am I now trying to win the approval of human beings, or of God? . . . If I were still trying to please people, I would not be a servant of Christ" (Gal. 1:10). This is where life is found, a mode of existence beyond and above the mistakes and failures we make. Christ is in control, and he has given us a new identity that no one, and nothing in this world, can ever steal or damage!

It's Not Necessary That the Underdog Wins

Some of you are saying, "Okay, so to truly soar and find joy and solve the problem of life, we need to discover both God and ourselves. I really want to do that, but I am not the person you have described here. I'm a failure. I'm the one so impacted by the sins of my fathers or of others, or my own that I have derailed my life beyond recognition, beyond what can be salvaged. There is no hope for me." I understand. But I want you to know there is *no* life beyond repair. Every day is another opportunity to turn it all around. That doesn't mean you'll end up getting back everything you've lost or become rich or healthy again or whatever else the self-help gurus, or your own mind, say is the goal. That *could* happen—because God is good and powerful and wants to do amazing things in your life—but even if it doesn't, that doesn't mean God has abandoned you. Your hope is in more than a worldly view of success and accomplishment. There is another way to look at life, and it is found in the most unlikely of places: *in how you fail.*

A documentary about the battle between Tiger Woods and Rocco Mediate for the 2008 U.S. Open at Torrey Pines presents a back-and-forth duel for the ages.[10] The unknown Rocco—looking like a fish out of water as he walks around the course, buttons his sweater, laughs, smiles, and talks to the crowd—is up against the greatest of all time. Tiger is a terminator: silent, focused, and resolved to destroy anyone and anything in his way. It is a true David-versus-Goliath matchup. Tiger is one behind as he walks up to the last hole of the tournament, and he has to make a birdie. He hacks his ball out of the long rough, and it lands on the green. To force a playoff, he now has to make a thirteen-foot putt. Rocco, watching on the TV from the tent, waits in anticipation. Will he win a major championship? A win would change his life. Tiger drains the putt. The two of them go on to a full-day playoff the next day.

To this day, Rocco says, he will be walking around with his wife and people will ask him about that experience. He says it is one of the great joys of his life—battling all day, back and forth. That day, Tiger made a birdie, which required Rocco to drain a twenty-foot putt to continue. He missed it.

In the documentary, just before they show him missing the putt by an inch and losing, they ask him about greatness. "Am I a great golfer?" he responds. "No. Good? Yes. But not one of the greats." This would have been Rocco's first and only major championship. But it was Tiger's fourteenth. Despite the loss, Rocco smiled and shook Tiger's hand and has since carried on with life as one of the most beloved golfers to ever play the game. In fact, Rocco later said he was on a personally destructive path before that tournament, and if he had won, it likely would have catapulted him down a bad road. In its own way, that loss is something he counts as a blessing. He believes he would have lost much more in winning, perhaps his family, his health, and all he holds dear.

Near the end of the documentary, the announcer, Bob Costas, says a line I will never forget: "It's not necessary that the underdog *wins*, only that the underdog *gives a good account of himself.*" I've remembered that statement because I believe it to the core of my being. Most of us are *not* winners. According to the rules of the world, you may be a loser. You aren't financially killing it. Maybe your marriage is mediocre. Your job is a job, but not something you saw yourself doing when you were eight years old and dreaming of what you would one day be. You have made mistakes. You've failed time and time again, sinned against God and others more than you can count. And you feel like your losses and failures and faults have no upside, no glory to them.

But maybe they do. Maybe life isn't about being a winner but about *giving a good account of ourselves* even in the losses, in the difficulties of life. What if the rewards come, in this life and the next, because of how we respond to loss and difficulty, who we are in the fire versus when we're standing on the podium? And when people gather around at church or the cemetery to celebrate your life in the end, it won't be the wins or successes they talk about, but the way you lived your life through those trials. When you were up against the worst, they remember the *way you carried yourself.*

This is what the famous Rudyard Kipling poem is exploring when it says,

If you can keep your head when all about you
Are losing theirs and blaming it on you,
If you can trust yourself when all men doubt you,
But make allowance for their doubting too . . .

If you can dream—and not make dreams your master;
If you can think—and not make thoughts your aim;
If you can meet with Triumph and Disaster
And treat those two impostors just the same . . .
Or watch the things you gave your life to, broken,
And stoop and build 'em up with worn-out tools:

If you can make one heap of all your winnings
And risk it on one turn of pitch-and-toss,
And lose, and start again at your beginnings
And never breathe a word about your loss . . .
If you can force your heart and nerve and sinew
To serve your turn long after they are gone,
And so hold on when there is nothing in you
Except the Will which says to them: 'Hold on!' . . .

Yours is the Earth and everything that's in it.[11]

That's what is amazing about *Rocky* and why that film connected with so many people when it came out. It was of course a classic hero's journey story and rags-to-riches tale, but at the end, where most films would have the underdog win the final boxing match, surprisingly—and people forget this—Rocky loses. And yet the audience is still satisfied because that is real life. They see themselves in Rocky's loss and hope they can simply carry themselves well when life beats them down. And life will beat them down. It is a guarantee.

Life knocks people down. And for some, the harder it hits, the *more* they become, not less. How? Because they admit to themselves that they have been victims—of misfortune, of their own sins and those of others—and that they have hurt others as well. But they also accept someone else's victory applied to them, changing their status before God and the world. Instead of victims, they now see themselves as victors, as "more than conquerors" (Rom. 8:37) because of who they are in Christ, no matter what they have done, no matter how much they have hurt or been hurt by others. They come to know what grace really is, who they really are and aren't, and how God still loves them, running to them and throwing a party at the first sign of their remorse. What a place to be in life, where all the failings we believe define us can't hold a candle to all the love we are shown.

This is why in the introduction of Brennan Manning's book *The Ragamuffin Gospel*, he writes that his book is "for the bedraggled, beat-up, and burnt out. For the sorely burdened, the weak-kneed who know they don't have it all together and are too proud to accept the handout of amazing grace. For the inconsistent, with hereditary faults and limited talents. For the bent and bruised who feel that their lives are a grave disappointment to God. For smart people who know they are stupid and honest disciples who admit they are scalawags."[12] Manning knows, as we all must, that God can do something with our lives when we meet him in humility.

In the 1960s, a psychologist named Marvin Eisenstadt started a project interviewing innovative people who had made a cultural impact around the world—artists, entrepreneurs, leaders—and he noticed an odd fact. A surprising number of them had lost parents in childhood. He combed through the lives of famous and impactful people through history, reading through the *Encyclopedia Britannica* and noting anyone whose life justified more than one column. He had 573 eminent people on his list. Of them, 35 percent had lost at least one parent by age fifteen, and by the age of twenty that number was 45 percent. Several of England's prime ministers were part of this group: 67 percent had lost a parent by the age of sixteen. He concluded that "gifted children and child prodigies seem to emerge in highly supportive family conditions. But geniuses have a perverse tendency of growing up in more adverse conditions."[13] It's a fascinating truth: that while we would never hope to be orphaned, it appears that those who find the strength to rise out of the ashes of despair can turn tragedy into virtue. It is *the advantage of disadvantage.*[14]

And that can be you. It can be any of us.

PART III

The Problem of
PAIN

You got to take the crookeds with the straights.
That's what Papa used to say.

—August Wilson, Fences

There are two trees on the roadside directly behind my house. No
bark is left on the bottom half of those tree trunks. It will take
years for it to grow back. And every year, around Christmas, you'll find
four small white crosses placed between the trees where four men, one
a respected doctor, the others businessmen—husbands, fathers, most
of them members of the golf club my family and I belong to—skidded
off the road one December night. They had been out together for
dinner and had decided to all ride together. The driver went too fast
around the corner, and his car—full of these men, these *souls*, with all
their histories, childhoods, hurts, highlights, favorite movies, love for
their kids and wives, dreams for the future—slammed into the trees.

My friend was driving to pick up his daughter from my house when it happened and was one of the first people on the scene. A raging fire had instantly engulfed the mens' car, and he tried desperately to douse the flames with a fire extinguisher. He attempted to pull them out, but it was too late. The roof had collapsed; the fire was too hot. Even if he could have pulled them out, the men were all dead on impact. Four lives were snuffed out in one second. And beyond that, the tragedy's effects rippled out to their wives, their kids, their grandkids, and many friends.

This is just one story, from behind my house. One day in the life of people in my small corner of the world.

Sadness, tragedy, death—we turn on the news and see them every day. Another shooting, a tsunami, an earthquake, a terrorist attack, a stabbing, a war, a rumor of a war. Yet most of us don't feel severe pain and grief in these big global events. We tend to feel it most powerfully in the small ones, when the people we know and love are affected. It's the diagnosis, the divorce, the loss of a parent or, God forbid, a child. It's the loss of a job, the repeated anxiety attacks, the burden of debt, the cancer diagnosis. It's the pain and suffering of our lives that no one ever reads about but that is nevertheless very real for us. Sometimes it is overwhelming.

Pain is such a part of life, so often the score in the background, that we may forget to ask why. Why is this our lot in life? How could a good God exist if this is the way things are? And more importantly, is there anything we can do about pain and suffering when it becomes an embedded, unalterable part of our story? The problem of pain, as it has sometimes been called, is an undeniable part of life, and we can't talk about the human experience and how to flourish without asking what it has to do with the bigger puzzle of life's purpose and meaning. We can't understand ourselves without addressing it. As the psychologist Dr. Gabor Maté has said, "Any movement toward wholeness begins with the acknowledgment of our own suffering, and of the suffering in the world."[1] Life is filled with joy and warmth and happiness but also pain and challenge. Existence kicks back, and sometimes its kick is deadly.

No one escapes pain; it is a basic fact of life. But it's no use just pointing this out. We must ask how to *think* about it and what to *do* about it as we journey through this life. All of this and more, we now turn our attention to, or as Shakespeare said in the prologue to *Romeo and Juliet*, a play defined by both love and tragedy, all of this

> Is now the . . . traffic of our stage;
> The which if you with patient ears attend,
> What here shall miss, our toil shall strive to mend.[2]

CHAPTER 6

Look Pain and Suffering
SQUARE IN
THE FACE

*Our cause as demons is never more in danger
than when a human, no longer desiring, but still
intending, to do God's will, looks round upon a
universe from which every trace of God seems
to have vanished, and asks why he has been
forsaken, and still obeys.*

—C. S. LEWIS, THE SCREWTAPE LETTERS

Recently we put down our beloved dog. That was preceded by a month of vet visits and bills, of cleaning up her vomit all over the house. She was our first dog, a beautiful boxer, and losing her was devastating to our whole family: to my wife, Erin, to myself, and especially to my three daughters, who had grown up with her. We felt the crack in creation that day and for many afterward. I confess that the day after she passed, when I was finally left alone and could stop being the rock my girls needed me to be, I cried deeply. *With volume.* I felt the loss at the core of my being.

Today we had to put down a beautiful horse that friends gave us a while back, which had also become like family to my daughters in the throes of moving to California from everything they ever knew. My middle daughter, Hayden, spent an hour just last week lying on the horse, talking about her fears and feelings about this new world and how the horse felt like her closest friend in it all. And then a week later, she held the horse's head in her arms as it breathed its last breath. She is heartbroken. And there is little I can do to help.

We all come to learn the vicious truth that grief is the cost of loving. We will be hurt, our hearts broken, our souls victimized. We will be used, forgotten, made fun of, talked about, lied about, built up just to be torn down. This life is filled with pain and suffering, challenge and despair, from the cradle to the grave. But it's not enough to know this. To flourish, we must face it. We must know how to think about it when we experience it, then frame it somehow so we can survive it and maybe even come out the other side in a way that multiplies blessing rather than cursing to those around us and those who come after us.

To do that we must explore the problem of life in terms of not only who we are but also the state in which we find ourselves.

If I want to win a race, I need to know the conditions. Is it a street race? Cross country? Am I healthy? Do I have an injury I need to protect? What are the weather conditions?

In the same way, in life we need to know *what we are up against.*

So what happened to the world? Why is life so difficult? Why is there endless evil, reckless hate, and pointless suffering? It's no good to throw up our hands (as most do) and say, "We don't know!" Any worldview worth living should answer these questions.

The Terror of Creation

First and most obvious: We are living not in the perfection of Eden or the glory of paradise but in the real world. And it's a fallen, broken place: a world of cancer and car accidents, of disease and danger, of love and loss at every level of our experience. "Taking life seriously," the psychologist Ernest Becker said, "means whatever man does on this planet has to be done in the lived truth of the terror of creation . . . of the rumble of panic underneath everything."[1]

History offers many explanations for why this is so. Some have said there isn't a problem at all, that we are still in a paradise that sort of works, but our role as human beings is to coexist and together make it better as we build a utopia. Others have said this world is just a *little* broken and needs a tweak, but we can probably fix things through education, technology, politics, and psychology. There are a hundred views on how to address the reality of pain and suffering, and each assumes a different starting point.

The biblical view is quite different from all the others. It says something that immediately connects with our felt reality and experience, which is that *we aren't in paradise anymore.* Yes, the Bible *starts* with humans in paradise, which is why we all still pine for it and know about it in the deepest parts of ourselves, but that isn't where we are now. Something happened, and the world broke. Paradise has been lost.

"Life is pain, Your Highness," says one of the characters in *The Princess Bride.* "Anyone who says differently is selling something."

Indeed.

We must face the reality not only of Genesis 1 and 2, as beautiful as they are, but of Genesis 3 as well—life *after* the fall. This is our reality now: We're imperfect creatures in a world of brokenness and vices and pain and loss and struggle. We were saints, the story tells us, but now we are sinners and sufferers.

The fact that life is painful is important because it affects how we understand life and our approach to it. Christian Smith notes that in the brokenness of our world, "flourishing is not automatic or guaranteed, but [dependent]. It must be purposively accomplished against resistance and obstacles, both internal and external. Achieving human flourishing requires a specific set of resources, experiences, and efforts. . . . People who take advantage of them stand a good chance of thriving. . . . But the default outcome for those who do not is personal failure, stagnation, and degeneration."[2] Our goal is to be the first kind of people: those who understand our situation and who take advantage of the resources and experiences and efforts of others to thrive versus being beaten by life.

So what is our situation, collectively? About sixty million people die every year—about 160,000 every day—from things such as traffic accidents, cancer, earthquakes, heart attacks, shootings. And those affected by the shock and grief that death leaves in its wake are innumerable. Beyond death are things that can sometimes feel worse: abuse, neglect, divorce, loneliness. We can't escape pain.

The world is filled with horrors. As a pastor, I am at the front lines of personal tragedy. Recently I did a funeral for a middle-aged father of three. He was a flight instructor and died when one of his students lost control of the plane he was flying. It is always hard looking out to an audience and seeing kids crying as they mourn the loss of a parent. Unfortunately, it was not the first time I'd had to do this, and it won't be the last.

In the last few years, multiple friends of ours have experienced the loss of a child: one to a car accident, another to murder. Others have lost a spouse to cancer; another to a brain tumor. We have friends in their thirties who have already lost both parents to tragic deaths and face the rest of their lives without them, and others who have gone broke, gotten divorced, or gone to prison. All of this is just what orbits around me—one person among billions. Not to mention the innumerable tragedies we see play out in our cities locally and around the world every week, which seem almost too much for the heart to bear. Again, as Shakespeare said,

. . . Each new morn
New widows howl, new orphans cry, new sorrows
Strike heaven on the face.[3]

Tragedy is with us every day and splashed across the news a hundred times over. We know it well, and when we see it enough, we become numb to it. But we aren't numb when it affects us personally. We feel that. Suffering and evil are not abstract problems. Life kicks back. Not in general, but against *you*. "Angels may weep because the world is filled with suffering. A human being weeps because his daughter, she and not another, has died of leukemia this very night."[4]

The headline-worthy pains aren't the only ones that hurt. It's knowing you should love your spouse but some days it feels so darn hard. They don't do what they said they would do. The relationship isn't what it used to be. There is disappointment where there used to be dreams. There is annoyance where there used to be passion and pleasure. They used to be the means of your joy, but now they just seem in the way of it.

And *work*. That always seems to be a frustration. Your boss demands so much from you but lets everyone else off the hook. You work and work but never get to the bottom of it, never arrive, never finish.

And there is never enough money in the bank.

And *life* is so fragile. You had to say goodbye to a loved one—a parent, a friend, a spouse. Death *stole* them. First came the diagnosis. Then the hospital visits. The bony hand that used to be so full. The last goodbye. The last breath. The unbelief the next day and for months afterward when their side of the bed remained still and the kitchen table sat quiet. It all feels wrong.

Or maybe, for you, it's the *kids*. You love them and want the best for them, but they fight and cry and mess up, and some days you wonder whether you are hurting more than helping. You are a worse parent than you thought you would be. But you don't want anyone to know. Some days nothing is more beautiful than being in their presence, watching them grow and discover the world and learn to love. Other days are filled with yelling, slammed doors, and screams of "I hate you!"

This isn't the way you envisioned it. But here you are.

Made for Another World

Atheism concludes in the face of all this something that on the surface seems logical but, as we will see, is not. "If God exists," the skeptic Sam Harris says, "either he can do nothing to stop calamities, or he doesn't care to. God therefore is either [weak] or evil himself. There is another possibility, of course, and it is the most reasonable: the biblical god is a fiction, like Zeus and the thousands of other dead gods who most sane human beings now ignore."[5] In other words, all the pain of our lives means there is no God.

There is the opposite view, however, which I think makes more sense. That the reason all this pain grates against us and frustrates us and saddens us is precisely because somewhere inside us we know, as C. S. Lewis contended, that we were made for another world. Our comparing and unrest and discontentment are evidence of God and our uniqueness among creatures, for if this is the only world there is, and if we are truly only animals, as Darwinism says, then what are we comparing this world with when we say it is filled with pain or suffering or evil or injustice? No such things exist if this world is all there is. The philosopher Alvin Plantinga said as much when reflecting on how pain and suffering as a category raises more questions about God than it answers:

> Could there really be any such thing as horrifying wickedness [if there were no God and we just evolved]? I don't see how. There

can be such a thing only if there is a way that rational creatures are *supposed to live*. . . . A [secular] way of looking at the world has no place for genuine moral obligation of any sort . . . and thus no way to say there is such a thing as wickedness. Accordingly, if you think there really is such a thing as wickedness, then you have a powerful argument for the reality of God.[6]

In other words, our longing and pains speak of another world, revealing truths in us we can't ignore when answering the questions of who, or what, we are as human beings and how we can flourish.

In the face of skepticism, this explanation at the very least makes the most sense of the data of evil and suffering. When our hearts are tempted to say the existence of evil means there is no God, we need only ask where we got the category called "evil" by which we are putting God on trial. If we are just animals and there is no God and thus no absolute moral standard, then rape and murder and genocide and cancer aren't wrong or tragic—they are just nature doing what nature does.

One needs an absolute moral category called "wrong" to even begin to question God, but where did we get that category if he doesn't exist? Certainly, it wouldn't be a product of naturalistic evolution, because there are times when death and murder would help you and your tribe, which should mean you and I never would have decided such things were "wrong." They might not be ideal for you or people you love, but "wrong" would be too heavy-handed a word. After all, such crimes may have benefited the perpetrator, so who are you to project your values on them?

To have any standard that compares the way things *are* with what *ought to be* points *toward* the existence of God, not away from him. Who are we to say a line is crooked if we don't know what a straight line is? Without God, the universe and all that happens (including to you and those you love) would be meaningless—*by definition.* As the atheist Bertrand Russell once described in an honest summary of things if God doesn't exist,

> Man is the product of causes which had no pre-vision of the end they were achieving; his origin, his growth, his hopes and fears, his loves, and his beliefs, are but the outcome of accidental [groupings] of atoms. . . . All the labors of the ages, all the devotion, all the inspiration, all the noonday brightness of human genius, are destined to extinction in the vast death of the solar system, and the whole temple of Man's achievement must be buried beneath the debris of a universe in ruins. . . . Only on the firm foundation of unyielding despair, can the soul's habitation henceforth be safely built.[7]

That is where Russell wants us to start, and then build on that foundation a robust moral life where we treat one another with respect and love. The problem is that if he was right, there is *no reason to do so* beyond it being his opinion. Beyond that, to try to build our lives on ourselves ends up working against us because we find out that while there are angels among us, there are demons as well. Writing years after Russell, and after the barbarity of the First World War, George Orwell, with a somber realism, reflected on our philosophical and scientific endeavor to find our own meaning and purpose without God:

> For two hundred years we had sawed and sawed and sawed at the branch we were sitting on. And in the end, much more suddenly than anyone had foreseen, our efforts were rewarded, and down we came. But unfortunately there had been a little mistake: The thing at the bottom was not a bed of roses after all, it was a

cesspool full of barbed wire. . . . It appears that amputation of the soul isn't just a simple surgical job, like having your appendix out. The wound goes septic.[8]

The wound of *soullessness* ends up affecting every part of us. Or, as the Bible tells us a hundred different ways, we're not good gods to build anything on. We are too self-interested, self-deceived, and self-destructive for our own good.

How Long, Oh Lord?

Most worldviews conclude something depressing in the face of all this pain. Atheism says there is no God. Other views such as deism say that if there is a God, he must have created the universe and then abandoned it. In the concluding words of Joan Didion's book recounting the sudden death of her husband, "No eye is on the sparrow." And then there are the conclusions of Eastern philosophies and religions, such as Hinduism, Buddhism, and New Age: the illusion is not that there are gods but that there is suffering. Evil and pain aren't real; they are only illusions in your mind.

The biblical view is different. Many have said the Bible doesn't give us direct answers to this question, and I agree: it does not always offer us definite answers to the specific painful moments of our individual lives. But neither does the Bible claim to give answers in the precise way we often look for them. God's people face pain and suffering throughout Scripture, and their constant cry is, "How long, Lord?" (Ps. 6:3)—yet there is rarely a specific answer to that question. The books of Job and Ecclesiastes were written to wrestle with the tension of how God can exist alongside our pain, and they don't give a ton of answers other than that God does exist, that he is in control of the universe, and that we need to be humbler in our approach to suffering because why would we assume we are smart enough to understand the ways of the universe?

As the philosopher Charles Taylor has pointed out, modern people have far more confidence in their reasoning powers and their ability to unlock the mysteries of life than did ancient people. The belief that because we can't think of a reason for something, therefore the gods don't have one, would have been seen as a fallacy. But today it is a way of life—the pinnacle of the great pride and faith we have in our own minds.[9]

The Fall

The Bible tells us exactly how the world ended up in the state it's in and what role we played in that. Once we grasp that, we are in a better position to fight the problem of suffering and evil so we can flourish. As Old Testament scholar Walter Brueggemann says, "The story [of the fall] does not want to aid our theologizing. It wants, rather, to catch us in our living."[10]

So why is the world this way? Instead of it being a result of the gods fighting, or a cold and empty universe with no purpose, the biblical explanation says we had a part to play in the way things have turned out and that there is hope for all of us in the midst of the mess.

One word summarizes the biblical view of all that went wrong in the world: *sin*. The word used all through the Bible literally means "to miss the mark or target" or "a failure to attain a goal." Five different Greek words are used for it in the New Testament alone, and they depict both passive and active failures: what theologians call sins of commission (things we do wrong) and sins of omission (right things we *don't* do).

The target we miss is a right relationship with God, one in which we stand before him naked and unashamed. Sin is less a lack of virtue than a failure to take God at his word, a failure to trust him, a failure to believe we are who God says we are. Knowing the reality of sin is our "first need," J. I. Packer says. "The subject of sin is vital knowledge. To say that our first need in life is to learn about [it] may sound strange, but in the sense intended it is true. If you have not learned about sin, you cannot understand yourself, your fellowmen, or the world you live in. . . . The Bible is an exposition of God's answer to the problem of human sin and unless you have that problem clearly before you, you will keep missing the point."[11]

While it is unpopular to speak of sin today, we must, or we won't see the gospel and all its implications in their proper light. When the apostles preached, they could assume even their pagan hearers had an understanding of sin. So in a sense, Christianity needs to unpack the diagnosis before it can win a hearing for the cure. We lack the first condition for understanding what the Bible is talking about as it relates to us personally, even if we feel it on the scale of culture, with all the death and pain and agony that are reported each day.[12] And we need to because, as Martyn Lloyd-Jones pointed out, a lot of people hold Jesus up to the world and think that is enough, but it's not enough because we will never fly to Christ if we don't understand why we need to.

I think that is why the Bible so quickly moves to the topic of our sin and pain and brokenness. The Bible begins with the creation of a good world and us as people in it serving God and working under him to make it flourish. Love, purpose, joy; spiritual and emotional vitality; no human death. And then we messed it up. We disobeyed. And we are only three chapters into the story.

So what happened? God made it clear that we could enjoy this amazing world, but there was one thing we could not do. One thing. "You are free to eat from any tree in the garden," he said, "but you must not eat from the tree of the knowledge of good and evil, for when you eat from it you will certainly die" (Gen. 2:16–17). People ask why God would give this option. It's a bit of a mystery, but I think it has something to do with creating a world and a relationship with us where there could be *obedience to God without there being sin*. Whatever the reason, fourteen verses later we did the one thing God told us not to. The result? That beautiful, radiant, loving, open relationship between God and humankind was ripped asunder. Furthermore, our relationships with *one another*, our relationship with *creation*, and our relationships with *ourselves* were destroyed. Thomas Aquinas said that the fall of Adam and Eve brought "four wounds" to human nature.[13] They are original sin (lack of sanctifying grace and original justice), concupiscence (the soul's passions are no longer ordered perfectly to the soul's intellect), physical frailty and death, and darkened intellect and ignorance. These negated or diminished the gifts of God to Adam and Eve of original justice or sanctifying grace, integrity, immortality, and infused knowledge.

Biblical scholar Christopher Watkin traces seven types of brokenness and separation that happened, all of which are still at play today:

1. God is alienated from us, and he is angry with us (Gen. 3:11).
2. We are alienated from God, and we flee from him (Gen. 3:10).
3. We are alienated from ourselves, and we experience shame (Gen. 3:7).
4. We are alienated from our bodies (Gen. 3:16).
5. We are alienated from each other (Gen. 3:12–13).
6. We are alienated from the rest of creation (Gen. 3:17).
7. Creation is alienated from itself (Gen. 3:18).[14]

Saint Augustine was right when he said, "The problem with humanity is not that we sin, but that we are in a *state of sin* that needs a comprehensive solution."[15] Sin reaches wide. It is a personal, psychological, spiritual, and physical matter, but also a social and political one. We are broken, and the world is broken, and when we understand that, we know that to try to solve only one of those (ourselves or the world) while ignoring the other is a grave error. It shrinks the gospel down to just getting souls to heaven while leaving the world unchanged and justice undone—something God strongly says he is against (Isa. 1:11–17). On the other hand, we must not "thin" the gospel out to nothing more than social change that feeds the mouth but leaves the soul untouched. What good is it to help people for eighty years while ignoring the eighty billion years they go on to live after that?

The story of our world, while often a comedy filled with pleasure and fun and delight, is also a tragedy. We will live "east of Eden," as Steinbeck put it, until the new world fully arrives. Until then, life will steal from us. C. S. Lewis captured it well when he reflected on what it felt like as a small child to lose his mother, who was his whole life: "All settled happiness, all that was tranquil and reliable, disappeared from my life. . . . It was sea and islands now; the great continent had sunk like Atlantis."[16] And later he reflected on the death of his wife, Joy: "No one ever told me that grief felt so like fear."[17]

Beautiful but Still Fallen

What does the story of the fall tell us about ourselves? First, that while we are made in the image of God, *we are also sinners*. This is the state we are born into, and it leads to every bad thing under the sun: "sexual immorality, impurity, sensuality, idolatry, sorcery, enmity, strife, jealousy, fits of anger, rivalries, dissensions, divisions, envy, drunkenness . . . and things like these" (Gal. 5:19–21 ESV). In other words, *sex, religion, relationships, and drink*: it's not an exhaustive list but a good one. I have a friend who is a police officer, and he says these cover almost every reason he has to visit someone's home to investigate or arrest someone.

The bottom line—and it shouldn't take much convincing for us to believe this if we are paying attention—is that we are messed up. We are broken. And we are capable of all kinds of awful things. As G. K. Chesterton once quipped, this teaching, of all the teachings of Christianity, is the easiest to prove. We murder and kill and mock and hurt one another on a mass scale. And all the technological, scientific, political, psychological, and educational advancements in the world aren't solving anything in us. We truly are what the ancients used to call us: *homo incurvatus*—humankind turned in on himself. That is our state of fallenness and has been since the day we chose disobedience over obedience and everything broke in us. Every day, we are driven by what Karl Barth deemed three primary forms of personal sin: pride, sloth, and falsehood. All constantly presented to us by our three primary enemies since the fall: the world, the flesh, and the devil (Eph. 2:1–3). These sins and these enemies make our lives miserable and, most importantly, disconnect us from the God who wants us to "live life to the fullest" (John 10:10 CEB).

The problems we face aren't only *in* us; they are *around* us as well. "Creation was subjected to frustration," the apostle Paul tells us, and is now in "bondage to decay" and "groaning as in the pains of childbirth" (Rom. 8:20–22). But the Bible lays out a picture wherein *it wasn't supposed to be like this*. So when we ask why God would create a world with natural disasters that kill and destroy the lives of hundreds of thousands around the world each year, the answer the Bible gives is, *he didn't*. It wasn't always this way. When sin cracked the world, creation went with it.

And so we are both broken and we add to the brokenness. God told us this would be our lot: if we ate from the tree, we would "[know] good and evil" (Gen. 3:5). Well, "knowing" in Genesis is more than mere cognitive recognition; it is intimate acquaintance. "Adam *knew* Eve his wife, and she conceived and bore Cain" (Gen. 4:1 ESV, emphasis added), meaning they had sex. They were acquainted in the most intimate of ways. And God warned us that rejecting his ordered world, the world we were made for, would lead to intimate knowledge of evil and pain. We would experience and know these as intimately as a husband and wife know one another in lovemaking.

The suffering that follows sin, while a consequence of disobedience, is not a *punishment* for sin per se (though that is not outside the realm of possibility) but the result of taking the first step to distance ourselves from God and his ways. If God is the source of life, and every good and perfect gift comes from him, what happens when you move away from that? In rejecting life, what is there but death? "If you want joy, power, peace, eternal life, you must get close to, or even into, the thing that has them. . . . They are a great fountain of energy and beauty spurting up at the very center of reality. If you are close to it, the spray will wet you: if you are not, you will remain dry. Once a man is united to God, how could he not live forever? Once a man is separated from God, what can he do but wither and die?"[18]

Carpe Diem!

Attempting to thrive in our humanity and find purpose without accounting for the effects of the fall is a sure recipe for disaster. But when we understand why we are the way we are and why the world is the way it is, we grasp an important truth that the modern story is shy to admit: *we have limits.* We can't build paradise without God. Nor can we construct Babel and become God. And while this means the death of our self-sufficiency, it's also freeing. How much unnecessary burden do we carry because we lack a good theology of sin and an understanding of our limits in this life? Ernest Becker in his famous book *The Denial of Death* describes the modern person as someone who knows they are "a sinner," but in our secular world they are "a sinner with no word for it" who goes looking for why they are this way "in a dictionary of psychology which only aggravates the problem of his separateness."[19]

When we deny our sin, we deny who we are, our fundamental problem in life, and the solution to that problem. Why do we fumble and stumble? Because we are sinners who miss the mark. We are mistake-ridden, narcissistic creatures, lost in a world that seems hell-bent on dealing us only pain and frustration. If we are living out of the biblical story, we are freed from the burden of being perfect, freed from being our own saviors and bearing the responsibility and weight of justifying ourselves. We know why we feel depressed and helpless and afraid and alone and lost: because our brains are broken and our souls are guided by vices instead of virtues. Our hearts are fallen, and contrary to popular opinion, they should *not* always be followed, for they lead us astray. Our hearts don't have only neutral impulses but sometimes corrupt and mistaken ones: Jesus says, "For out of the heart come evil thoughts—murder, adultery, sexual immorality, theft, false testimony, slander" (Matt. 15:19). None of this is good news per se, but it helps us to frame our experience and navigate our lives.

Realizing that we are born *where Adam finished*, not where he started, changes everything about how we view ourselves. Even the brevity of life can be received as a gift, one that liberates us to live in the moment. "The untiring siren call of the future—with its grand plans to be accomplished, vacations to be had, retirements to be enjoyed—can become so strong it swallows our ability to live in the *now* . . . which means people fail to be fully present. We neglect spouses and children, disregard care for our bodies, and dismiss relationships."[20] Reflection on our limits awakens us to the present moment. This is why it's so powerful when Robin Williams's character in *Dead Poets Society* tells the boys in his class that one day they will be "food for daffodils." Thus, they must *"carpe diem"*—seize the day, make their lives extraordinary. The vulnerability and shortness of life drive us to make each day mean something.

This shift in our perspective—from viewing life as something we are *owed*, as if we deserve health, wealth, and goodness, to something we *receive as a gift*, a grace—makes all the difference. Lewis is again helpful here, asking us to imagine a group of people all living in the same building. Half of them think it is a hotel; the other half think it is a prison. Those who think it is a hotel regard the whole experience of their stay as "intolerable" when things occasionally aren't as they had hoped; but those who think it is a prison see it as surpassingly comfortable, expecting it will involve difficulty and suffering.[21] In the end, how you view the world determines whether you respond with gratitude or bitterness.

I for one fall on the gratitude side of things. Or I try to as best I can as I make my way through life. I try to take in every wonderful sunrise I see because I know life's end is coming faster than a freight train. When I stand beside the ocean or cry at a movie or listen to a beautiful piece of music, I try to be fully present and to take it all in. I'm thankful every time I look over and see my wife, her blonde hair strewn over her pillow; or feel her touch, her kiss; or see her smile. And I'm grateful that she is still, at least for today, alive and chooses to love me. This is the greatest gift anyone has ever given me, and I try my best to live in light of it. I watch my kids come down from their bedrooms, sleepy but excited about another day in this amazing world, or I see them singing and dancing in a play or around the house, or swimming in the ocean, or composing a song, or leading worship, or laughing, or hugging me, or telling me they love me. All of these are undeserved gifts, not things to be expected. They should be digested with gratitude to God. Consumed within an inch of their life. Savored. We should meditate on them and store them away. Because they will be gone in an instant. They are but a visit and a crack of light in the prison of my life.

There is another freeing thing about seeing ourselves as sinful and learning the lessons of the fall. In the end, only one standard matters—and it's in relationship to God, not other people. Theologian Millard Erickson points out, "If our intent is to reflect the nature of God, a human being is to be judged not by comparison with other humans, but by conformity to the divine standard."[22] So failure does not mean being less successful than colleagues or siblings, or not keeping to the standard of people on social media. Our biggest problem is not the need to make more money or to be smarter or prettier. Failure is failing to meet God's standard. *Failure is when we sin.* Comparing ourselves to others is a lost cause, a toxic venture that kills contentment at every turn. When a woman compares her husband with the richer, more successful man down the street and starts to daydream about what her life *could have been*, it replaces any gratitude for what she has and chips away at her satisfaction in her marriage. When a man endlessly scrolls the internet fantasizing about women he sees as more beautiful than his wife or wonders if he made a mistake with the woman he ended up with, it steals his joy.

Because we were created to receive what we have as a gift from God, comparing ourselves with others corrodes our soul. We were never designed to function that way. There is always someone better than us, ahead of us, cooler than us, whose kids are more successful, whose home is larger, or whose vacations are more extravagant. It's a game we can never win.

The only thing that matters in the end is how we measure up to the standard of God. Paul says we all "fall short of the glory of God" (Rom. 3:23), not short of other human beings' expectations, or our potential, or whatever else we tell ourselves. This puts us in the humble position of admitting that we don't measure up in the only way that really matters.

Never Lose Sight of the Bigger Picture

As necessary as it is to understand our sin, creation and the fall are not equal. Evil and sin are not original to the story—they are parasites that will one day be eliminated altogether. This is why "nature has the air of a good thing spoiled."[23] We can't understand the fall story and how it affects us without the creation story first. Behind and underneath and above all the sorrow and pain and guilt and suffering, there is a different way to be human. A different way the world was supposed to be. That's what we feel under the surface of ourselves. A kind of nostalgia, or fuzzy memory, as if built into our DNA, of a different world than this one that reeks of death and murder and racism and child abuse. Sin is part of our present, but it wasn't always. And it will not be in the final chapter of the story of the world, or your story within that.

Surprisingly, then, the story of the fall is important because it tells us that evil and suffering are *limited*, not original. They had a beginning and are not "natural" to this world. In the same vein, then, it's *not natural* for us to receive a cancer diagnosis, or to have our loved one stolen from us in the rubble of a car crash, or to have our home become the place we fear and dread because of the unspeakable things that happen there. None of that *belongs* in this beautiful world. And one day it will no longer be a part of it. "There will be no more death or mourning or crying or pain" (Rev. 21:4), God tells us.

This world was meant to buzz with God, and it will again. Jesus's miracles are not only throwbacks to a time before disease and death and fear but also pointers forward to the day when he will make this world whole again. They are "not *supernatural* miracles in a *natural* world, they are the only truly 'natural' things in a world that is unnatural, demonized, and wounded."[24]

The ancient Greek philosophers Socrates and Plato believed that all learning was a form of remembering. They taught that the soul, immortal in its essence, knew everything before it was born.[25] And while that is not the biblical view, it hovers around it: under all the pain and loneliness and fear and tragedy of this life, there is a good that we recognize somehow, and we can hear and feel the bubbling under the surface, however quiet. "It is as though we can hear, not perhaps a voice itself, but the echo of a voice . . . about things being put to rights, about peace and hope and prosperity for all."[26] Our hearts beat for all of this in the face of a universe that seems to suggest everything but these things. The world is as it is, but that is not all it is. There is more to it all than appears to be the case. The music critic Francis Spufford, reflecting on one of Mozart's pieces, once said, "It is not music that denies anything. It offers a strong, absolutely calm rejoicing, but it does not pretend there is no sorrow. On the contrary, it sounds as if it comes from a world where sorrow is perfectly ordinary, *but still there is more to be said.* Everything you fear is true. *And yet.* Everything you have done wrong you have really done wrong. *And yet.* And yet."[27]

The Bible begins with a vision of the good life—the wonder and awe of life with God in the garden—to help us make sense of the bad parts when death and pain and tears are the norm. As Jordan Peterson powerfully reminds us,

> When you are visited by chaos and swallowed up; when nature curses you or someone you love with illness; or when tyranny rends asunder something of value that you have built, it is helpful to know the rest of the story. All of that misfortune is only the bitter half of the tale of existence, without taking note of the heroic element of redemption or the nobility of the human spirit requiring a certain responsibility to shoulder. We ignore that addition to the story at our peril, because life is so difficult that losing sight of the heroic part of existence could cost us everything.[28]

Knowing we are made in God's image with a great task before us—to bring his rule and reign and love and justice to bear on the ugliness of the world—is exactly what we need when that ugliness visits our doorstep, which it will. When Galadriel hands Frodo the light of Eärendil in Tolkien's *The Fellowship of the Ring*, knowing he has a perilous journey before him, she says, "I give you this, our most beloved star. May it be a light for you in dark places, when all other lights go out."[29] And the lights do go out, and the star is needed in the dark caves as the great monster Shelob tries to kill Frodo and his companion Samwise.

In the darkest of moments of life, when the lights of health, family, and friends, or perhaps your own skills or knowledge or beauty have gone out, you still have the light of the earlier part of the story to make you get up in the morning and press on: the vision that you have a great quest before you, to be a co-laborer with God, and you are needed. To do your part and bring his kingdom on earth as it is in heaven in whatever square inch of the story he has given you until you breathe your last. You were made for this. To bring order to the chaos and, in so doing, soar.

Then when you wake up in the middle of the night, sweating and fearful that you haven't done enough, or been enough, you have some defense: for all your flaws, at least you are doing *this*. At least you are taking care of yourself. At least you are useful to your family. To a few of the people at work. At least you are moving, stumbling forward and upward.[30]

We are fallen *but still beautiful*. We are living, walking contradictions. "We are the pinnacle of creation and its greatest danger. We are Rembrandt and Hitler, Mozart and Stalin, Ruth and Jezebel."[31] Yes, there is corruption in us, but there is also good. You still mourn when you see the things that break the heart of God. You still fight evil and recognize beauty when you are lucky enough to behold it or create it. You trace the memory of wonder that gets beaten down every day and can still hear the voice, however small, that seems to be calling you from the other side. If it's true and is really there, it's worth living for because it means that our "momentary troubles" are just that— momentary versus forever—and "are achieving for us an eternal glory that far outweighs them all" (2 Cor. 4:17), as painful as they are. That promise, unique to Christianity, is not just a pat on the back from God in the midst of our pain but a reordering of the world in a way where we get back what we have lost and more.

Contemplate Your Beloved

The way through the pain and suffering we face in this life is holding to this vision of the future, having our eyes and hearts fixed on that heavenly reality, that assured joy. Viktor Frankl experienced the worst of humanity when in September 1942, he, his wife, and his parents were driven out of their home in Vienna and sent to a Nazi concentration camp. Over the course of the war, his wife was killed at Belsen, and his father and mother at Auschwitz. He said there was only one thing that staved off hopelessness: "My mind clung to my wife's image, imagining it with an uncanny acuteness. I heard her answering me, saw her smile, her frank and encouraging look."[32] From this he came to a powerful conclusion: "I understood how a man who has nothing left in this world still may know bliss, be it only for a brief moment, in the *contemplation of his beloved*. In a position of utter desolation, when man cannot express himself in positive action, when his only achievement may consist in enduring his sufferings in the right way—an honorable way—in such a position man can, through loving contemplation of the image he carries of his beloved, achieve fulfilment."[33]

The same is true of us as we live in this world. When we hold on to the image of Jesus himself, our wonderful groom, or heaven itself, the place of profound and eternal joy because we will be with God, we can face anything and, through any experience, achieve fulfillment in light of that overwhelming vision. I think that is in part why God ever bothered to tell us about it. You'll notice Jesus seems shy about heaven most of the time (he teaches about it in different places but not in as much detail as one might expect). The Bible as a whole doesn't give us much detail, except a few pictures now and then, but even they are symbolic. The glimpses God does give are mostly to suffering people (the Sermon on the Mount, the book of Revelation). Heaven and the treasures and pleasures therein are held out to weary and struggling disciples, those feeling squeezed under the pressure of persecution and the fire of the world, wondering how to push through, yet Jesus keeps lifting their chins. It is exactly to this kind of heart that he says, "If I go and prepare a place for you, I will come back and take you . . . where I am" (John 14:3). It's almost like he knew all the pain and torture they would endure in this life, and millions of disciples after them, some suffering actual death and torture, others the torture of a cancer diagnosis, a tumor, the loss of a child or spouse, but they all received the same promise. Jesus says, one day, if you have trusted and treasured me above all things, something is coming that will make all this sadness and pain come *untrue*.

In a climactic passage in Fyodor Dostoevsky's *The Brothers Karamazov*, this exact sentiment is explained. He writes,

> I believe like a child that suffering will be healed and made up for, that all the humiliating absurdity of human contradictions will vanish like a pitiful mirage, . . . that in the world's finale, at the moment of eternal harmony, something so precious will come to pass that it will suffice for all hearts, for the comforting of all resentments, for the atonement of all the crimes of humanity, for all the blood that they've shed; that it will make it not only possible to forgive but to justify all that has happened.[34]

CHAPTER 7

Transform Struggles into
STRENGTHS

"But the moon came slowly up in all her gentle glory, and the stars looked out, and through the small compass of the grated window, as through the narrow crevice of one good deed in a murky life of guilt, the face of Heaven shone bright and merciful. He raised his head; gazed upward at the quiet sky, which seemed to smile upon the earth in sadness, as if the night, more thoughtful than the day, looked down in sorrow on the sufferings and evil deeds of men; and felt its peace sink deep into his heart."

—CHARLES DICKENS, *BARNABY RUDGE*

We know we are separated from God and the world is broken. We are sinners and sufferers. But what can we do about it?

There is something we should *not* do: *make the story about us.* "When the woman saw that the fruit of the tree was good for food and pleasing to the eye, and also desirable for gaining wisdom, she took some and ate it" (Gen. 3:6).

Instead of basing our identity and flourishing on God and his ways, we only look to and ask questions about ourselves. The modern person has become "preoccupied with psychological therapies" at an almost religious devotion level.[1] This is what the philosopher Philip Rieff prophetically saw in his 1966 classic, *The Triumph of the Therapeutic*. He said the focuses we've had throughout the ages (theology, science, philosophy, politics) would give way to psychological exploration as the key interpretive grid for our lives. He posited that Western civilization had gone through three stages and was headed for a fourth:

- the *political* man (the age of Plato and Aristotle),
- the *religious* man (the Middle Ages),
- the *economic* man (trade, production, industry, capitalism, Smith, Marx),
- and the next stage would be the *psychological* man (Freud, Jung, Skinner).

In this fourth stage, for the first time we would begin "finding identity not in outward directed activities as was true with the previous [eras] but rather in the inward quest for personal psychological happiness."[2] In this shift, all meaning and truth and value would be shaped around personal taste rather than any external order. The inner psychological life of the individual would be sovereign. And that's exactly where we've arrived today. The modern person is a "figure whose very psychological essence means that he can make and remake personal identity at will."[3] Or as Ernest Becker said, "It is when psychology . . . offers itself as a full explanation of human unhappiness, that it makes the situation of modern man an impasse from which he cannot escape."[4] Because all the psychological analysis in the world "doesn't allow the person to find out who he is and why he is here on earth, why he has to die and how he can make his life a triumph."[5] In other words, if *we* are the ultimate authority in the universe, there is no one else to appeal to when things go awry. So we bear the burden and look inward only to find our own insecurity and brokenness, and deep down we *know*—and hope—that we can't be it. We keep making the same mistake as our parents in the garden. We decide that *we*, rather than God, should be in charge of our lives. We have spent a generation trying to "find ourselves," and in the finding have not flourished but withered.

As social theorist Max Scheler wrote, "An essential part of the teachings and directives of the great religions the world over have always been on the *meaning of pain and suffering.*"[6] Why? Because our pain seems to find meaning only when it is connected to what people have traditionally called "religion" (what we would call God himself), or when we see it in light of the transcendent versus just in light of a material, natural, disenchanted world. Take away the enchantment of existence and we are left looking only to ourselves and one another. We're left with what we have today: one of the worst cultures in history at dealing with suffering and evil.[7] We have no way to understand or absorb pain when it visits us, and it produces not only sadness but despair. As Viktor Frankl reminds us, "Despair is suffering without meaning."[8]

Removing our reliance on the transcendent, making us follow not what *is*, or *should be*, but only what we want to be the case, has led us only into a prison of our own making. "Religious man was born to be saved," Philip Rieff says, but the modern "psychological man is born to be pleased."[9] And we are pleasing him. We are entertaining him to death. Allowing him all the wide-open laneway he wants, to be whoever he feels himself to be at any given time of day. There are no absolutes to guide him, no virtues to call him to. Such things would assume something above him.

This sense of absolute authority makes us feel lost and alone, feelings that we then try to solve in a million ways outside our spirits connecting to God's. "Modern man is drinking and drugging himself out of awareness, or he spends his time shopping, which is the same thing. He buries himself in psychology; in the belief that awareness all by itself will be some kind of magical cure for his problems."[10] But it doesn't work. It was never designed to. Self-realization and "self-definition are not capable of bearing the full weight of human personality."[11] We learn to know about ourselves rather than know ourselves. No matter what modern secular therapy tells us, we can't construct ourselves by ourselves.

Christianity offers something different; it poses a problem for modern ideologies: "It insists upon the absolute *incapacity* of human beings to solve their most pressing problems by themselves and thus denies the central tenet of modern political ideologies, namely, faith in the possibility of autonomous human control over the world."[12] This modern view of humankind is the fall in microcosm: the way to freedom is to self-govern. But God has been warning us from the beginning: "Without God man can only organize the world against man. Exclusive humanism is inhuman humanism."[13] If I have the right to decide my own law and you your own, then we need a law that trumps us both and can provide for our common life.

The Long Defeat

One of the controlling questions we keep returning to is the purpose of human life. If the answer is to win the survival of the fittest, or to accumulate more stuff than the other guy, or to be enlightened or succeed or be beautiful, then *suffering has no place*. It is the worst thing that can happen to a person and is to be avoided at all costs. It is antithetical to our purpose.

But if a person's life has a grander goal—of doing God's will, of bringing the kingdom on earth as it is in heaven, of carrying a load for the sake of another—then "suffering can, despite its painfulness, be an important means of actually *achieving* your purpose in life."[14] It can play a crucial role in propelling you toward life's most important goals. Instead of being an aside, suffering becomes part "of what human life is all about . . . an important chapter . . . of that story."[15]

Forgive me for yet again dipping into the deep well of Tolkien's Middle-earth mythology, but one of the most poignant themes in *The Lord of the Rings* is that heroes are made *through* suffering rather than by avoiding it. The Elves have been fighting what Galadriel calls "the long defeat" against their enemies in Mordor for several thousand years. Even though they *know* they will lose the fight against Sauron, they *keep fighting until they are defeated*. Because courage is shown by plodding on even when you have no hope of victory at all. There is no courage without fear. You can't assess the likelihood of success as part of your venture. That's what makes the heroes in these great stories what they are. Even in the face of suffering, they keep going.[16]

We have a further advantage when we frame our lives within the great story of God. We find steel in our spines because we are fighting for something bigger than just ourselves. Our challenges and pains and tragedies are real because we have very real enemies—Satan, sin, and death, and so we keep fighting, even if it doesn't feel like we are ever going to win. Because the long defeat is guaranteed. But in this story, it's not our defeat but theirs. And yet we don't fight alone.

The Suffering God

Christianity is the only worldview that says all this pain and agony and suffering is not only part of our story but, amazingly, *part of God's story too*. The way God saves us is not by distant commands or occasional encouragements. Instead, he became one of us.

"No one has ever seen God," John says, "but the one and only Son, who is himself God . . . has *made him known*" (John 1:18, emphasis added). God doesn't just explain himself; he exposits himself.

According to theologian Frederick Buechner, God explaining himself would be like trying to explain Einstein to a clam. So "God doesn't reveal his grand design. He reveals himself."[17] And he did this in Jesus, a man remembered not for his military prowess or worldly extravagance but as "a man of sorrows" (Isa. 53:3 ESV), born not as rich nobility but as a poor commoner in a backwater town, experiencing all the pain and agonies of normal human life. He experienced weariness and thirst (John 4:6), distress, grief, and anguish (Mark 3:5; John 12:27). Throughout his life he prayed with "loud cries and tears" (Heb. 5:7 ESV; cf. Luke 22:44), wept at the death of his friends (John 11:35), was rejected by his family (John 7:3–5), was tempted and assaulted by the devil (Matt. 4:1), and ultimately was beaten half to death and then crucified and killed.

And this pain wasn't something peripheral that lightly touched him or something accidental to his primary purpose and calling in life. Suffering was central to *who he was* and *what he was here to do*: "He was pierced for our transgressions; he was crushed for our iniquities; upon him was the chastisement that brought us peace, and with his wounds we are healed" (Isa. 53:5 ESV).

Jesus said mysterious things: The son of man "*must* . . . suffer many things . . . [and] *must* be killed and on the third day be raised to life" (Matt. 16:21, emphasis added). Has that word ever stuck out to you? *Must*. I *must* be delivered, *must* suffer, *must* die, *must* be raised. I might be tempted to say, "Jesus was a good man and a great example, so be like Jesus," thinking that if I too am a good person and do good deeds and don't swear, if am a good mother, or man, or I go to church, or give to charity, then God will save me. But that doesn't make sense of him saying he *must* die. Jesus would not have had to die if we could be good enough.

But we can't be, and so he must.

We sinned and replaced God as the authority in our lives; so to save us God had to replace us, making Christ to be "sin for us," as the apostle Paul says (2 Cor. 5:21), that we might become the "righteousness of God." As the theologian John Stott said, "The essence of sin is man substituting himself for God, while the essence of salvation is God substituting himself for man."[18] Jesus "plunged himself into the furnace so that, when we find ourselves in the fire, we can turn to him and know we will not be consumed but will be made into people great and beautiful."[19] In reflecting on this most scandalous of ideas, we see that while we don't fully know the reason God allows evil and suffering to continue in our world and in our lives, we know one thing for certain: it is not because he doesn't love us or doesn't care about us. This much is clear: that *in love* God suffered immensely for us. The cross is a place of deep suffering where Jesus experienced physical, psychological, emotional, and spiritual pain at levels we can't even imagine, all to make sure we wouldn't have to experience those things forever.

God with Us

At this point some may say, "But that's only *half* of the answer to the question of why there is suffering and pain." I admit that is true, but as Tim Keller has said, it is the half we need.[20] And this is why Christianity has always thrived among the poor and the "least of these." Because it presents us with a God who connects to *every person* in our pain, suffering, trials, and difficulty. As Dorothy Sayers wrote, "For whatever reason God chose to make man as he is—limited and suffering and abject to sorrows and death—he had the honesty and courage to take his own medicine. Whatever game he is playing, he has kept his own rules and played fair. He has himself gone through . . . the trivial irritations of family life and the cramping restrictions of hard work and lack of money to the worst horrors of pain and despair and death."[21] No other religion or worldview offers this: not Islam, atheism, agnosticism, Judaism, Buddhism, Hinduism. Such is the amazing gem that is *God with us.*

This truth doesn't remove pain from our lives, but it tells us that God doesn't sit idly back and watch. Whether you are a single mom trying to provide for your kids, living in a slum in India, part of the underground persecuted church in China, suffering through cancer, or going through a divorce, Jesus *knows* and understands. The universe is not chaotic and meaningless; there is a God at the center of it who knows suffering and will reverse it at the end of all things. "Blessed are those who mourn," Jesus said, "for they will be *comforted*" (Matt. 5:4, emphasis added). This is in the future tense. We taste it at times in this life, but for most of us it is never finally resolved until we see God face-to-face. But the fact that he has promised that means we can get up and face the day, for the One who himself faced every trial we do, made the day.

God identifies with us in our pain, and Jesus gave us a promise with his parting words: "I am with you" (Matt. 28:16–20). The most powerful thing he can offer is not fancy answers to deep philosophical questions but *his presence.* What more beautiful and important thing is there? This is, after all, what we lost in the garden. It's what you need at 2:00 a.m. when the stresses of life come flooding at you with no easy solutions. It's what you need when you are in a hospital bed and your family is at home in their beds, while the monitor beside you beeps and the hallways are quiet and you have nothing but your own thoughts. "I will be with you" is far better than "Here are some instructions to live by."

I was thinking about this when I read of the submarine with five people in it that went down to see the sunken remains of the *Titanic.* The submarine was missing for three days, and during that time I pictured what it would be like to be down there, cold and afraid in the darkness. Our modern story says to us, "This life is all there is. There is nothing to comfort you, nothing to hold on to; your life is fleeting, and the universe and this ocean are just vast darkness." But what a comfort we have to know that even way down there in the depth of the ocean, in a little cramped sub, in the cold and endless expanse of darkness, we can hear God say, "I am *with you*." Nothing matters more than his presence, and certainly nothing is more important in our pain.

Tony Campolo tells a story of when he went to a funeral home to pay his respects to the family of a friend but by mistake ended up in the wrong funeral parlor. It was the funeral for an elderly man, and his widow was the only mourner there. She seemed so lonely that Campolo decided to stay for the man's funeral. He even drove with her to the cemetery for the graveside service. As they drove back Campolo admitted to her that he hadn't known her husband. "I thought as much," she said. "I didn't recognize you. But it doesn't really matter." She squeezed his hand. "You'll never, ever, know what this means to me."[22] What did it mean? Why was it helpful? Because he was there, he was present. He was a warm body, something more powerful than a text or a list of ideas for coping with loss. Saying "God has wounds" is an offense and a blasphemous idea to most religions of the world, but Christianity says it is only in this way that we truly understand God—and ourselves—in the end. Suffering is not a detour from our "real" life. As with Jesus, it is part of the way we *fulfill who we are*.

Our Lover's Quarrel with the World

The New Testament says we will "suffer grief in all kinds of trials" and that "these have come so that the proven genuineness of [our] faith—of greater worth than gold, which perishes even though refined by fire—may result in praise, glory and honor" (1 Peter 1:6–7). Suffering, as much as we hate it, produces something good when we suffer in hope. It "produces endurance, and endurance produces character, and character produces hope" (Rom. 5:3–4 ESV). Suffering refines us by removing all that is not of ultimate, lasting value and worth. It reveals what lasts and is used by God to transform us and train us into people fit for his kingdom. In life, whether it is the experience of muscle being built through the pain of working out, or the depth of knowledge that comes only through the struggle of persistent study, the things worth having come at a cost.

In Tim Elmore's work on generations, he notes generational patterns, starting with the differences between the Builder Generation (born 1929–1945) and Boomers (1946–1964), namely that the hard times the Builders faced—the Great Depression, the Spanish flu, World War II—created a "strong generation." Further, he says, a strong generation then creates "good times," and the result of those good times is a "weak generation," which then creates "hard times." Why do hard times create strong people? "They become resourceful because they have fewer resources."[23] While none of us would ask for or desire the difficulties of war, no one can argue with the truth that difficulty produces strength.

Of course, this is the exact opposite of how we all live, myself included. I try to avoid any experience of pain and loss. I want to be conformed to the image of Christ *without* such things. I want the kingdom without the cross. And yet Paul seems pretty clear that while God may not *cause* our hardships, perhaps it simply is not possible to treasure Christ with any depth or intensity if we do not expand our capacity for more of God through the furnace of pain and difficulty. "Christ learned humanhood from his suffering (Heb 5:8). And we learn Christhood from our suffering."[24]

Could it be that "our homelessness, our alienation, our misery, our confusion, our lover's quarrel with the world—that this is our greatest blessing, next to God Himself"?[25] Not because these things in themselves are good but because they are the *means* by which we grow more dependent on God, seeking him and finding him as the only good that is greater than the things we love dearly in this life. In our loss, we discover the rest and joy and consolation that come with finding God himself.

Blaise Pascal came to see this truth, humbly realizing it in a prayer that I find hard to pray. Yet it is profound in its implications for us:

> I ask you neither for health nor for sickness, for life nor for death; but that you may dispose of my health and my sickness, my life and my death, for your glory. . . . You alone know what is expedient for me; you are the sovereign master; do with me according to your will. . . . I know but one thing, Lord, that it is good to follow you, and bad to offend you. Apart from that, I know not what is good or bad in anything. I know not which is most profitable to me, health or sickness, wealth or poverty, nor anything else in the world. That discernment is beyond the power of men or angels, and is hidden among the secrets of your Providence, which I adore, but do not seek to fathom.[26]

These words could have been those of Jesus in Gethsemane before he died. The gospel writers tell us he didn't want the suffering cup of God's judgment, but in the end he was settled: "Not my will, but yours be done" (Luke 22:42). Over and over in the Bible we find that God uses suffering to release us from dependence on other loves, and God knows that our greatest need is to know and love him more than life itself. Sometimes he keeps us from pleasures and prosperity that he knows will ruin us. In our encounters with hardship, there is a profound difference between the unbelieving world and the followers of Jesus. For the world, pain is fundamental and joy is superficial—it won't last. Yet for the believer, pain is superficial and joy is fundamental—it will be our ultimate reward.

I learned He never gives a thorn without this added grace,
He takes the thorn to pin aside the veil which hides His face.[27]

Our trials and pains will produce in us a good that is like nothing in this world—if we let them shape us rather than melt us. We must trust, somehow, that the pain is making us what he intends us to be: holy, like him.

What Princess Leia Taught Me about Pain

Our moments of pain and stretching are then always being *used* by God to do nothing less than bring us to himself, and thus closer to finding ourselves. Jesus repeatedly taught this truth: "Unless a kernel of wheat falls to the ground and dies, it remains only a single seed. *But if it dies,* it produces many seeds" (John 12:24, emphasis added). When we die (or experience discomfort, pain, or challenge), we grow, we expand, we multiply. As Martin Luther King Jr. used to say, "The cross we bear precedes the crown we wear."[28]

Recently, I read a memoir of Carrie Fisher, the actress who played Princess Leia in *Star Wars* at the age of nineteen. In her book *Wishful Drinking*, she shared about her addiction to drugs and alcohol over the span of her life. The first time she entered rehab was in her twenties, and she would go on to battle addiction for much of her life until she passed away suddenly in December 2016. In the book she reflected on her addiction, saying it was driven by a desire for happiness. "Happy," she said, "is one of the many things I'm likely to be over the course of a day and certainly over the course of a lifetime. But I think if you have the expectation that you're going to be happy through your life—more to the point, if you have a need to be *comfortable all the time*—among other things, you have the makings of an addict."[29]

Fisher says it was a revelation to her that what she needed to do first to find freedom from addiction was to get her compulsion for comfort under control. One day, she had to go to an AA meeting that was three hours long, and she didn't want to go because she didn't like the meetings. Her friend said she didn't have to *like* meetings, she just had to go to them. "Well, this was a revelation to me! I thought I had to like everything I did. And for me to like everything I did meant that I needed to take a boat load of dope. But if what this person told me were true, then I didn't have to actually be comfortable all the time. If I could, in fact, learn to experience a quota of discomfort, it would be awesome news."[30] You find a similar truth in the stories of many other addicts. In a recent interview with Howard Stern, Ben Affleck, who was an alcoholic during his marriage to Jennifer Garner, said that his early days of trying to be sober were really hard, but for him *"the cure for addiction was suffering . . .* When I felt it impacted my kids, it was the worst day of my life . . . Since that day, I have not ever wanted to drink once. Ever. So it's the easiest thing in the world."[31]

Both Fisher and Affleck are saying what the Bible points out again and again. *Pain is the way forward.* As Tolkien says about Sam Gamgee after he goes through trial after trial in his journey to destroy the ring of power in *The Lord of the Rings*: "But even as hope died in Sam, or seemed to die, it was turned to a new strength. . . . And he felt through all his limbs a thrill, as if he was turning into some creature of stone and steel that neither despair nor weariness nor endless barren miles could subdue."[32]

Pain is not something we enjoy, but in a fallen world it is the way we grow strong. And while I don't seek after it (who does?), I know that the most important lessons I have learned in my life have come through difficulty. I have asked God many times to take away my mental challenges (Tourette syndrome and OCD): "Save me from the embarrassment of being on a stage twitching and making weird faces and noises. It is distracting and annoying for all those forced to watch and listen!" And yet he doesn't. But even more than my present struggle, as hard as it is at times, I wonder about the teenage Mark. I wonder why God would allow that pain and struggle. Those uncontrollable tics, the weird noises, the bashing of my knees. Or the year I spent alone in my room having lost most of my friends, just living in my imagination. I remember my dad leaving, his death, and the feeling of being abandoned, alone, and scared.

What was the *purpose* of all that pain? I don't know, but I can honestly say as I look back that I wouldn't ask for my life to be one iota different. Because something in all that struggle has made me who I am today. If God had saved me from all that pain, I would be a different person with different experiences. It would mean that my loneliness never would have driven me to meet a friend named Chris, who led me to Jesus, which then led me to a guy named Rob, who invited me to church, where I met Erin, whom I then married and entered this crazy adventure called life with. I've had experiences with her I never could have dreamed of. My obsessive personality, while hard to live with, also makes me pretty good at my job. I obsess over my work: whether it's preaching or writing or leading or pastoring, I pore over these tasks with extra attention and effort. But I am not sure I would have been able to do these things any other way. My brain is broken, but aiming that brokenness at the right things can have great results.

Charles Spurgeon, the nineteenth-century preacher who struggled deeply with depression, often spoke of the role of pain and suffering. In one of his reflections, he said something I believe with all my heart:

> Even our mercies, like roses, have their thorns. . . . The trials which come from God are sent to prove and strengthen our graces, to test the genuineness of our virtues, and to add to their energy. Our Lord in His infinite wisdom and superabundant

love, sets so high a value upon His people's faith that He will not screen them from those trials by which faith is strengthened. You would never have possessed the precious faith which now supports you if the trial of your faith had not been like unto fire. You are a tree that never would have rooted so well if the wind had not rocked you to and fro. Worldly ease is a great foe to faith; it loosens the joints of holy valor, and snaps the sinews of sacred courage. The balloon never rises until the cords are cut; affliction does this sharp service for believing souls. While the wheat sleeps comfortably in the husk it is useless to man, it must be threshed out of its resting place before its value can be known. Thus it is well that Jehovah trieth the righteous, for it causes them to grow rich towards God.[33]

Do the fires of life melt us or make us? The latter can be true. And I think Scripture and our experiences point to this.

A few years ago, a grizzly bear mauled a friend of mine in the mountains of British Columbia while he was out hunting. The bear pounced on his chest while slashing at his body, and the pain caused my friend to pass out—which likely saved his life. He later told me that his scars and that harrowing experience shaped him into a different, deeper man—someone who, after the attack, loves and follows God *more* rather than less. Of course, such an attack could also have led to the opposite: a depressed and lost man. What makes the difference? Understanding what our pain is—that it has some place and purpose in the ongoing story of our lives.

Safe in Dying

But what if my friend had died that day? Would that mean God is not good or powerful, or that he doesn't exist? The church has often fumbled its response to pain and suffering. We preach or have theology that makes people feel that their suffering is somehow their fault because God wants only health and safety for their lives. If that is the case, then every death and sickness and financial struggle is outside of what God is trying to do. We visit sick friends or relatives in the hospital and say things like, "These things don't just happen. Somewhere, you must have stepped outside of God's will." Some faith movements within Christianity teach that if we have enough faith, we won't (or shouldn't) experience suffering. "Sickness is never God's will!" they say.

I had a pastor friend who believed this and told me not to say the word *cancer* around him because saying it would "welcome it into his house"; he preferred to deny its reality. I assured him that this belief was more akin to witchcraft than Christian theology. As a pastor, he didn't appreciate that, but it was true.

The Bible doesn't shy away from talking about pain and agony, but it also doesn't blame us for it as if it's all a form of karma. When people ask Jesus who is to blame for the suffering of the blind man in John 9, they give him two options: "this man or his parents" (v. 2). But Jesus outright denies both, saying, "Neither this man nor his parents sinned" (v. 3). He is clear that their sinning hadn't directly caused this man's suffering. Such ideas belong to religious or superstitious views of the world, not the way of Jesus. Instead, Jesus says this suffering is for God's glory to be displayed, and then he compassionately heals the man, speaking nothing of his mistakes.

That story has something important for all of us—namely, that faith in God offers no insurance against tragedy. Repeatedly, the Bible makes this clear. Faith in Jesus doesn't mean we won't die but that we are *safe in dying*.

Do our pain and suffering mean we are just weak animals, grasping at straws in times of need? I don't think so, though we do tend to lean on God when we have nothing else. As the old saying goes, you don't realize Jesus is all you need until Jesus is all you have. God becomes more visceral to us when we are stripped of distractions. C. S. Lewis's famous phrase rings true: "God whispers to us in our pleasures, speaks in our conscience, but shouts in our pains."[34] It's not that God actually turns up the volume, but more that we turn up the intensity of our listening when we are in pain.

Modern science and academia agree with this understanding of pain and suffering in our lives. Psychologist James Davies calls it the "importance of suffering," saying that it is a mistake to interpret a patient who suffers from "low self-esteem" or "feelings of worth-lessness" as simply suffering from "distorted thinking patterns" or "thinking errors." Instead, what if our negative thoughts about ourselves are actually right? The feeling of being cowardly may not be faulty thinking at all but an accurate appraisal of part of us that *is* *cowardly*. Facing that reality, he says, rather than denying it, is the prerequisite to changing. He then points out that many people, instead of being plagued with low self-esteem, are actually plagued "with self-love," so much so "that they are unable to love others and cannot see beyond the horizon of their own needs and concerns."[35] The prevailing view that the depressed person tends to distort reality in a negative way may be wrong: "Recent research has turned this received wisdom on its head [saying] that it is not the depressive who distorts reality but the so-called healthy population . . . because they remove the positive self-biases that are seen in the non-depressed."[36]

It is like the message of the Pixar film *Inside Out*, wherein the characters learn that to be healthy, sometimes joy needs to give up the controls and hand them over to sadness, that being sad is actually part of life for a reason.

Perhaps we are just catching up to something God has been telling us all along: that sometimes happiness and prosperity are what lead us astray, sending us into an echo chamber far from reality and far from what is best for our flourishing. As hard as this is to swallow, I believe it may be true. And it leads us to the last reality we will explore regarding the question of our pain.

Why Is God Silent?

The last thing I want to tackle is not so much what God does in regard to our pain in life but what it seems he *doesn't* do—namely, the question of his silence. If God is good and loving, his apparent refusal to answer our specific questions about our suffering—as the books of Psalms and Job and Lamentations and Revelation point out again and again—leads us to more questions. Why is God silent in the face of our diagnosis, the loss of our spouse, the mental strain we feel and wouldn't wish on our worst enemy? Smarter thinkers have wrestled with this question, and I wish I could say I have found a great answer (I haven't). But I want to offer one way of thinking about this that hit me recently, an insight that came from an unlikely source, a novel written by the brilliant Jewish writer Chaim Potok called *The Chosen*.

The main character, Reuven Malther, makes friends with Danny Saunders, the brilliant (think Matt Damon's character in *Good Will Hunting*) son of a Hasidic rabbi named Reb Saunders. Both Reuven and Danny are raised in conservative orthodox Jewish homes in Brooklyn during the 1940s. Danny's father is raising him in strict silence, meaning he doesn't talk directly to him at all.

Danny goes through many trials and finally grows up, chooses a college, and is moving on with his life away from his father and his bizarre silent treatment, which has been torture. In the last pages of the novel, Danny and Reuven finally have a meeting with Danny's father the rabbi. He talks to Danny only through Reuven, never once looking at his son. But he explains why he raised Danny the way he did. And as I read it, I found myself crying uncontrollably.

Reb, the father, explains that early in Danny's life, he could see that Danny had an unbelievably brilliant mind but possessed *little soul*. "I looked at my Daniel when he was four years old, and I said to myself, How will I teach this mind what it is to have a soul? How will I teach it to *want* to take on another person's suffering . . . while not abandoning the Master of the Universe and his Commandments?" As a young boy, Danny felt no compassion for the suffering of others, no empathy, no sense of mercy. "Ah, what a price to pay . . . ," Reb says, "the years when he was a child and I loved him and talked with him and held him when I prayed . . . 'Why do you cry, Father?' he asked me once. 'Because people are suffering,' I told him. He could not understand. Ah, what it is to be a mind without a soul." He then says, "You can listen to silence. I've begun to realize that you can listen to silence and learn from it. It has a quality and a dimension all its own."[37]

Reb tells the story of his own brother, who forsook Jewish observance in favor of intellectual pursuits and then died in the gas chambers of Auschwitz. He explains that only knowledge of the immense suffering in the world can redeem one's soul. Reb reveals that the silence he imposed on Danny was a way to teach him compassion, to teach him to feel the suffering of others. He then confesses that his own father raised him that way. Reb himself learned through silence to turn inward, to feel his own pain and, in doing so, to suffer for his people. He says that bearing this burden is a fundamental part of being a *tzaddik* (a truly righteous man in the world). Reb finishes by telling Reuven that while of course with Danny's brilliant mind Reb always wanted him to be a rabbi like he is, he does not care what profession he chooses—he knows now that his son has a soul and "will be a tzaddik for the world" no matter what job he holds. Reb finally turns to his son Danny, speaking ever so quietly, and asks him if he will shave off his beard and earlocks for graduate school given that he is not choosing to be a rabbi; Danny nods that he will. He asks if Danny will continue to observe the Ten Commandments; Danny nods that he will. Stuttering, Reb shuffles out of the room. Danny bursts into tears, and his friend Reuven goes over to him, puts his hand on his shoulder. "I was crying too," he says, "silently, for his pain and for the years of his suffering, knowing that I loved him, and not knowing whether I hated or loved the long-anguished years of his life."[38]

I wonder sometimes whether this story gives us a hint. It doesn't explain the reason for our suffering but perhaps explains God's silence in it. Maybe God's silence has a reason similar to Reb's: To help us, in all our brilliance and strength and arrogance, to be able to connect to the pain of our neighbor. To teach us compassion and empathy. To let us connect to the suffering of others in a way we otherwise wouldn't. To ensure we have a soul and not just a mind.

To teach us how to be *tzaddik*—righteous—for the world.

The medical doctor Dr. Paul Brand made a similar point about the human body: that cells need to care about other cells or the whole body dies. "In human society," he said, "*we are suffering because we do not suffer enough.* . . . Due to the selfishness of one living organism that simply doesn't care when the next one suffers. In the body . . . we call it cancer . . . and if it is allowed to spread the body is doomed."[39] This is the concern Danny's father had all along, and the only way he thinks Danny can ever lean in and feel for others is for him to *not always be protected and insulated* from the elements of this harsh world. In the long run, he believes some semblance of pain will result in a better Danny and, more importantly, a better world.

Or maybe Spurgeon was right when in one of his sermons, through pain and agony, he looked out on his congregation and said, "God does not need your strength: he has more than enough power of his own. He asks for your weakness: he has none of that."[40]

I will add that all that silence, of course, caused Danny many years of confusion and pain, which is hard to justify in my mind. But the book does close in an interesting and profound way. Danny comes to Reuven's house, and Reuven and his father are saying goodbye as Reuven heads off to college. Reuven's father, reflecting on the brutality of raising a son in silence, says to Danny, "When you have a son of your own, will you raise him in silence?"

Danny says nothing for a long time.

And then . . . "Yes, if I can't find another way."

PART IV

The Problem of
PURPOSE

*Yes, a key can lie forever in the place where the
locksmith left it, and never be used to open the
lock the master forged it for.*

—LUDWIG WITTGENSTEIN

I recently read a story about a group of amateur mountain climbers who were climbing Mont Blanc in the French Alps. Their guide told them to leave all their belongings behind and to bring only what was necessary for the climb. One of the guys thought he could make it with all the extras he had always dreamed of bringing to the top of the mountain: a block of cheese, a bottle of wine, two or three extra camera lenses, a nice blanket. So he brushed off the guide's advice and packed it all. Halfway up, he couldn't carry everything anymore. It was too heavy, too cumbersome. Now he had a decision to make: either leave the stuff behind or give up his dream of making it to the top of the mountain. He sat down, opened the bottle of wine, laid out the blanket, and bid farewell to the group, and they went on without him.

I can't help but see some of us and our journey through life in this story. Human beings make decisions every day, and some of them are grand blunders. When we find we can't make it to the top of life with all of our accessories, or when life doesn't work out the way we thought it would, instead of facing the hard truths—maybe we miscalculated or are trying to carry too much or are taking the wrong path—and adjusting plans, we *let the top go* and pitch our tent in the plain.[1] We settle for sex and drink and money as if these things were *the thing* itself, not realizing they are just pointers to a far greater glory. And in doing so, we trade in our shot at the greater glory. As C. S. Lewis once said, we are far too easily pleased and content "making mud pies in a slum when we are being offered a holiday at sea."[2] We settle for mediocrity in shiny things that promise life but never deliver. The good life is the enemy of the great life.

We avoid this mistake by knowing not only who we are, as we have explored, but also *what we were made for*, which we will now explore, and going after nothing less than that, never settling for less than the life God intends for each and every one of us—and the joy that follows.

CHAPTER 8

Live Out What You
Were Made For,
NOT
SOMEONE
ELSE

*The reason death sticks so closely to life isn't
biological necessity—it's envy. Life is so beautiful
that death has fallen in love with it, a jealous,
possessive love that grabs at what it can. But life
leaps over oblivion lightly, losing only a thing
or two of no importance, and gloom is but the
passing shadow of a cloud.*

—YANN MARTEL, LIFE OF PI

I will always remember the day I first heard my daughter's heartbeat.
With excitement, Erin and I went to the ultrasound appointment,
and I remember the monitor sending out the echo of that little beating
heart. "I *will* be born, I *will* be born, I *will* be born," it seemed to say.
And then months later, as Erin delivered her through pain, blood, and
near-death, the baby came.

But came *where*? To do what? And why?

Why do we live? Why do we cherish life with such passion? Why, when there is every reason to despair, do we continue? Why are we on this planet? Why are *you* on this planet? And how do you flourish rather than flounder in this life? Or as the philosopher James Loder puts it, "What is a lifetime? And why do we live it?"[1]

These are the central questions of our lives, and it is impossible to answer the question—or problem—of life and the deep longings of the soul without answering them, as well as the question that orbits them all—namely, What is my purpose?

What We Do in Life Echoes in Eternity

The creation story tells us many things about ourselves as human beings. Contrary to many modern versions of self-help, it says that we flourish not by sitting around pondering who we are in a vague way, exploring our personality profile in a vacuum, but by *doing what we are given to do in the world*. Scholars sometimes call this the "cultural mandate," which is found in the first chapter of Genesis: "Be fruitful and multiply and fill the earth and subdue it, and have dominion" (Gen. 1:28 ESV).

Rather than attributing something to the first human pair regarding their *essence*, or "inner identity," as we tend to emphasize, God assigns them something to *do*. He gives them a *role*—not a particular talent or trait or Enneagram number so they can figure out their "personality" or specific bent, but something more profound. He gives them a role in managing the chaos—a task in which we all can partake and find our fulfillment. It's a broad cultural mandate and a specific personal mandate.

No other creature God made has this. Humans are to be *fruitful* instead of just takers and consumers. They are to *have dominion* so the world around them flourishes rather than flounders.

In other words, no matter who you are or what you do, whether you are a doctor, a stay-at-home mom, an artist, an accountant, a CEO, or a prisoner, there is important work for you to do.

One chapter later the writer of Genesis sets the stage for our grand task: "Now no shrub had yet appeared on the earth . . . for . . . there was no one to work the ground" (Gen. 2:5). Wherever will God find someone to help make the world flourish and work? That, it turns out, is the task for both Adam and his wife, Eve. It's a work that J. R. R. Tolkien once called *subcreation*.

"The earth was an empty waste and darkness was over the deep waters" (Gen. 1:2 NLV). Here we see that while the world is good, it isn't perfect. There are words in Hebrew for "perfect," and they aren't used here. The world is wild, created with massive potential that can be turned into an amazing reality.[2] Nancy Guthrie summarizes the creation account by noting that "Eden was unspoiled but also unfinished."[3] And it was humankind's job to finish it—to make the "wild and waste" of Eden and what lay beyond it into order and beauty, to bring the loving, perfect rule of its Creator over the whole earth so it would sing. Unlike the other high mammals, who are born as essentially completed organisms, "man is curiously 'unfinished' at birth, and we are impelled to impose meaningful order on reality."[4]

As we look to the future, contrary to what many Christians might think, this unique and compelling vision for our lives *does not end with the end of this world* but continues with the dawning of the new world—the new heaven and new earth. We catch hints of this continuation when the picture of redemption in Christ comes full circle back to this picture in Genesis wherein in heaven human beings don't just exist but reign with Christ over a renewed earth (Eph. 2:6; Rev. 3:21; 5:10). Instead of us sitting around singing forever or being in blissful contemplation in a disembodied spirit world, the Bible says we are embodied, resurrected people carrying forward the original task

God gave us in the garden at a cosmic level we cannot fully imagine! This is what is behind the parables of Jesus wherein he promises to his followers, "You have been faithful in the smallest of things, now take charge of ten cities," "five cities," "many things" (See Matt. 25:21; Luke 19:17). Dallas Willard says, "In due time, I can only imagine it will be some while after our passage into God's full world—we will begin to assume new responsibilities."[5] If this is true, he says, it is quite different from the vision of heaven that we often have in our minds: "Perhaps it would be good for each of us to ask ourselves: Really, how many cities could I now govern under God? If, for example, Baltimore or Liverpool were turned over to me, with power to do what I want with it, how would things turn out? An honest answer to this question might do much to prepare us for our eternal future in this universe."[6] It is an amazing and startling vision of our future, perhaps closer to what Russell Crowe's character Maximus in *Gladiator* lays in front of his soldiers: "What we do in life echoes in eternity!" Indeed. So Willard continues,

> We will actively participate in the future governance of the universe. We will not sit around looking at one another or at God for eternity but will join in. . . . We will "reign with him" (Rev. 5:10) in the endlessly ongoing creative work of God. It is for this that we were each individually intended. . . . A place in God's creative order has been reserved for each one of us from before the beginnings of cosmic existence. His plan is for us to develop, as apprentices to Jesus, to the point where we can take our place in the ongoing creativity of the universe.[7]

What an amazing vision and foundation for your life: That every day you wake up, you are living toward this great future. That the new creation will be an eternal reality filled with creativity, responsibility, and new experiences versus this short-lived, temporal time we currently inhabit. Eternal life isn't disconnected from this one, but like walking through a door from one room in your house to another, it continues on in the same vein, with wider expanse. Our eternal experience in heaven, as Willard says, "will not fundamentally be different in character from what it is now, though it will of course change in significant details. The life we now have as the persons we now are will continue in the universe in which we now exist."[8] There is continuity with what we are tasked to do in the here and now that goes on and shapes eternity.

This is all part of the larger point we are homing in on here. As Christopher Watkin said, "A Christian philosophy of meaning could do worse than to begin with a meditation on Adam's naming of the animals."[9] Why? Because in that act God grants to humankind, he is giving us authority over the world. It is similar to God's naming of Adam and speaks fundamentally to something we were *made for*: ruling and reigning as good stewards of the world. We have work and it has purpose. We toil to see the world around us taken from where it is presently to a better version of itself. We are meant to shape it, to improve it. Biblically, this is our calling, and it is essential to knowing ourselves.

On the flip side, to not wake up in the morning to significantly contribute to and shape the world—or even our little worlds—is to have no joy at all. It is to be lost in the wide expanse of things, to quite literally have no identity and hence to have the feeling of emptiness we all glimpse from time to time, and which devours many of us. The call to engage in this world and leave it different from when we awoke this morning goes straight to our "why" as human beings. It's why our hearts beat. It's to know why God placed us, and not another, on planet earth at such a time as this. This gets at Paul's point in his famous sermon in Athens: "From one man [God] made all the nations, that they should inhabit the whole earth; and he marked out their appointed times in history and the boundaries of their lands" (Acts 17:26). The fact that you exist *now*, in the place you do with the people who surround you and the opportunities in front of you, is all part of a grander plan. As C. S. Lewis once said, this applies even right down to your friendships:

> In friendship . . . we think we have chosen our peers. In reality a few years' difference in the dates of our births, a few more miles between certain houses, the choice of one university instead of another . . . the accident of a topic being raised or not raised at a first meeting—any of these chances might have kept us apart. But, for a Christian, there are, strictly speaking, no chances. A secret master of ceremonies has been at work. Christ, who said to the disciples, "You have not chosen me, but I have chosen you," can truly say to every group of Christian friends, "You have not chosen one another but I have chosen you for one another." The friendship is not a reward for our discriminating and good taste in finding one another out. It is the instrument by which God reveals to each of us the beauties of others.[10]

In other words, our lives are no accident. You are not an accident. And you have work to do. To make the world sing. To leave it better than you found it. God has appointed you for such a time as this.

And when I say you, I mean *you*. Not *them*. Never compare yourself to anyone else. Their story is not your story for a reason. The thing that eats away at our contentment most in life is comparison. We scroll social media and compare our bodies, our jobs, our spouses, our houses, our kids, and every time we do we shrivel a little inside. My grandfather lived until he was one hundred years old, and he didn't struggle with health issues in his life almost at all. He just died of old age. On the flip side, I have done funerals for thirty-year-olds and younger, or people who have had multiple cancers and sicknesses throughout their lives. In our minds, none of that is *fair*, and of course I don't pretend to understand why it happens, but the book of Ecclesiastes assures us that everyone has their set time and life according to what God is doing, and we can't completely understand it.

It is why when you read the Gospels not everyone is treated the same. A rich guy comes to Jesus and says, "What do I need to do to get eternal life?" Jesus says, "Give all that you have to the poor," and yet to the guy on the cross who asked him, he said, "You don't need to do anything; I will see you in paradise this very day." What is that? I don't know, but I know that God never writes the same story twice. And that is freeing. You aren't them, so don't try to be.

He has things for you to do in this world that no one else can do like you. Never compare yourself—your looks, your talents, your spouse, your income—to anyone else. It will only drive you to darkness. Instead, go after what God has given *you* to do and you will find a joy that nothing can steal from you. Your unique and special place in the world is needed. Right now.

Bearing a Load

The calling to do all this, however, is lived out not in the paradise of Eden, of course, but in a fallen, broken world. We are in a world of debt and divorce, tsunamis and taxes, poverty and parasites. The task has not changed, but it has been made more difficult.

Modern psychology has finally caught up with the biblical vision. The academic and clinical psychologist Jordan Peterson says the very "purpose of life" is found in exactly this tension: "To do good. And the only way to do good is to find the biggest burden you can carry, and then carry it. . . . The only way to achieve lasting fulfillment and a sense of true and unwavering peace is to carry our burdens and carry on with our missions."[11] Some might object and say that a load or burden is something to avoid. Why would I want to carry it and disrupt my comfort? Shouldn't we avoid hard things to truly flourish?

As we saw in our look at the purpose of pain, the Bible is clear that the work of shaping the world comes with adversity. God tells us what life will be like in this fallen world: "By hard work you will eat food from [the earth] all the days of your life. It will grow thorns and thistles for you. . . . You will eat bread by the sweat of your face because of hard work, until you return to the ground" (Gen. 3:17–19 NLV).

God designed us for the hardship he knew we would face. Peterson is on to something when he frames our burden-carrying as he does. People have been designed to overcome struggle and fight adversity, he says, but when there's no adversity to face, either we create some fake adversity or we become useless and suffer. Without challenge, we don't grow. Struggle is one of nature's ways of strengthening us. Some even quit comfortable, well-paying jobs in which they're not challenged. They come to a place where they think, "It's a good job. It gives me security, and yet I can't stand this. It's eating away at my soul. It's all security and no challenge." Part of the reason we feel this way is because adversity is what we were built for—it's what strengthens us. We need to be strong because life is extraordinarily difficult:

> Because the evil king is always whittling away at the structure of
> the state. And you have to be awake and sharp to stop that from
> happening so that you don't become corrupt. And so that your
> family doesn't become corrupt. And so that your state doesn't
> have to become corrupt. You have to have your eyes open, and
> your wits sharp, and your words at the ready. And you have to
> be educated. And you have to know about your history. And you
> have to know how to think. And you have to know how to read.

And you have to know how to speak. And you have to know how to aim. And you have to be willing to hoist the troubles of the world up on your shoulders. . . . Then the second part of that is the better part, and it's the optimistic part, which is despite the fact that life is a tragedy tainted by malevolence, at every level of existence there's something about the human spirit that can thrive under precisely those conditions, because as difficult as life is—and as horrible as we are—our capacity to deal with that catastrophe and to transcend that malevolent spirit is more powerful than that reality itself.[12]

Living out your purpose in life requires taking on responsibility. We know there is something wrong with the world that needs to be set right, and perhaps the one to do that is you. Your life is not about drifting without an end goal but responding to a calling from a divine voice.

We are built for action and adventure, living under God's order and plan in a contested cosmos. "Go from your country," God told Abraham, "your people and your father's household to the land I will show you. . . . I will make your name great, and you will be a blessing. . . . And all peoples on earth will be blessed through you" (Gen. 12:1–3). The blessing in our lives, like Abraham's, is found in the going and the stretching. It's in the risk of responding to the call and walking by faith, trusting in the One who calls us. When you wake up in the middle of the night and the doubts crowd in, you will have this as your defense: For all my flaws, I am doing *this*. I am responding to the call, fighting for my family, serving my church, working for the good of my city, being there for my coworkers—and though I am not perfect and I stumble about, this is the load I have been given to carry.[13]

When I was twenty years old, I didn't have much responsibility for others. My life revolved around going to school, dating, playing video games, and working. In my early twenties I got married, we moved across the country, we had our first child, and I started working as a pastor. When I was twenty-seven God called me to do something I had never considered before. He asked me not just to *lead* an existing church but to *start* one from scratch. Initially, I was confused. Aren't there enough churches? Most of them are half empty. Eventually, though, I saw that the data was clear: new churches are more effective at reaching new people and new people groups than established ones. With so many people who didn't know Jesus in my city, why not try everything we could to reach them? Over the course of a year, we gathered a core group of thirty-five people, moved our family, found a gymnasium at a local elementary school, and started our church. The first year wasn't the success we wanted it to be. We had 162 people on our opening Sunday, dropping to around 90 halfway through that year. It was a grind. We fought hard for every person we reached, every dollar we raised, every ministry we started, every volunteer we wooed. During those first years, every sermon, every wedding, every funeral, every counseling session, every staff hire and fire, every decision made about everything came through me.

Over time, the church grew. One hundred became three hundred and then twelve hundred. We moved locations, and twelve hundred became three thousand and on and on. Now with three young daughters, a wife, a master's degree to finish, and an entire church on my shoulders, I—maybe for the first time in my life—felt the burden of carrying something that pushed me to my limit. But it was a good burden. The kind that defines a person. I felt the weight of paying the bills and running the daily operations of a church, but more than that, the weight of reaching people in our city, teaching well, casting a vision, helping the poor, fighting sex trafficking, and building schools and hospitals overseas. I forced myself to look beyond myself and to take responsibility for the world. And while it was all harder and more exhausting and more stressful, it was also *better*.

All the wins and successes of our church—all the marriages saved, addicts set free, people baptized, kids discipled, poor served—are things that made me who I am. They were all a product of a burden carried. Yes, there were years of long hours, burnout, exhaustion, criticism, backstabbings, and people leaving. Yes, I had to pastor people through the death of their kids, fire staff for adultery, fall on my sword for people who fumbled the ball but who needed to be protected, and on and on it went.

The hurts have been numerous, but I tell you about them only to say that while it was complicated and weighty to do all this, it was also all worth it. It was what I was supposed to do. It was part of my calling, my identity. It was a chance to have lasting impact on the world, because I refused to just keep sitting around playing video games, with my eyes and heart closed to the corruption of the world around me.

Real, lasting joy, the kind that comes from doing fulfilling, God-given work, is often birthed in us from the decision to take the harder road. To feel pain because we chose to get close to it to heal whatever little bit of it we can. Such is the calling of us all: to bear a burden almost too heavy for us to bear. To go to bed tired because we took up the task of bringing heaven to earth in whatever small way we could.

The Curious Case of Dieter Zander

When we take on responsibility and follow our divine callings, our lives take on meaning in ways they didn't previously. While my story meant starting churches and pastoring, finding meaning is not limited to that. It can be found in all of life, in every little thing *you* do every day. We honor our divine calling by raising kids; being a coffee barista, a teacher, a realtor; or running a company—it's all sacred work. Martin Luther recaptured this biblical idea during the Protestant Reformation—and also got in a lot of trouble for it. At that time, the work of priests was the only thing seen as spiritual and divine, but Luther disagreed, saying,

> It is pure invention that popes, bishops, priests are to be called the "spiritual estate"; while princes, lords, artisans, and farmers the "temporal estate." That is indeed a fine bit of lying and hypocrisy. . . . If a little group of Christians were taken captive and set down in a wilderness, and had among them no priest . . . and if there they were to agree in choosing one of themselves, and were to charge him with the office of baptizing, and preaching, such a man would be as truly a priest as though all bishops and popes had consecrated him. . . . There is really no difference between laymen and priests, princes and bishops, "spirituals" and "temporals," as they call them, except that of office and work. . . . A cobbler, a smith, a farmer, each has the work and office of his trade, and yet they are all alike consecrated priests and bishops.[14]

When the mundane or ordinary things of life are framed in light of our divine calling, they take on a new meaning. What did Jesus do with his time on earth? Was most of his time spent preaching in a synagogue or hanging out with the religious folks or reading books in a library? No, as R. Paul Stevens points out in his book *Down-to-Earth Spirituality*, Jesus was Jerusalem's favorite dinner guest. He also spent three years rubbing shoulders with tax collectors, was touched by prostitutes, went fishing, and worked as a carpenter. In other words, true spirituality and walking in God's purpose for our lives doesn't make us angels. It makes us *fully human* in the everyday things of life, infusing those ordinary moments with meaning. It's in naming a new baby, eating a meal, working hard, being present with friends around a warm fire, telling and retelling stories, falling in love, getting married, making love, having children, and facing head-on the sufferings of life and the ultimate problem of life, our own death.[15]

You are on a meaningful path whether you are a priest or a politician, a lawyer or a loan officer, a teacher or a truck driver. "Whatever you do, do it from the heart for the Lord," Paul says (Col. 3:23 CEB). The key idea is that whatever we do, we do it with excellence and intentionality, as an offering to God. This verse kept me going through many hard days of work in my life, especially when I served as a janitor, worked at a Michaels Arts and Crafts store, washed dishes at local restaurants, or was the guy collecting carts in the parking lot of a department store in the middle of January when it was twenty below zero. I would literally play this verse over and over in my head to get through the day because it infused that seemingly insignificant work with a sense of worth. This verse also reminds me of how Steve Jobs, as he was growing up, would spend hours making sure screws looked a certain way inside a cabinet he was building, even though no one would ever see them. For him, everything was art and it *mattered*. As the preacher and theologian Jonathan Edwards once said, "Worldly business attended to with great cheerfulness, as part of the service of God 'tis found to be as good as prayer."[16]

Dieter Zander was a musician and preacher at one of the most influential churches in the United States. He would tour all the big conferences where thousands of youth and young adults would worship Jesus. God was using Dieter for the most amazing things.

One morning, Dieter woke up and learned he had suffered a stroke. It affected his ability to move his face and use his voice—leading him to resign as a pastor. Instead, he got a job at Trader Joe's mopping floors in obscurity, stocking shelves, and taking extra food to the Salvation Army. Reflecting on his new reality, Zander said that when he was doing ministry, "God was my boss, but God is my friend now. God says, 'Dieter, you are not going to work. Now we play.'"[17]

You see, there is no audience in Dieter's world now, but that's okay. Because *he's not performing* anymore. He lives and works for an audience of One—the only One whose applause and approval really matter.

Listen to the Disenchantment in You

When we understand this, it is then and only then we are truly free to live and be ourselves. Jesus invites us to find the peace we are all looking for by coming to him with our burdens rather than looking to ourselves, our output, our talents, etc.: "Come to me, all you who are weary and burdened, and I will give you rest. . . . For my yoke is easy and my burden is light" (Matt. 11:28–30). "Easy is a soul word, not a circumstance word. Aim at having easy circumstances and life will be hard all around. Aim at having an easy soul, and your capacity for tackling hard assignments will actually grow. The soul was not made for an easy life. The soul was made for an easy yoke."[18] And that yoke needs to be God's and not your own, or the yoke of things around you, or the people around you, or the myriad other things that could be controlling your life.

Coming to God is a relief, not a burden. This is why he came.

Whatever is crumbling around you, wherever you feel stuck in life, know that his heart is for you. What the theologian Thomas Goodwin said so many years ago is just as true today: "That which keeps men from Jesus is, that they know not Christ's mind and heart. . . . The truth that he is more glad of us than we can be of him."[20]

We will remain unsettled and disappointed and unfulfilled until we heed the call of God and shoulder responsibility, but do so knowing that if and when we fail, he doesn't crush us but was crushed for us and bears the burden alongside us as we labor in the world. The task we were handed in the garden is now reinterpreted in light of the work God has done through Jesus. With Jesus, we bring order to the chaos of the world and beauty out of the ashes. Through him, we *set the world to rights in whatever way it seems set aside for us to do.*

In that sense, ironically, the *disenchantment* we have with the way the world is serves as an indicator of our specific and personal destiny and calling: your annoyance with your job, the government, your parents, your spouse. The part of yourself oriented toward the highest good highlights the gap between the ideal you imagine and the way the world is presently. These are hints to what you are being called to turn around, to give your life to fix and make hum. While it would be far more fun to tell you that your flourishing is found in the successes and the inward tranquility of "finding yourself," I think it is in the tension and the imperfection of the world that we understand why we were made the way we were.

Think of Jesus turning over the tables in the temple. His discontentment and frustration with the religious leaders of his day and the way they were enslaving people led to one of the central acts of his life.

Our purpose and calling are found not only in perfect moments of bliss and meditation. They're not always in the serenity of the mountains or forests where we tend to escape. Often we discover our purpose in the midst of pain and challenge. Smack-dab in the midst of those times, it becomes as clear as blue crystal: This is why I was born. This is what I was put on this earth to do.

We know this as we stare at life and ask what principles it has for us. If we are paying attention, we may understand it after all: a new world is born not only through the pleasures of romance and what it takes to conceive but also through the blood and sweat and pain and fear and pushing and gasping and crying of labor itself.

CHAPTER 9

Become the Best
in the World

AT THE
FOLLOWING
THREE
THINGS . . .

The secret of man's being is not only to live but to have something to live for.

—FYODOR DOSTOEVSKY, *THE BROTHERS KARAMAZOV*

A few years ago, we took our three daughters to Disneyland. One of the rides had a two-and-a-half-hour-long wait. We began walking away, then a thought struck me: *I will model good parenting for my kids and show them the sacrifice of what it means to be a parent.* I said, "I'll wait in line. You guys go have fun." They all hugged me and said they would be back in a couple of hours. My phone ran out of battery at about the one-hour mark, so for the rest of the time I just stood there. I stuck my hands in my pockets and was just looking at people, talking to strangers, glancing around. Today's equivalent of a psychopath.

The minutes slowed and seemed to start moving backward until my family finally arrived. They had been enjoying a great time: cotton candy had been eaten, soda consumed; and they had gone on a bunch of other rides. And there I was missing it all—but my sacrifice had taught them a deep and profound truth about parenting. As they got in line beside me, I said, "Now remember, kids, one day you will do this for your kids. That's what sacrifice is."

There it was. Point made. Worth all the agony.

My oldest daughter, Sienna, looked at me and without missing a beat said, "No, I won't. My husband will!"

What an adventure in missing the point.

We laugh at such moments and tease people for missing obvious things about the world, without realizing we are in the same boat, ever so close to grasping and knowing and living out our clear and resounding purpose but often missing the point. We fall for models that emphasize inward introspection almost exclusively and so set us up to miss the point because they are too individualistic and not oriented to the world around us and our calling to it, or what the ancients called "vocation." As we have been discovering, having a vocation or calling is key to finding fulfillment in life. As the respected thinker Jonathan Haidt says, "Buddha may have taken things too far." It turns out that "happiness in our lives comes in part from *outside of yourself,* if you know where to look."[1]

So what are we supposed to *do?* That is one of the many mysteries in the universe, but the search is worth it because the anxiety and flailing and insecurity and uncertainty and sleepless nights and paranoia cease to control us once our purpose is realized.

Who Am I?

It could be argued that every story we tell—in literature or music or painting or dance or whatever—is a story about *identity*. The protagonist under the surface is trying to answer the questions, *Who am I?* and *What is my place in the world?*

These are the questions beating under the surface of all our lives if we are honest. Every morning, in every encounter, in every conversation with a stranger, it is the question pulsating through our veins. And every beat of our heart is pounding different answers. Who am I in regard to God (if there is one), to others, to my family and friends, to the world around me? Am I a hero or a villain? Am I a winner or a loser? Am I more powerful or influential than them or are they more so than me, and what does it matter anyhow? Am I cool? Am I pretty? Am I successful? Am I a failure? Am I a sinner or a saint? Am I both?

But while these questions bubble underneath our lives and our decisions, they aren't the ones we consciously spend our time asking. The philosopher Christian Smith argues that few people today in fact spend much time deliberately pondering the question of what we are as human beings. Instead, we spend our lives attending to what we see as more pressing matters—money, sex, family, relationships. Yet none of us can finally avoid, at a personal level, answering the big questions, "for the choices, trials, routines, and tragedies of human life require some assumptions and beliefs about human beings to guide our decisions, responses, and commitments."[2]

If what we have been exploring so far is even half true, then so much of what we thought we knew about how to find and keep our true purpose in life has been wrong. We've been duped. We've been told the secret to our life is either *indulgence* (atheism)—get more pleasure and adventure and sex and money and power and beauty and brains—at any cost and you will find yourself, and in so doing find peace and tranquility. Or the secret is *denial* (religion)—deny all forms of pleasure and worldly experience and only then will you find yourself and flourish. But of course, these and all the other narratives in between have failed to answer our deepest longings.

Here is what I have come to realize. We must abandon cynicism and doubt about whether we will ever find these things and lean into the journey, because the reason we were made *can* be discovered. We *can* find truth. We can finally find the answers to the longing we have for peace that "transcends all understanding," as the apostle Paul described it (Phil. 4:7). We can finally gain understanding and revelation: about ourselves, our loved ones, our neighbors, our enemies. About love and why it is the best and worst of things. About pain and sadness and why they seem to write themselves into our story time and time again uninvited. About joy and pleasure. About having meaning and purpose each day versus just existing, like so many who just live for the weekend, finding happiness only in fits and starts—like blades of grass growing up through concrete, showing themselves only once in a while. Without this revelation, we're lying to ourselves that we are content, that we have actually found the foundation of our lives, while knowing deep down that we haven't and wondering why.

I think all this lostness and confusion is solved by leaning into, indeed mastering, three things in life: sex, God, and gardening.

Let me explain.

Sex, God, and Gardening

As we have seen, finding ourselves and our place in the world isn't just about *what* we are but also about what we *do*: our purpose. We truly find ourselves in a *doing*, not just a *being*. And what is that doing? The biblical story says we have been assigned as human beings to a "dominion." We're called to shape the world in three basic ways: *relationship*, *worship*, and *stewardship*, or in N. T. Wright's words, sex, God, and gardening.[3] We were made for each other, for God, and for the world around us. This is the central reality of our identity, which, if missed, leaves us lost and confused about why we wake up in the morning and, when we do, what we are supposed to be doing. What we are here *for*.

RELATIONSHIP: MADE FOR ONE ANOTHER

In one of her books, Sue Johnston explores the world of baby orphans who have been ignored and abandoned by the adults in their lives. She says the most haunting part about these orphanages is that while they are filled with newborns, the rooms are dead silent. The babies don't cry, because no one is coming to help them anyway.[4]

One of the most popular spheres of psychology today is attachment theory, the idea that most issues in our lives can be traced back to issues of attachment: to our parents when we were children and to other human beings as we grow up. Even when we're adults our emotional life is often defined by connection or disconnection with others.

It is amazing how much the core of our being pines for connection to others. "It is not good for man to be alone," the Lord said when he made us (Gen. 2:18 NLV), and nothing could be truer. Even for introverts, social connection is essential to what it means to be human at the deepest levels of ourselves.

What Wright means by "sex" isn't just literal sexual intercourse; he is using it as an image of us being made for one another, with sex being the pinnacle of human-to-human relationship, to be shared with one person in the context of marriage. We are fundamentally designed for others.

It was not hyperbole when C. S. Lewis wrote, "Is there any pleasure on earth as great as the circle of Christian friends by a good fire?"[5] He, of course, had an amazing circle of friends, including J. R. R. Tolkien and several writers and thinkers we still love and read today. They would meet at their favorite pub and read to one another the poems and books they were all working on—now some of the best and most beloved works of the twentieth century! But the same is true even in our lesser-known lives. I can sincerely say some of the greatest and most enjoyable times of my life have been spent laughing, telling stories, traveling, just being together with other people. These were times when it wasn't just about me, it was about our attachment, our connection. There was a shared energy, something not fully reproducible no matter how hard we try. Nonetheless, we lean in day in and day out, hoping for a glimpse of those moments.

Among the many things the global pandemic of 2020 taught us was the importance of human connection. It is essential, and when we lack it, we despair. All the negative mental health impacts of that time are evidence that we're wired this way, though even those who admit this is true don't ask *why* this is the case. Scripture tells us exactly why: because we were made for one another and, ultimately, for relationship with God. Life without seeing the grocer, the mail carrier, or our teacher is not life—it's far from the ideal, and it's not the way we were made. When the pandemic first hit (and we were all wiping down our grocery bags), my wife and I would go over to friends' houses, sit out on their driveways, bring our own drinks, and chat about life and laugh. We stayed a safe distance away from one another because who knew? But the connection was worth the risk, wasn't it? And over time, it was worth more risk. Sooner or later, we started to live as if the pandemic had never happened. We returned to shaking hands, hugging, blowing out candles on the birthday cake and eating it without a care in the world. Not because the science had changed or we had grown immune to getting the disease but because we knew life wasn't worth living without these things.

So "love your neighbor as yourself" turns out to be not advice but a road map for your own soul's flourishing. Don't get lost in your own reflection but in the serving of others. As I tell my kids as they navigate life: Don't try to be interest*ing* but interest*ed*. Ask questions, be curious.

Show up to your friend's play. Be a nurse to those who are sick and dying, or those just coming into the world. Call a family member you have been estranged from. Visit someone in prison who is sitting there wasting away, who made his mistakes but is still human—even he still has something to offer.

Show the world a better way. Don't just talk about it. This is our task.

Human beings were made for each other like puzzle pieces meant to slide into one another's contours to make the whole. Anything else is incomplete.

WORSHIP: SURPRISED BY JOY

The second thing Wright says we were made for is God himself. We relate to God through everything we do, and when our lives and affections place him above all things, we flourish and find joy. It may surprise you that I use the word *joy* here as the defining characteristic of properly focused worship, but this is overwhelmingly the message of the Bible. The Westminster Confession, written in 1646, offers one answer to what life should be all about. Its opening line asks the question, "What is the chief end of man?" In other words, what is the main purpose of humans in this world? What were we made and designed for? The answer: "Man's chief end is to glorify God, and to *enjoy* him forever."

I would venture to say this is the best answer to the question of human purpose ever given. The first half of the sentence may not surprise us, as it sounds like something Christians should say. Yes, we exist to glorify God. But the second half may be one of the most forgotten, neglected, and misunderstood ideas in all of Christianity. In that small answer—to enjoy him forever—lies the precious truth your heart needs to navigate life. Because it tells us that when we center ourselves in God, the result is our own joy and the joy of those around us. In honoring God, we find the thing we want most.

The most motivating factor in our lives, driving everything we do therein, is our own joy. Blaise Pascal said it powerfully when he wrote, "All men seek happiness. This is without exception. Whatever different means they employ, they all tend to this end. The cause of some going to war, and of others avoiding it, is the same desire in both, attended with different views. The will never takes the least step but to this object. This is the motive of every action of every man, even of those who hang themselves."[6]

We try to find joy in everything this world has to offer, but it never satisfies. It has been said that every man who walks into a brothel is looking for God, and nothing could be truer. And that is because "there once was in man a true happiness of which now remain to him only the mark and empty trace, which he in vain tries to fill from all his surroundings, seeking from things absent the help he does not obtain in things present. But these are inadequate, because the infinite abyss can only be filled by an infinite object; that is to say, only by God himself."[7]

Instead of tracing pleasure along a path that leads us to God, we end up chasing it down pathways that lead away from him. Sexual urges lead us to cheat on our spouse, an appreciation of money leads to greed, a love of wine leads to alcoholism, a desire to raise our kids right ends in us suffocating them. On and on go the examples of a good thing distorted. Saint Augustine captured this tragedy in his *Confessions*: "My sin was this: That I looked for pleasure, *beauty*, and truth not in Him but in myself and his other creatures, and the search led me instead to pain, confusion, and error."[8]

The fool's errand is trying to derive joy from created things, but this is a story we all know too well. We elevate life above God, gifts above the Giver. But it never works because "good motives for idolatry cannot remove the objective fact that the idol is an unreality. You can't get blood from a stone or divine joy from nondivine things."⁹ Cambridge philosopher and atheist Roger Scruton described it this way:

> To understand the depth of the *"as if"* is to understand the condition of the modern soul. We know that we are animals, parts of the natural order, bound by laws which tie us to material forces which govern everything. We believe that the gods are our invention, and that death is exactly what it seems. Our world has been disenchanted and at the same time, *we cannot live* as though that were the whole truth of our condition. . . . We therefore see others *as if* they were free beings, animated by a soul, and with more than a worldly destiny.¹⁰

In the realm of fact, Scruton says, we *know* people are the unintended products of material necessity, plus time, plus chance. We *know* God is a figment of our imagination. We *know* there is no objective value in truth or beauty. "However, *we cannot live as if all this were true.* Therefore, we must be inconsistent and live the lie of 'as if.'"¹¹ What Scruton is amazingly admitting is that science only goes so far. It does not help us address the *moral* perspective in its description of the world.

Naturalistic explanations of the world give us no reason to expect beauty or pleasure or joy. I would argue that an explanation that includes rather than excludes God has greater credibility. And it should. This offer of true joy as a product of aiming our lives at God versus the world, or ourselves within it, is one of the things we must rethink our way into at the most fundamental level. Because what if the very thing we have been fighting our whole lives to attain turns out to be found in God all along? What if he, being the one who made us, can offer us the joy and contentment we have always been seeking?

"Ask and you will receive," Jesus taught, "and your *joy* will be complete" (John 16:24, emphasis added).

STEWARDSHIP: MADE FOR THE WORLD AROUND US

The last thing Wright says we were fundamentally made for is stewardship: the amazing calling to shape and impact the world under God. God tells Adam and Eve to "fill the earth and subdue it" (Gen. 1:28; see also 2:15). We have a responsibility to shape the chaos into order, to make our own future to some degree, rather than simply being products of determinism or the will of the gods. Contrary to secular theories, we're not just hapless creatures clawing around mindlessly or at the mercy of the stars. We were created for a purpose "to do good works, which God prepared in advance for us to do" (Eph. 2:10). To work and make the world amazing is core to how we feel fulfilled and happy as human beings.

In this context, then, we see a haunting aspect of AI, which we talked about earlier. In his book *Sapiens,* Yuval Harari looks at a future wherein AI eliminates thousands of jobs. After exploring how humanity has developed over millions of years—moving through a cognitive revolution, an agricultural revolution, and a scientific revolution— Harari predicts we are heading toward a future where technology has replaced us in every sphere of society. There will be what he calls a "useless class," who are not only unemployed but *unemployable.* "In the twenty-first century we might witness the creation of a massive new unworking class," he says, "people devoid of an economic, political, or even artistic value, who contribute nothing."[12]

Oxford professor John Lennox cites Harari's prediction and adds his own chilling conclusion: "The world already experienced a slave economy where the very few were served by the very many. . . . When society collapsed . . . they had no idea how to rebuild. Some suggest it was for that reason that the Roman Empire eventually collapsed."[13] In other words, as we are exploring, part of our purpose as human beings is *to work* and to influence the world to make it better. To not produce, to not imprint our ideas and influence on others and the world around us, is dehumanizing in ways we can't imagine.

We are not merely consumers or critics—though we spend most of our time doing these two things. We are called to be culture *makers.* We were born to shape the world, and we have an amazing capacity to do so. We are hardwired for this quest. When we hold lanterns up to cave walls, we see evidence that our ancestors were artists and storytellers. They drew pictures not only to document things but to create, adding to the world in some way.

Culture is quite literally what we make of the world.[14] As Andy Crouch says, "We make sense of the world by making something of the world."[15] So create! Learn languages. Build roads. Invent technologies. Compose songs. Make films. Pass laws. Build hospitals. Save a marriage. Teach a kid how to throw a football. Make an omelet.

Fashion, commerce, infrastructure, government. The arts, the sciences, religion. Philosophy, psychology, sports, health, education, raising a family. These aren't something *other* than what we are called to be and do in the world but the very heart of it. Not that we all are called to do all of these (some will never raise a family; others will never be involved in science, or psychology, or music), but these, collectively, are all part of the human project. What a way for us to wake up in the morning—to say, Today is another opportunity to *add to the world*!

The question is, Will we use this capacity for good or ill?

Practically speaking, how does one find this specific purpose in their life? My wife and I were talking to our girls recently about how excited we are for them to find their voice and place in the world. They asked us how they were going to do that. There are of course many strategies, but studying ourselves and how who we are connects to both God and the world around us is central to it. I couldn't help but think of the bestselling author Rick Warren's S.H.A.P.E. strategy. He says you really begin to know your purpose when you see it through five things:

Your Spiritual gifts—if you are a believer, God gives you spiritual gifts to serve people that are supernatural, that shape what you end up doing with your life: teaching, hospitality, leadership, etc.

Your Heart—what you are passionate and excited about when you wake up in the morning.

Your Abilities—distinct from your spiritual gifts, these are the natural abilities you were born with and that you hone and develop over time. These are competencies that people see in you and agree that whenever you are doing this or that, you are in your sweet spot.

Your Personality—the unique way you end up doing your calling. There are a lot of bankers or pastors or teachers or musicians or stay-at-home parents, but this is the unique and specific flair you bring to your role. Introverted, extroverted, loud, quiet, people-oriented, task-oriented—there a million ways to do whatever we are called to do, and we should know our own way of doing things.

Your Experiences—the way you do what you end up doing in this world is going to be colored and shaded by how you were raised, your experiences good or bad. It all helps define what you end up doing and how you do it.[16]

We need to see it all as what God uses to shape our purpose and calling.

Overcoming the Monster

One of my goals in writing this book is to encourage us to recapture the vision of our potential impact on the world so we can flourish as human beings. But again, as inspiring as that sounds, that calling is lived out in the real world, which unfortunately is a post-fall world of death, disease, dysfunction, and pain at every level of existence. The goals of relationship, stewardship, and worship are noble, but they have been derailed by evil. In Genesis, Satan, our enemy from the beginning, distracts us, and then pain and resistance enter the story. And that reality keeps most of us from going through with the great dreams we have for our lives. Or after bumping into a few experiences of resistance, many of us quit trying and settle. But that is to fail at the great task we have before us.

The Bible is about how the people of God, empowered by God, face all that pain and resistance and exile and death and yet push on and emerge victorious in the end. While sin and death have entered the story, as with Cain, God places a mark of protection on his humans so they can still live under his grace and make something of the world, even if that world is now filled with murder and strife.

It is the great story we tell repeatedly as human beings, a theme literary scholars call "overcoming the monster." Think *Beowulf, Moby Dick, James Bond, Harry Potter, Jurassic Park, Mission Impossible, The Avengers*. At their core these stories are about the power of friendship to defeat evil in the world and inside each of us. A group of people band together and use their skills to defeat a narcissistic evil that is threatening the village or city or world, and once it is accomplished, things go back to the way they once were, to the peace these places once enjoyed.[17]

This isn't just fantastical talk; this is core to our identity as humans. Our job is not to sit back and bemoan the way the world is. We must *do* something. We must fight to birth a new and beautiful world, even in the face of certain death. And most of the time, this is done by showing those around us a different and better way to be human. "The only way to change culture is to create more of it. . . . We must create something new in order to persuade our neighbors to set aside their existing set of cultural goods for our new proposal."[18] All of this upends the other views we are tempted to adopt wherein we are just victims of a system we can never change and thus we must just give up and play our part in the corruption. No, the Bible says, all human beings are called to great things. Even if those great things are small things.

Even if you find yourself powerless and without hope, God has a calling for you: to be not a culture *follower* but a culture *former*. As Dr. Martin Luther King Jr. said, God's people need to be thermostats, not thermometers. Shaping the cultures they live in instead of merely feeling out the temperature of the world and its ways, they should be looking to regulate the shape of society.

What does God tell Jeremiah the prophet to do amid the crisis he faces in exile from his homeland, oppressed and suffering in Babylon, which feels like the end of all things? Lock yourself away from the world? Take your money out of the bank and hide it under your mattress? Get your bunker ready? That is what many Christians say. We should *run from the world*. But God has a different plan. He says, "Build houses and settle down; plant gardens and eat what they produce. Marry and have sons and daughters; find wives for your sons and give your daughters in marriage, so that they too may have sons and daughters. Increase in number there; do not decrease. Also, seek the peace and prosperity of the city to which I have carried you into exile" (Jer. 29:5–7). In other words, sometimes the work of restoring the world in the face of the end of history is not running from it but investing in it by doing normal, ordinary things that please the Lord. Buy real estate, love your neighbor, have children (a profound act of hope when faced with cultural crisis)—all of which are ways of saying, "Even in the midst of this malaise, collapse and brokenness, this is still God's world and he will, indeed, restore it."[19] It's called *active waiting*.

We believed the lie of the serpent in the garden that knowledge, endless progress through technology, and scientific discovery would heal us. And now we have come to the beginning of the twenty-first century and realized we were sold a dark and dangerous deception founded on an illusion: that progress by itself was all-competent and could solve any problem. We should have known, though, that we would bump into reality at some point. Collide with the givenness of things—in this case, history. And we have with a vengeance. "The twentieth century was the most barbaric in history, and makes the myth of progress read like a cruel joke: 160 million human beings slaughtered by their own kind; more people dying of starvation in a single decade than in all of history; AIDS epidemics in Africa and elsewhere; the widening gap between the rich and the poor; the environmental crisis; the threat of nuclear holocaust—the list goes on and on."[20]

In the place of this failed experiment, we as human beings must look to God, his order and beauty and grace and peace, as the only path to the paradise we thought progress (or secularism or scientism or hedonism) would bring us. This vision of our lives, even if you are a skeptic, is inspiring. Because it says that reality is far more—far bigger and more expansive and wonderful and interesting and magical—than anything we can put in a test tube. That the stories we have been drawing on walls since we could, aren't nonsense but are *artifacts of the soul*.

There is a humility when one comes before the transcendent God who oversees all of life and who is over and above the complexity of all that is, including that which J. Robert Oppenheimer (the creator of the atomic bomb) found when exploring the electron: "If we ask whether the electron *changes with time*," he said, "we must say no; if we ask whether it *remains the same*, we must say no; if we ask whether it is at *rest*, we must say no; if we ask whether it is in motion, we must say no."[21] I guess, as one writer has said, if it isn't a paradox, it isn't true. We in our modern minds scoff at this or react against it, but what else could be more beautiful? In other words, true reality is so vast and complex and mysterious and wonderful. How could we not need lightning and music and sex and art and colors and transcendence to catch glimpses of it? There will always be mystery because we are limited and subservient to the One who is without limits in every way.

Have we ever stopped and thought, "Why would we want to reduce God to make him understandable?" That perhaps we are better off standing where the apostle Paul stood when, after explaining the complex plan of God for eleven chapters in the book of Romans, he exclaimed,

> Oh, the depth of the riches of the wisdom and knowledge of God!
> How unsearchable his judgments,
> and his paths beyond tracing out! (Rom. 11:33)

How wise and unsearchable and awesome are these ways? Enough to define our lives around God versus ourselves and to wake up every day mastering the three things he made us to master: relationships, worship, and stewardship. All of this we are to carry out and lean into every day until our dying breath.

But even that raises an interesting question. What exactly is that? Death, I mean.

While we explored our origins earlier, now it is time to ask, Is death really our ending? Is there life after it? If so, what is it like and how does it shape how we live our life now?

To all this we now turn our attention as the final, and most important, leg of our journey.

PART V

The Problem of
DEATH

To die will be an awfully big adventure.

—J. M. BARRIE, PETER PAN

Here on the shores of the sea comes the end of our fellowship,"
Gandalf says to Sam, Pippin, and Merry in J. R. R. Tolkien's
The Return of the King before he and Frodo board the ship to the
Undying Lands (Middle-earth's version of heaven). The hobbits cry
and embrace Frodo. They are happy he is going to a place of unending
joy and delight, but sad for themselves, for they will miss him dearly.
Gandalf looks them each in the face and says wisely, "I will not say do
not weep, for not all tears are an evil."[1]

Every one of us, some sooner than others, will face a day when
our fellowship with the world and everyone in it—everyone you have
loved, laughed with, played with, hugged, watched a movie with,
fought with, danced with, shared a meal with, and a million things
in between—will come to an end. Tears will be shed. But not all tears

signal evil or sorrow. Death is the edge of a blade that cuts two ways. If those we know and love live on in a higher realm and a better place, then those tears are merely for us who live on, who can't follow where they have gone quite yet. We grieve, but not "like the rest of mankind, who have no hope" (1 Thess. 4:13). If eternity is not secure for them, however, our tears are a deeper mourning for that person and the dread they may face. Or if, as secularism suggests (but can't prove), there is nothing after this life, the tears are only selfish in that we are upset only for ourselves. We will miss them, but the implications for them are nothing, as they don't know one way or the other. All of this and so much more is what we will now wrestle with in this exploration of life—namely, death itself.

Death is the end of life.

Or is it?

All of biblical history and most of human history, across all cultures and times, suggest not. They suggest something far more interesting and compelling that, if true, works backward to change everything we do in our lives now as we live. As Dallas Willard says, "The life we now have as the person we now are, will continue in the universe in which we now exist."[2] I believe this with all my heart.

If this is true, what are the implications?

It changes everything.

Now, some may wonder why in an exploration of life we would end with the topic of death, but nothing could be more important. As Charles Spurgeon once said, "To be prepared to die is to be prepared to live." And after we stare the topic of death in the face for the last two chapters, I think you will see why this is exactly the case and why it is the most exciting thing we could do.

CHAPTER 10

You Only Live Twice,
NOW LIVE
LIKE IT

Death destroys a man: the idea of Death saves him.

—E. M. FORSTER, *HOWARDS END*

Several years ago a friend took a trip with his family to Hawaii. They were enjoying themselves immensely until one morning, as he and the kids were hanging out on the beach, his phone gave off an awful noise. He looked around and noticed that every phone around him was emitting that same noise. People began screaming, covering their mouths in horror. Grabbing his phone from his pocket, he read in disbelief a warning from the US government (January 13, 2018): "BALLISTIC MISSILE THREAT INBOUND TO HAWAII. SEEK IMMEDIATE SHELTER. THIS IS NOT A DRILL."

Televisions broadcasted a scrolling banner: "The U.S. Pacific Command has detected a missile threat to Hawaii . . . impact on land or sea within minutes. THIS IS NOT A DRILL. Remain indoors well away from windows. If you are driving, pull safely to the side of the road and seek shelter in a building or lie on the floor. We will announce when the threat has ended. Take immediate action measures."

Immediately, my friend called his wife, but there was no answer.

Not knowing where she was, he collected the kids, ran up the beach, and loaded everyone into the elevator of their hotel. They shot up to their floor and ran to their room.

"Honey!" he yelled.

"Mom! Mom!" the kids screamed.

All to no avail. The room was empty. He texted and called her phone over and over, but she didn't pick up. He went down to the hotel lobby, now packed with hundreds of people from all different cultures, praying to their gods, crying, hugging their loved ones. He prayed with his kids (made sure they were right with Jesus!), and they gathered in a huddle as they waited for the missiles to light up the sky. After a few minutes of chaos in the lobby, they decided to walk back down to the beach, staring heavenward for signs of the approaching threat.

What else was there to do? There was nowhere to go. This was Hawaii—a small speck of land protruding out of the Pacific Ocean, with no escape. Their deaths were likely imminent. And so they waited for what felt like an eternity.

But then something unexpected happened.

Another text came through thirty-eight minutes after the original: "There is no missile threat or danger to the State of Hawaii. Repeat. False Alarm." Everyone who was gathered on the beach and in the lobby broke out in applause and celebration. My friend hugged his kids. They cried and prayed and thanked God for this fresh shot at life. Making their way upstairs, he found his wife coming out of the shower and dressed for the day. The children ran to her and hugged her close. "Mom! Mom! Where have you been?" they cried, laughing and crying and everything in between.

"What are you talking about? I've been right here," she said, laughing.

They stared at her as if she had two heads. "You don't know?" they said.

"Know what?" she asked.

They looked to their father to explain. "I don't know where to start," he said. "I guess let's start with: Where have you been?" She told them she had been working out in the hotel gym. She met a nice woman and the two of them were chatting about life, kitchen remodeling, how the kids were doing in school. Their phones were in their bags, so she hadn't heard any calls. They finished up, came up in the elevator together, and then went their separate ways. She had immediately jumped into the shower and was still a little confused about why everyone was so emotional.

She had not felt the breath of death on her neck as they had. She had not known the end was upon them—that they had mere minutes left to live and make peace with God. She had not sensed that pressure on her soul—the knowledge that she was about to pass into the next life.

When my friend shared this with me, part of me realized that in many ways this is the story of our world. Of everyone reading these words. Some people look at the big questions of life; they tap into the deeper, spiritual, soulish, eternal things. They let them rise to the top; they face them head-on. They pray and lean into the question of eternity, sense how close death is, how fragile they are, and then allow that to give way to faith and life. They seek to settle the questions of God and the state of their soul.

And then there are those who just run on treadmills. They never come to the end of themselves or face their vulnerability. They avoid the big questions or are distracted by the cares of life and never bother with them. They scroll on their phones, buy new cars, redo their kitchens, talk about the real estate market, gossip about the next election, make observations about the weather, discuss their Enneagram number, boast about how many followers they have, and brag about the school their kids got into.

Some of these are important things, of course, but they're things that keep people from the *most important* things.

The apostle Paul calls all this getting "entangled in civilian affairs" (2 Tim. 2:4).

In a matter of minutes, my friends lived out a stark picture of all of history and of everyone who draws breath even now. Some settle the questions of God, eternity, and their own souls, and others never do. The difference between these two kinds of people is often the same exact difference between my friend and his wife: *one knew and believed the threat and the other was oblivious to it.* One had faith that their end was real and coming soon and that eternity was part of the question they were facing that very day, and the other paid it no heed.

———

In the end, every person reading this will die—100 percent guaranteed. There are no false alarms. No "Sorry, we made a mistake" text we get at the last minute.

Nevertheless, some people just aren't interested in the question of death and eternity. They believe it is an irrelevant question that has no bearing on daily life. "We will never know for sure what happens after we die, so why worry about it?" they say. For others, it's not a *timely* question. There is no urgency. We have plenty of time to figure out the big question of life, we say. Those who are younger, full of spunk and vinegar and a feeling of invincibility, often feel this way. They look into the future and can't conceive of a world without them in it.

But we must face the harsh fact that both of these approaches are misguided, even dangerous. Instead, we need minds and hearts awakened to eternal things. The Bible tells us that our life is but a vapor (James 4:14); we are here for a moment and then we fade, like morning mist. It's why Robin Williams's character in *Dead Poets Society* brings all of his students into the hallway to stare into the faces of the past students at their school. As they stare into those black-and-white photos, he says, "They're not that different from you, are they? Same haircuts. Full of hormones, just like you. Invincible, just like you feel. The world is their oyster. They believe they're destined for great things, just like many of you. Their eyes are full of hope, just like you. Did they wait until it was too late to make from their lives even one iota of what they were capable? Because you see, gentlemen, these boys are now fertilizing daffodils."

That's why as we finish our journey together through the problem of life, we end by talking about death. My goal is not to dwell on the morbid reality of being dead but, more importantly, to think about how we should *live our life in light of death.* And even more, live in light of what comes *after* it.

There is a popular saying—YOLO (you only live once). But it turns out, it's not true. Every one of us faces a far more interesting, scary, and overwhelming truth—YOLT. Admittedly, it's less catchy, but it's far more real: you only live *twice.* The first life we live in this temporal, earthly, this-world life for an average of seventy-seven or so years. But when this life ends, there is another life to live, a life that will *never* end—an eternal, next-world life.

So first things first. When this life stops, what starts? And what is that second life like? Is there anything we can do now that will shape or affect that next life? We must face these questions head-on. Not to do so is malpractice. These two lives are intimately related in such a way that if we want to have a strong and flourishing life in this world, we must have our minds firmly fixed on our ultimate future. In other words, to solve the problem of (this) life, we must think not only of this life but also of the one we will live beyond it.

What happens when we walk through the door to the next world? We began this journey by exploring our origins—where we came from—and now we end by asking, Where are we going? What, ultimately, will become of humans and, more pressing, to each of us individually?

The Most Personal of All Things

The problem with death is that it is the most *personal* of all things. Yet it is common to everyone and ties every human life together. Someone once said all the wars and plagues and disasters the world has ever seen have never raised the death toll. It's a 1:1 ratio—every person who has ever lived has ended up dead. About 120 people die every minute, 7,000 every hour, 170,000 every day. But those numbers don't get our attention. What does get your attention is thinking deeply about the reality that one day, it will be *you*.

It is guaranteed.

This is why the *fear* of death is also inescapable, no matter who you are. It's why whenever there is suddenly an earthquake, or a shooting, or a fire, people scatter. We naturally run away from danger; we seek to preserve our lives and fight to survive. And when we sense the end is near, we grow afraid. A friend recently watched his father die, and he shared with me that as his dad lay on the hospital bed, nearing the end, his breathing intensified, his eyes opened, and he started gasping for air harder and harder—as if he were reaching for one more breath and then another. It was violent, a fight for life. And his father did this right until the bitter end, until that last fought-for breath simply eluded him.

In John Bunyan's masterpiece, *The Pilgrim's Progress*, toward the end of Christian's journey to the Celestial City, he and his companion Hopeful come to a river symbolizing death. There they are informed, "You must pass through this River or else you cannot arrive at the gate of the City."[1] Bunyan is reminding us that death is the only way to heaven. You would think that knowing what lies on the other side would be enough, that Christian would have nothing to fear. But as they enter the waters of the river, Christian is immediately overcome with panic, screaming, "The billows go over my head, all his waves go over me . . . the sorrows of death have totally compassed me, so that I shall not see the land that flows with milk and honey."[2]

If we are honest, even with our eyes fixed on God, death can still arouse feelings of fear and panic. I feel it every time I fly. I know the statistics say I could take a commercial flight every day of my life for one hundred thousand years before I was in a plane crash, but I still fear it to some degree. Why? Because of what it means: my certain death.

Beyond ourselves though, death is also personal because it visits those closest to us, and for some of us, that is even scarier. This is very real to me, personally, even today as I'm writing this. My wife, Erin, visited her doctor for some tests a few days ago, and the doctors didn't like what they saw. A few masses might be cancerous, they said. News like this is hard to accept and difficult to believe. They did a biopsy and we wait for her test results, and while we hope and trust the masses are benign, our minds inevitably wander. We begin planning for the worst. I think about life without her, and I can't even fathom it. Even the thought of losing their mom had my daughters crying themselves to sleep for several days, wondering what life without Mom would be like. They think about the daily comings and goings—the cuddles and laughs and moments of wisdom about what it means to be a godly woman—but also the big days: celebrating weddings, having kids of their own, and knowing she would be the very best grandmother. All gone with the wind.

It struck me today that what would be hard, among so many things, is that while I would still have lots of videos and pictures of her, and I would be able to listen to her voice at any moment I wanted to (unlike many in previous generations), there would be nothing *new*. There would be no response to something I said or did. No conversation, no progression, no new ideas or advice, no reports on something

I didn't know yet—just old memories, frozen in time. There would be nothing *alive* about any of it, nothing novel, nothing for today—all of which makes our human experience together what it is, the things that make her my wife but also my best friend. Death robs us of all this—the ongoing imprint people's lives make on our own.

I share all of this because, as we will soon see, this is where Christianity as a way to do life has the corner on the marketplace of ideas. Christianity tells us that all of that fear and hopelessness, while it is very real and natural, doesn't have to be the final verdict. It tells us there really is life after death, an eternal state after this temporal one, and that if we are restored in relationship to our Creator, this life is the most wonderful state one can ever imagine, a world of "pleasures forevermore" (Ps. 16:11 ESV) where God "will wipe every tear from our eyes . . . [and where] there will be no more death or mourning or crying or pain, for the old order of things has passed away" (Rev. 21:4). We will get to be face-to-face with God, the author and source of all pleasure, goodness, beauty, and love, and reunited with those we knew and loved who knew God as well.

But that's not true of everyone. You see, there is more than one option. The Bible is clear there is also an eternal existence for those who have not received Christ—but the description of that is much different. It's a world of isolation and pain where we live out the consequences of the choices we have made in this life.

But we're getting ahead of ourselves. Let's first reflect on what death even is.

The Great Insult

Most of us live unprepared for our death. We think we have plenty of time to deal with whatever eternal issues we may be delaying. But we never know. Just last week I was in a car with someone who shared that his dad had passed away in an airplane accident when he was two years old. There was no plan for that. I came home from being with that friend and that very same night was checking social media, and I was stunned to learn that a girl I went to high school with, one year my senior, who was in several classes with me and always the brightest light in the room, so encouraging to everyone she knew, had been beaten to death by her boyfriend. She was forty-five years old with two sons.

In both of these cases—and thousands upon thousands of others every day—there is no runway, no hint or heads-up, no weeks or months or years of goodbyes. Just here one day and gone the next—sudden and final in the worst kind of way. The way that says, "If they had only . . ."

If they had only left the house two minutes later, listened to that advice, not met that person, then maybe I would still have them.

But alas, that's the thing: We can't do anything about it. We can't reverse what has happened, and we can't wake up from the nightmare once it has become reality. All of this is why death is the Great Interruption, tearing loved ones away from us, or us from them. It's the Great Schism, separating us soul from body, which was never the plan. It's the Great Enemy, hideous and frightening and cruel. It's the Great Insult, wherein as mighty and powerful and invincible as we feel in life, in the end, as Shakespeare says, we are food for worms.[3] As human beings we are split in two: "We have an awareness of our own splendid uniqueness in that we stick out of nature with a towering majesty, and yet we go back into the ground a few feet in order to blindly and dumbly rot and disappear forever."[4]

If I Had My Life to Live Over Again

Secular culture sees death as all of these things—an interruption, an enemy, a schism, and an insult—yet Christianity has an additional element that changes how death fits into our lives. It's another chapter in a coherent life story, it says, the *crucial* chapter. Because it lasts far longer than *this* life. It lasts forever.

The secular take that sees this life as all there is explains why we are far less prepared for death than our ancestors. Death in our contemporary framework has no meaning. It has no place in our lives and is rejected outright, replacing sex as the new unmentionable.

Throughout most of human history, however, death was up close and in your face, part of normal experience, not hidden away in the lonely halls of poorly painted hospitals. It was something that regularly occurred in your village and in your home. You cared for those you loved until their dying breath, and for many, death often took them young. The British pastor and theologian John Owen (1616–1683), considered one of the great theologians of the church, outlived every one of his eleven children as well as his wife. Can you imagine what that was like? All of them died at home as he sat by their bedside, caring and praying, doing what he could. Yet even his best efforts collapsed under the unbearable weight of death, the one thing none of us can control.

Seeing death regularly provides a unique perspective, one that encourages us to suck the marrow out of life while we still have time. As Viktor Frankl said, "Live your life as if you were living it already for the second time."[5] Live as if you have the chance to correct your mistakes, your regrets, your sins and missteps. Live so that on the day when you breathe your last and death finally comes, whether you lay alone or are surrounded by loved ones, you don't look back and say, "I wish I would have _____."

The novelist Erma Bombeck once wrote a column called "If I Had My Life to Live Over Again," in which she concludes,

I would have waxed less and listened more . . .

Instead of wishing away nine months of pregnancy and

complaining about the shadow over my feet, I'd have cherished every minute of it and realized that the wonderment growing inside me was to be my only chance in life to assist God in a miracle.

I would have taken the time to listen to my grandfather ramble about his youth. I would've invited friends over to dinner even if the carpet was stained and the sofa was faded.

I would've sat on the lawn with my children and not worried about grass stains. When my child kissed me over and over, I would never have said, "Later. Now go get washed up for dinner."

There would have been more I love you's . . . more I'm sorry's . . . more I'm listening's . . . but mostly, given another shot at life, I would seize every minute of it . . . look at it and really see it . . . try it on . . . live it . . . exhaust it . . . and never give that minute back until there was nothing left of it.[6]

Live life backward. Philip of Macedon had his slave awaken him every morning with the same reminder: "Philip, remember that you must die." Psalm 90:12 calls us to "number our days, that we may gain a heart of wisdom." In other words, not recognizing the inevitability and implications of our upcoming death is very *unwise*.

I've named this book *The Problem of Life*, and while some would rather just focus on life *without* considering death, that would be a tragedy. As J. I. Packer reminds us, "If you cannot make some sense of death, you cannot make sense of life either; and no philosophy that will not teach us how to master death is worth two cents to us."[7]

This is because, like it or not, each one of us is dying right now—albeit some at a faster rate than others. But death is part of life, perhaps the most important part of it.

Reflection on death prepares us to take responsibility for our life—our life now and our forever life. Because as much as we might want to believe we cease to exist upon our death, that is (most likely) not the case. "The truly brave person is the one who can cheerfully face the prospect of an unending existence. Suppose you are never going to stop existing and there is nothing you can do about it—except possibly make your future existence as desirable as possible."[8] This is the task before us in the end.

Before we continue, I want to finish my earlier story about my wife's health. The test results came in, and she is cancer free. While we are happy to receive good news, we are conscious that this is not everyone's story. And it reminds us that ultimately this good news just pushes the question back to a further date. For *now* my wife isn't dying, but one day she will.

So when that day comes, what will she step into?

The Afterlife

The biblical story is clear and compelling: we all die, and yet we continue to live on. Death was the result of humankind sinning in the garden, but we were already made "forever creatures" when we were breathed on by God in such a way that we possess a living soul that never ceases to exist, even when our bodies do. "The dust returns to the ground it came from, [but] the spirit returns to God who gave it" (Eccl. 12:7). Both the Old and New Testaments teach this.

- "Jacob . . . yielded up the ghost, and was gathered unto his people" the writer of Genesis tells us (49:33 KJV).
- Over and over people are described as sleeping, or resting, with their ancestors—to be reunited with their forebears (1 Kings 2:10).[9]
- Jesus tells the man on the cross beside him, "Today you will be with me in paradise," and tells a parable wherein the righteous upon death go to be with Abraham, while the unrighteous experience torment yet are also conscious.

- Paul teaches that, for believers, "to be absent from the body" is "to be present with the Lord" and that to "die is gain," for this means they are "with Christ, which is better by far."[10]

All of this tells us that when our physical life ends, we still exist, though now in a different place and in a different state of being. Some go to be with the Lord, while others go to what the Bible calls "Sheol" or "Hades" (which we will explore). But for now all deceased people exist in what is called the *intermediate state*, which will then give way to the final state of every person who ever lived.

A Faith Position and Judgment

At this point I know those who are atheist, agnostic, or generally skeptical about Christianity are saying, "All of this is just your faith position! You don't have any evidence of this. That's your view of the afterlife, but you have no proof!" To which I would respond this way.

Years ago, my grandmother died after years of pain. After she passed, my friends and family—many of whom are atheists—said to me, "At least she's not suffering anymore." You may have thought something similar about a loved one in the past. And I understand the sentiment. The problem with believing this though is that *it too is a faith position*. How do you know this person isn't suffering *more*? The idea that our loved ones no longer suffer after death is a view and belief about the afterlife. It is a belief that after we die, nothing happens. We go extinct and cease to exist. But how do we know that is true? If we are honest, we just don't. We can't prove it one way or the other. We've never been to the afterlife and come back with evidence to say this is what it is like. And if we are honest, every view of the afterlife is one of faith—especially the atheist view.

I say that because while we have the same amount of evidence, the biblical position about the existence of a soul and of heaven and hell, etc., is based on data: the teachings and claims of Jesus, who really existed in history and who according to the best evidence really rose from the dead. In other words, there are good historical and rational reasons to believe that what Jesus said about the afterlife is true versus atheism, which just says that according to nature or our experience there is no afterlife.

Near-Death Experiences and Judgment

Even if you aren't willing to accept the word of Jesus, we see some correspondence to his claims and those of the rest of the Bible (not to mention Greek and religious thought from around the world) from the growing field of *science* investigating near-death experiences. This includes the work of Emily Williams Kelly, a psychologist at the University of Virginia with degrees from Duke University and the University of Edinburgh, as well as many other people who explore the reports of people who experienced death (in a clinical sense) and then returned to life. These researchers conclude that at least some of the experiences provide "evidence that consciousness seems to exist even after normal brain function ceases."[11]

To me, there is better evidence that there is something after death than that there is nothing, and if this has even a small chance of being true, I'd rather have some kind of plan for an eternal future than literally *nothing*, based on a vague hope that this is all there is. And if we are honest, something deep within all of us tells us that there is more. "We know deep down that we are not like trees or grass. We were created to *last*."[12]

Beyond us just continuing to exist, Scripture says that it is appointed for every person to face *judgment* at some point (Heb. 9:27). That what we do with our lives today will affect our experience of life forevermore. Jesus taught it this way: "A time is coming when all who are in their graves will hear [my] voice and come out—those who have done what is good will rise to live, and those who have done what is evil will rise to be condemned" (John 5:28–29).

In other words, we will all live, die, and go to an intermediate state—with God or not—and then there will be a day of resurrection when this intermediate state gives way to a resurrection of all people. It will be a final judgment with an assignment that lasts forever. Some to life in a new heaven and a new earth (what is typically called "heaven"), and others to a place of condemnation, a place of no rest, continual regret, and no grace—where people plead for a drop of water but it is withheld (what is called "hell").

This is life *after* "life after death"—the final state of all things. If you are anything like me, you likely have a hundred questions at this point. What will these places be like? How does a person get to heaven versus hell? Are these literal places? Is hell really a thing, or is that just some weird old religious idea? And if it is, how is that compatible with a loving God?

Let's explore these questions, beginning with heaven.

The New Earth: Rethinking Heaven

The Bible tells us that heaven is a place of unending delight and pleasure. That the greatest joys in this life are just dull pointers to the joys of this amazing place and state of being. We will be present with God and Christ and all those who have gone before us who trusted Christ. We will "be his people, and God himself will be with [us] and be [our] God" (Rev. 21:3–4). The biblical imagery provides pictures of the best of the natural world too, with rivers "as clear as crystal" (Rev. 22:1) and bountiful trees, leaves, fruit, and crops. With the Bible coming full circle to return to the Genesis story, we see the tree of life standing on each side of the river that runs down the middle of a great city, a place where "no longer will there be any curse" (Rev. 22:3). Sin and death, the very things that derailed our relationship with God and poisoned our experience with him and every other living thing, are now fully defeated. They can never create pain again.

And it is this way forever. A million days are like an hour, and an hour like a million days. As the hymn "Amazing Grace" says,

> When we've been there ten thousand years,
> bright shining as the sun,
> we've no less days to sing God's praise
> than when we'd first begun.

This doesn't mean that all we do in heaven is *sing*. I know many have been turned off by that picture, especially those who aren't into music or who can't wait for the worship portion of a church service to be over. You need not worry, because, as with most things in the Bible about heaven, these images are largely symbolic. "For many people . . . music is the thing known in the present life which most strongly suggests ecstasy and infinity."[13] Singing represents the voice of the soul, a pure and endless joy that erupts from within us, and this is certain to happen when we are in the presence of our Savior—the one who made us, died for us, and has pursued us throughout history to remove all the obstacles to this true and lasting joy.

That's what all those Scripture passages about praising God are all about: "Delight yourself in the LORD," "His praise will always be on my lips," "Enter his gates with thanksgiving . . . praise his name" (Ps. 37:4 ESV; 34:1; 100:4). This isn't religious mumbo jumbo but a natural outworking of a heart and life that has found its joy and the satisfaction of all its desires in God. C. S. Lewis mentioned that this was lost on him for the longest time, until one day it all made sense:

The most obvious fact about praise—whether of God or anything—strangely escaped me. I thought of it in terms of compliment, approval, or the giving of honor. I had never noticed that all enjoyment spontaneously overflows into praise. . . . The world rings with praise—lovers praising their mistresses, readers their favorite poet, walkers praising the countryside, players praising their favorite game—praise of weather, wines, dishes, actors, horses, colleges, countries, children, flowers, mountains, rare stamps, beetles, even politicians or scholars. . . . *Praise almost seems to be inner health made audible.* . . . People spontaneously praise whatever they value, so they spontaneously urge us to join them in praising it: "Isn't she lovely? Wasn't it glorious? Don't you think that magnificent?"

Lewis then said what we so often miss: "I think we delight to praise what we enjoy because the praise not merely *expresses but completes the enjoyment*; it is its appointed consummation. It is not out of compliment that lovers keep on telling one another how beautiful they are; the delight is incomplete till it is expressed. . . . Fully to enjoy is to glorify. In commanding us to glorify Him, God is inviting us to enjoy Him."[14]

This is what makes heaven so great. It is a place of vibrant *life*. D. L. Moody, the great evangelist, looked at his congregation one day and said, "One day, you will read in the newspaper that I am dead. Don't believe it for a second; for in that moment, I will be more alive than I have ever been!" Moody knew the true picture of those who die in Christ: joy, delight, pleasure; people pulsating with a kind of energy and vitality that nothing in this world could capture. What else is there to do but glory in that?

Heaven will, of course, include deep and joyous singing and worship of God, but it will not be an unending church service. It will be far *more* than singing. There will be many things to do. Remember, the biblical picture of heaven is not a place of disembodied spirits sitting around floating on clouds. Our future is a resurrected *re-embodiment*, not a disembodiment! This is why Jesus was resurrected bodily, and he serves as the prototype of what will happen to all of us—and to the earth itself. "The creation itself will be liberated from its bondage to decay" (Rom. 8:21). Heaven is described as a city (Heb. 11:10), and what comes to mind when you think of a city? Buildings, culture, art, music, events, work. Heaven is also described as a country (Heb. 11:16). Again, what is that? Territories, rulers, national interests, citizens, rivers, trees, mountains, flowers. God doesn't promise us a *non*-earth. He promises a *new* earth (Rev. 21–22).[15] "God promises that the glory of his people will demand a glorious creation to live in. . . . When God makes all things new, he makes us new spiritually, morally, physically, and then he makes the whole creation new so that our environment fits our perfected spirits and bodies."[16] This is why Paul speaks of "the redemption of our bodies" (Rom. 8:23).

Peter preached this as well, that Christ must remain in heaven "until the time comes for God to *restore everything*" (Acts 3:21, emphasis added). Humans living in a disembodied spiritual realm would not qualify as a "restoring" of all things. This is why the clearest and grandest picture of heaven in the last two chapters of the Bible is an image not of us "going to heaven" but of heaven coming down to earth. "I saw the Holy City, the new Jerusalem, *coming down out of heaven* from God, prepared as a bride beautifully dressed for her husband" (Rev. 21:2–3, emphasis added). What a picture of renewal and restoration! Rather than us going away to live in God's home forever, God will come down to live with us in our home forever. "The new Jerusalem . . . does not remain in a heaven far off in space, but it comes down to the renewed earth; there the redeemed will spend eternity in resurrection bodies. So, heaven and earth, now separated, will then be merged."[17]

The biblical vision of the future is less of an ending and more of a new beginning. It is not *other* worldly; it is *new* worldly. So Eugene Peterson says, "The biblical story began, quite logically, with a beginning. Now it draws to an end, not quite so logically, also with a beginning. The sin-ruined creation of Genesis is restored in the sacrifice-renewed creation of Revelation."[18] Our destiny is an earthly one: a new earth. It is a city, with a garden, full of life and likely architecture, art, culture, and travel, with people of many nations and languages. It is not nonphysical, bland, and colorless. We were made *physical*, which is why we have no appetite for a heaven that is nonphysical and purely spiritual. "Trying to develop an appetite for a disembodied existence in a nonphysical Heaven is like trying to develop an appetite to eat gravel."[19]

You won't ever love that cloudy picture of heaven because you weren't designed that way. Just as we were made *from* the earth, we were made *for* the earth. This is why we have an appetite for a "resurrected body and being with people we love on a resurrected Earth with gardens and rivers and mountains and untold adventures."[20] For this, and nothing less, we were made. As J. I. Packer says, "As life in the 'intermediate' state for the believer between death and resurrection is better than life in this world that preceded it, so the life of resurrection will be better still. It will, in fact, be best. . . . Hearts on earth say in the course of a joyful experience, 'I don't want this to ever end.' But it invariably does. The hearts of those in heaven say, 'I want this to go on forever.' And it will. There can be no better news than this."[21]

At the center of this wonderful picture of the new world is Jesus, who calls himself "the bright Morning Star" (Rev. 22:16). Revelation is sometimes so wordy these images pass me by and I don't stop to think about them, but I was intrigued recently to learn about how the morning star works and its relationship to night. "The morning star often appears between two and three at night, when the darkness is complete, and the faintest sign of morning is not yet visible. When you see the star, you know that the night has been defeated. For the morning star pulls the morning in behind it."[22]

God is saying that in the darkest days and moments of our lives, no matter how long the night feels, we can look toward this new world, for Jesus himself pulls the new heaven and earth with all its peace, joy, and pleasure in behind him as surely as the morning dawns every day of our lives.

Your Life's Work

Why new bodies? To do what? I think New Testament scholar and historian N. T. Wright is right when he says, "The purpose will be to *rule* wisely over God's new world."[23] Forget those images of lounging around on clouds or playing harps. There will be work to do and we shall love doing it. What that work will be is not entirely clear, but it will be the work of co-laboring with Christ in creating and expanding the universe in some way—work of cosmic importance. Or at least that is what we infer from the many references to "reigning" with Jesus in the new heaven and new earth.[24]

There will likely be continuity with our life now, as we explored earlier. Dallas Willard suggests, "In due time—I can only imagine it will be some while after our passage into God's full world—we will begin to take on new responsibilities. 'Well done good and faithful servant,' our Master will say, 'you have been faithful in the smallest things, take charge of ten cities,' 'five cities,' 'many things' or whatever is appropriate (Luke 19:17). How many cities could you see yourself leading? Answering this question will do much to prepare us for our eternal future in the universe."[25]

Notice the giving of responsibility in the parable is connected to what the servant had already accomplished previously, implying there is some kind of continuation with our lives now that carries on into eternity. The great writer Victor Hugo, who wrote the novels *Les Misérables* and *The Hunchback of Notre-Dame*, was reflecting on this and said, "For half a century I have been translating my thoughts into prose and verse: history, drama, philosophy, romance, tradition, satire, and song; all of these I have tried. But I feel I haven't given utterance to the thousandth part of what lies within me. When I go to the grave I can say, 'My day's work is done.' But I cannot say, 'My life's work is done.' My work will continue the next morning."[26]

Recapturing this vision is key to the re-enchantment of our lives! We must learn to make our present life extraordinary because it builds into the new creation in some mysterious way. Paul, as he ends his longest and most extensive teaching on the nature of the resurrected life in 1 Corinthians 15, closes with these seemingly off-topic words: "Your labor in the Lord is not in vain" (1 Cor. 15:58). And now we begin to see why he says that. Nothing we do in this life, no matter how small or insignificant, is wasted. The good we do lasts and stands and somehow makes its way into shaping the new creation God will create some day.

In *The Last Battle*, C. S. Lewis portrays the girl Lucy mourning the loss of Narnia. As she and her siblings are on the threshold of Aslan's country (representing heaven), she looks back at Narnia and feels a sense of profound loss. But as she gets deeper into Aslan's country, she notices something unexpected. Narnia is not dead; what they are now experiencing *is* Narnia. Though Narnia was destroyed and the sun went out, that Narnia was a shadow and a copy of this real and better one. Old Narnia mattered, yet all the dear creatures have now been drawn into the real Narnia through the Door. And of course it is different, as different as a real thing is from a shadow, or as waking life is from a dream. The new is a deeper country: every rock and flower and blade of grass looks *as if it means more*. And all the good things are there because in this final and amazing place, no good thing is destroyed.

Closing, the narrator says, "I can't describe it any better than that: if you ever get there, you will know what I mean."[27]

Indeed.

CHAPTER 11

Prepare Yourself for
DEATH

*It seems to me that if you or I must choose
between two courses of thought or action, we
should remember our dying and try so to live that
our death brings no pleasure to the world.*

—John Steinbeck, *East of Eden*

It was May 2013, and I was preaching through a sermon series on the different stages of life and how to find purpose and meaning in each of them. The last message of the series was simply entitled "Death." It was about the fact that we will all inevitably face the crooked and rotten face of death at some point.

What are we to think of it? And what happens *after* it visits us?

At the end of the message, I shared the hope the Bible gives us, reading to the congregation parts of the great passages of Scripture that describe the new heaven and new earth—a place where there is no more death and every tear and sadness has been wiped away (Rev. 21:4). People were crying as we were confronted with the amazing hope of being with Jesus, being back together with loved ones we had lost, living fully in a world that no longer has murder, sickness, or suffering—only life and love and joy.

Fast-forward a little less than two years to February 2015. A young woman named Shiloh Johnston had started coming to our church.

She was filled with faith, was part of a small group that met weekly, and was regularly serving—and then she experienced a tragedy: her sister, Keziah, passed away suddenly. Shiloh was devastated but sought to remain hopeful and strong for her friends and family. Then, just ten days after Keziah died, Shiloh herself was tragically hit by a car while on a walk during a work break and died. The funeral for both girls was held on the same day.

A few weeks after the funeral, Shiloh's aunt and cousins were at church and I spoke with them. It was distressing to see the pain in their eyes, yet there was also hope. They knew Shiloh had trusted in Jesus and lived for him, and they believed that because she knew Jesus she was more alive now than she had ever been. As they began to leave, Shiloh's aunt turned to me and said, "Oh, I wanted to let you know something. When we finally collected her belongings after the accident, we saw that she was listening to your sermon on Death as she was walking that day, when she was hit and killed." Her boyfriend, Justin, who had been planning to propose to Shiloh in a couple of months, messaged me saying, "The accident happened on her lunch break, and on her breaks, she would always listen to one of your sermons. On that day, that was the sermon that was up on the app when the police gave her phone to us—completely shattered."

It hit me hard that this young woman, processing the death of her sister, was listening to that message on death and seeking comfort and understanding, not knowing she would experience death herself in just a matter of minutes. I asked myself, "What are the odds of this?" Extremely high. And again I was reminded that there are no coincidences. And I also knew it was a kind of grace that the words she was hearing between this life and the next were about the hope and beauty of the new creation, as she herself stepped into it.

During that sermon, I quoted the words of Jesus: "Whoever lives by believing in me will never die" (John 11:26). Jesus is not referring to our passing on from this world. Obviously, everyone dies. He is speaking of continuing on to *another kind of life*, an even fuller and brighter kind that this one only points to. After saying this, Jesus immediately asked a question: "Do you believe this?" It's a profound and interesting question we all must face. Shiloh believed and trusted in the One who could give her this new kind of life. And I pray you do too. It's the only hope we have.

A Changed Perspective

If everything Jesus says is true, death is transformed from the scariest and most hopeless thing we can imagine to the next step in our unfolding story—a necessary step toward greater glory. "Dying is but getting dressed for God / Our graves are merely doorways cut in sod."[1] This isn't just positive thinking or a way to comfort ourselves; it is literally true if indeed Jesus rose from the dead and what he says about life after death is true. Those who trust Jesus no longer need to fear those who can only "kill the body" (Matt. 10:28); they will not *experience* death (John 8:51–52) and will, in fact, not die (John 11:26). The millisecond their heart stops beating in this life, they simply continue on the journey home and enter God's realm.

This is why the Bible calls death a "shadow" nineteen times, implying that it is a passing thing, something that is nothing at all compared to the reality that awaits us with God. Donald Grey Barnhouse was a pastor of a well-known Presbyterian church in Philadelphia for many years when his wife, who was in her late thirties, died of cancer. He was left to raise their four children, all under the age of twelve. As they were driving to the funeral, a truck pulled up beside them, casting its shadow over their car. As the children cried in the back seat, Barnhouse looked at them in the rearview mirror, his eyes filled with tears, and asked, "Children, would you rather be run over by the actual truck, or just the shadow of it?" One of his kids spoke up: "The shadow of course." Barnhouse replied, "Kids, that's what has happened to your mother . . . only the shadow of death has passed over her, because death itself ran over Jesus in her place."[2]

This changes not only how we experience our *own* death but also how we mourn as we lose *others*. When we lose someone we love, we feel the pain and mourn, but if they knew Christ we mourn only for ourselves, for those left behind without them. I'm reminded of something an old priest shared at a funeral I recently did. The family had grown up at his church but had started coming to ours a few years earlier, and they wanted us to do the service together. The mother had passed away, and her two teenage kids sat in the front row crying. The priest encouraged the kids with this story:

> I'm standing on the seashore. A ship at my side starts out for the blue ocean, spreading her white sails. I stand and watch her until she is just a speck of white in the distance, where the sky and sea meet. And then I hear someone at my side saying, "There, she's gone."
>
> Gone where?
>
> Gone from my sight, that is all.
>
> Her diminished size is in *me*, not in her. Just as I say, "There, she's gone," there are other eyes watching her coming, and there are other voices saying, "Here she comes!"
>
> And that is dying.[3]

Jonathan Evans, the former NFL player and son of pastor Tony Evans, was similarly wrestling with God about his mother's death. At her funeral Jonathan shared how angry he was with God because he had prayed for his mother to be healed and continue living, to be able to know her friends and family for many years to come. He believed that if God allowed her to die, that would be unfair. Yet in the days leading up to the funeral, God gave him a clear message that changed his perspective, saying to him,

> Number one, you don't understand the nature of My victory. Just because I didn't answer your prayer *your* way doesn't mean that I haven't already answered your prayer *any way*. Because victory was already given to your mom. . . . There was always only two answers to your prayers—either she was going to be healed or she was going to be *healed*. Either she was going to live, or she was going to *live*. Either she was going to be with family, or she was *going to be with family*. Either she was going to be well taken care of or she was going to be *well taken care of*. Victory belongs to Me. The two answers to your prayer are yes and yes.[4]

The apostle Paul said Jesus will not return alone but "with all his holy ones" (1 Thess. 3:13), referring to people all through history who have given their lives to Jesus. Those who are still alive at his coming will be "caught up together with them" (1 Thess. 4:17). As the Puritan theologian Richard Baxter said, "I know that Christ is all in all; and it is him that makes Heaven to be heaven. But yet it much sweetens the thoughts of that place to me that there are such a multitude of my most dear and precious friends in Christ."[5] Saint Augustine had a dear friend, Nebridius, whom he would constantly spar with and laugh with, who died. Augustine wrote that his friend, in the state of heaven, "avidly drinks as much as he can of wisdom, happy without end." And yet, Augustine said, "I do not think him so intoxicated by that *as to forget me*, since you, Lord, who he drinks, are mindful of us." In other words, Nebridius will never not be someone who was Augustine's friend.[6] Redemption does not undo the relationships or history we have with others. It is not an erasing but a "gathering up" of our lives and histories as this world is birthed into the new world.

To Die Is Gain

That wonderful, perfect place of pure love and delight in God is *what we were made for.* It is the home we have been searching for all our lives. In every moment of pleasure and delight, our souls catch a taste of heaven. It is like an imprint on our memory, or as C. S. Lewis said, "I must keep alive in myself the desire for my true country, which I shall not find till after death. . . . I must make it the main object of life to press on to that other country and to help others do the same."[7] This perspective helped him when his world came crashing down and he lost his only true love, his wife, Joy. Lewis heard someone say, "She's in God's hand now," and suddenly had a picture: "'She's in God's hand.' That gains a new energy when I think of her as a sword. Perhaps the earthly life I shared with her was only part of the tempering. Now perhaps He grasps the hilt; weighs the new weapon; makes lightnings with it in the air. 'A right Jerusalem blade.' . . . How wicked it would be, if we could, to call the dead back."[8]

The life of those dead in Christ is still far better than ours alive in this world.

David Watson, a leader in the charismatic movement, received a terminal diagnosis and thought he would be healed, so he began writing a book to document his experience, claiming throughout the book how he trusted God was going to heal him, yet he died. J. I. Packer wrote the foreword for the book that was eventually published, and he said something we all need to hear. Packer urged us not to focus on the fact that David thought he would be healed while he was writing the book. That's not what matters, Packer said.

In the providence of God, who does not always show his servants the true point of the books he stirs them to write, the theme of [this book] is the conquest of death, not by looking away from it, nor by being shielded from it, but by facing it and going down into it. David's theology led him to believe that God wanted to heal him. Mine leads me rather to say that God wanted David home, and healed his whole person. . . . Health and life, I would say, in the full and final sense of those words, are not what we die *out of*, but what we die *into*.[9]

What a beautiful and subversive perspective, knowing that in God's hands even our death is a victory, an upgrade over our present condition. God is claiming his victory: "This vale of tears is but the pathway to the better country: this world of woe is but the stepping-stone to a world of bliss."[10] All of which leads the apostle Paul to taunt death as he considers the wonder of the resurrection:

"Where, O death, is your victory?
Where, O death, is your sting?" (1 Cor. 15:55)

The hope of the resurrection relativizes our fear of death, which works backward into our lives in a million different ways. In his book *Future Grace*, John Piper draws on the work of psychologist Ernest Becker and the denial of death in our modern culture. "Have you ever asked yourself," Piper says, "how much addiction and personality dysfunction and disordered lifestyles may originate in the repressed fear of death?"[11] His point is not that people are enslaved to a constant, conscious fear of dying but that we are enslaved in a thousand ways by trying to avoid this fear itself. Instead of facing it as an unchangeable reality, we avoid it in every way possible and are enslaved in our avoidance.

The writer of Hebrews says it this way: "[Christ] too shared in their humanity so that by his death he might break the power of him who holds the power of death . . . and free those who all their lives were *held in slavery by their fear of death*" (Heb. 2:14–15, emphasis added). Death looms for each of us—that much is certain—and we become its slaves in many ways. When we deny the reality of death, we are enslaved to an illusion. When we succumb to fear, we are enslaved to terror. Our only hope is to reject these options for the assurance of being rescued by a Savior, and so these options impact all of us as we journey through this world. God desires that our ultimate safety and security, our final hope, be in him. And he wants that to have an immediate effect on our lives.[12]

Even if you are a skeptic and approach life as if there is no God and all this religious talk is nonsense, I hope you'll admit this hits a nerve. Because even if we don't think any of this is true, we still *want* it to be. We all want there to be a way in which the sadness and injustice and pain the world has experienced will somehow be rewound or renewed or restored. It sounds too good to be true, and yet that is the story we are invited into. As the Bible says, "Plan your life, budgeting for seventy years (Ps. 90:10), and understand that if your time proves shorter that will not be unfair deprivation but rapid promotion."[13] In the end we want to declare along with the apostle Paul—as many have engraved on their tombstones—that "the time for my departure is near. I have fought the good fight, I have finished the race, I have kept the faith" (2 Tim. 4:6–7).

That is the way.

Death as a Grace

If all of this is true, that death for the believer loses its sting and is something different than the understanding most of us have had, then we can begin to understand why the apostle Paul, in prison and facing imminent death, could write to his friends and say, "To die is gain," and "To depart and be with Christ . . . is better by far" than remaining in this world (Phil. 1:21–23). The secular take is that death is the worst thing that can happen to a person. It means you lost the game of life. But what we see in the Bible is something radically different. As Charles Spurgeon contended about the topic, "The best moment of a Christian's life is his last one, because it is the one that is nearest to heaven." As a pastor, he said, "The only people for whom I have felt any envy have been dying members of this very church." We must realize that "he who learns to die daily while he lives will find it no difficulty to breathe out his soul for the last time."[14] For those who belong to God, death is a mild interruption in our lives, simply the next, but not final, step we must take.

I remember a few years ago hearing a story about the author and preacher Francis Chan. Chan had said that he pleads with God that he would rather the Lord take him in death than he would ever cheat on his wife. That may be jarring to hear at first, but once you have a Christian perspective on death, you can understand where he is coming from. Chan is simply reminding us that there are *worse things than death*. In this his intentions are like Jesus telling us that if our habitual sins are at risk of destroying us, we must destroy them first. If that sin is lust, Jesus says, it is better to enter heaven with no eyeballs—having plucked them out—than to go to hell with two eyes (Matt. 5:29). If stealing, we should want to go to heaven with one hand rather than hell with two. Before you hurt yourself, know that Jesus wasn't being literal, but he was making a very real and literal point: eternity must take priority over and above this temporal life. Eternal life is worth whatever sacrifice we need to make in this life.

One of the most profound paragraphs I have ever read comes from C. S. Lewis's book *The Screwtape Letters* on this exact topic. A young protégé demon says he is excited at the thought of the death of the man he has been assigned to. He feels he could die any day in a bombing in London (it is set during World War II), but the older, wiser demon strongly opposes his plan. His reason is quite chilling:

> If he dies now, you lose him. If he survives the war, there is always hope. . . . If only he can be kept alive, you have time itself for your ally. The long, dull monotonous years of middle-aged prosperity or adversity are excellent campaigning weather. The routine, the gradual decay of youthful loves and hopes, the drabness which we create in their lives and the resentment with which we teach them to respond to it—all this provides admirable opportunities of wearing out a soul by attrition. If, on the other hand, the middle years prove prosperous, our position is even stronger. Prosperity knits a man to the World. He feels that he is "finding his place in it," while really it is finding its place in him. His increasing reputation, his widening circle of acquaintances, his sense of importance, the growing pressure of absorbing and agreeable work, build up in him a sense of being really at home in earth which is just what we want. . . .
>
> . . . That is why we must often wish long life to our patients; seventy years is not a day too much for the difficult task of unravelling their souls from Heaven and building up a firm attachment to the earth.[15]

Lewis here affirms what Paul and so many other biblical writers teach: that this life feeds into the next one in such a way that our choices here have real consequences for our future. This life may end with a tumor or a car accident, without any notice or our ability to prevent it. But the decisions we make today will affect the millions of years we face in the next life.

Having this perspective also changes how we cope with the death of those we love. Viktor Frankl, the psychologist and sole survivor of his whole family through the Holocaust, tells a story to this end.

Once, an elderly man consulted me because of his severe depression. He could not overcome the loss of his wife who had died two years before and whom he had loved above all else. Now, how can I help him? What should I tell him? Well, I refrained from telling him anything but instead confronted him with the question, "What would have happened, if you had died first, and your wife would have had to survive you?" "Oh," he said, "for her this would have been terrible; how she would have suffered!" Whereupon I replied, "You see, such a suffering has been spared her, and it was you who have spared her this suffering—to be sure, at the price that now you have to survive and mourn her." He said no word but shook my hand and calmly left my office. In some way, suffering ceases to be suffering *at the moment it finds a meaning*.[16]

The same is true of death itself, which is why we must decide before it ever visits us what we want it to be like, for that will then forever be its meaning for us. And God's desire and invitation for us all is that our eternity would be with him and the sweetest of all experiences.

The Great Divorce: Rethinking Hell

The opposite experience is also an eternal reality, though very different from the one we have been looking at. As Jesus says, it plays out the exact opposite of heaven. It is a place that has come to be known as *hell*, which is a translation of the word *gehenna*, the garbage dump outside the city of Jerusalem in Jesus's day. Jesus uses a reference to a place they knew, and likely one that other rabbis and prophets used as well, to speak of the judgment of God as a place and experience of darkness and fear and terrible things. Jesus provides us with many images about this place or state of being throughout his teachings. It is a place, he says, of "fire," "darkness," "weeping and gnashing of teeth," "and "eternal punishment" (Matt. 5:22; 22:13; 25:46); but not the mercy of *nonexistence*, for it is a place where nothing dies, Jesus says, even though it wishes to cease suffering (Mark 9:42–48). Of course, all these images are symbolic in some way, just as those of heaven were. That is how apocalyptic literature works, through symbolic language and metaphor. But these images are symbolic *for something*, and whatever that something is, it is the opposite of flourishing and life and joy—all the things we long for. They are symbolic for a kind of eternity that is scary and lonely and filled with emotional, spiritual, and potentially even physical pain. Just as heaven will be better than we could dream, where our bodies feel sensations of pleasure this life can only hint at, hell could be the opposite and will certainly be worse than we can conceive, worse than these images can paint for us.[17]

We of course scoff at all this as modern people, but the reality is that the kind of existence we find in hell is the result of a life that finally receives the autonomy and distance from God's grace that it always fought for. Hell is the answer to us falling for the serpent's promise in the Genesis story. God grants us our desire forever: "I would rather be God than have God be God. I would rather be my own person, do my own thing, than to accept his free offer of grace." Hell is the final answer to that posture, and thus a place where all trace of God's grace has been removed. For in rejecting God, we reject his gifts, things like love and beauty and wonder and joy. We will no longer experience the rain when there has been nothing but drought and death; the sun when there has been too much rain; the laughter of our child as they walk for the first time; our newborn baby when we hold them and they look up at us and we wondered how we ever lived before; the absolute bliss when a score or song hits us at just the right time; our spouse when we see them walking down the aisle with our whole lives ahead of us; a frame from a film, or a painting, or a sunset as it touches us in a way that transports us. All the moments of knowing the enveloping of love and peace around us like a warm blanket gone forever. Hell is a place devoid of these graces. It is Mordor because we rejected the goodness of the Shire.

This is not as absurd as some would say. The person who rejects the offer of God in this life will over time enter a state wherein, as C. S. Lewis says, "the taste for the *other*, the very capacity for enjoying good, is quenched in him except in so far as his body still draws him into some contact with an outer world. Death removes this last contact. He has his wish—to live wholly in the self and to make the best of what he finds there. And what he finds there is Hell."[18] This is the inevitable result of refusing to embrace the offer of self-abandonment. Those who refuse are "successful rebels to the end . . . enjoying forever the horrible freedom they have demanded."[19]

So the first thing we can say is that hell is the end of the trajectory of a heart that does not follow God. It is a punishment, but it is also the natural result of an unforgiven life echoing into eternity. Heaven is filled with forgiven people, but "forgiveness needs to be accepted if it is to be complete and a man who admits no guilt can accept no forgiveness."[20] So in the end there are only two kinds of people. There are those who look to God and say, "Your will be done." And there are those to whom God says, "Your will be done," who go on to live out the freedom they have desperately demanded.[21] Will you receive the gift of God and allow him to save you, or will you stubbornly repeat what our first parents did in the garden— decide you are better off on your own, making your own choices and seeking your own future?

Darrell Johnson summarizes this well: "We are all going to die. And each of us is going to give an accounting for our lives. On that day we have two options. The first option is to take our stand on the basis of what *we* have done with our lives. The second option is to take our stand on the basis of what *Jesus Christ* has done with his life. I shall exercise option two. I find no hope in option one."[22]

Note carefully that these eternal questions revolve around Jesus in particular. Our culture is saturated in God-talk, yet that is inadequate. It may be a win when someone says they believe in God, or want to align their life with him, but what "god" are we are talking about? The life we desire isn't ultimately found in a generic god, or one who fits into whatever flavor of religion we want to try. No, life to the full is found specifically in the God *revealed in the person and work of Jesus.* Nothing else will do because "there is no other name under heaven . . . by which we can be saved" (Acts 4:12 NLV).

This isn't narrow-minded or judgmental, as many say; this is simply consistent with what we've been seeing all along. The explanation of reality I've been giving you is unique to the God revealed in the Bible in Jesus, and once we see that, we come to understand that "God without Christ is no God. And a no-God cannot save or satisfy the soul. Following a no-God will be a wasted life. God-in-Christ is the only true God and the only path to joy."[23]

Security and a Trapdoor

And so we end our exploration of life with what matters most. If we live forever, we have a decision to make between what God invites us into and its opposite. What matters more than this? I am not talking about taking our eyes off the concerns of this world, but rather readjusting our perspective to truly see this life for what it is. Our purpose is not to live our days plucking blackberries, but to take off our shoes every chance we can, in recognition that our life is a gift, a sacred and enchanted thing to be treasured and stewarded wisely unto the glory of God, not ourselves.

When we accept that this is true, the things of this world—things that promise to provide meaning and joy and purpose—appear different. Priorities adjust and we experience a new freedom. Like when seminary professor Addison Leitch was speaking at a missionary conference many years ago, and he inspired some young girls to leave home and go on the mission field. Their parents were not happy about it, and they approached Leitch arguing that these young women should "get some security first: like go to seminary and get a master's degree or something before they go off and do this missionary thing." Leitch's response perfectly captures our situation in this life: "We're all on a little ball of rock called Earth, and we're spinning through space at millions of miles an hour. Someday a trapdoor is going to open up under every single one of us, and we will fall through it. And either there will be millions and millions of miles of nothing—or else there will be the everlasting arms of God. And you want them to get a master's degree to give them a little security?"[24]

Most of the people who don't end up in heaven aren't evil, malicious people in the way we typically think of them: tyrannical rulers like Hitler, serial killers, or sociopaths who hurt others. Often they are just ordinary run-of-the-mill people who squandered their opportunity in life on temporary pursuits without really asking the most important questions of life: Why am I here? And do the things I do in this life have any impact on my long-term future after my time here is over? They neglected the eternally important questions because they were busy doing other things. One preacher I recently listened to put it this way: "Do you know what the devil uses to destroy your life? It's not visitations at night, or blatantly evil experiences, or even temptation to outright sin; those are obvious. It is the device in your front pocket or your purse. That phone that just keeps you scrolling, distracted and entertained all the way to the grave."

Again, Lewis in *The Screwtape Letters* suggests this is our real problem. The uncle demon, writing from hell to his nephew, says, "Once you have made the World an end, you have almost won your man. . . . Provided that meetings, policies, movements, causes, all matter more to him than prayer, he is ours. I could show you a pretty cageful of people like that down here."[25]

Let us then resolve not to be distracted. And if you have been, decide right now, from this day forward, to consider the ultimate questions that will affect you forever. This world matters a great deal, but we cannot live the way we were designed until we put the concerns and priorities of this world in their place and embrace the perspective of the reality of the next world.

The Great Story

Like ships heading into the unknown, we are heading into an eternal future with the God who makes all things new. What will that world be like? How will we feel and think? Honestly, I don't know. We have a few hints, but that is all the Bible gives us. Tolkien tried to capture some of the heavenly future in *The Lord of the Rings* when Frodo, after all his suffering to destroy the ring of power, was given the gift of going to Middle-earth's heaven across the sea: "The grey rain-curtain turned all to silver glass and was rolled back, and he beheld white shores and beyond them a far green country under a swift sunrise."[26] This was his reward for all the difficulties and suffering he experienced, for remaining faithful to his task until the end. And one day, when we stand before Jesus, our reward will be to hear him say, "Well done, good and faithful servant!" followed by the invitation, "Come, you who are blessed by my Father; take your inheritance, the kingdom prepared for you since the creation of the world" (Matt. 25:23, 34).

To get a taste of what that will be like, think of the most glorious, wonderful, joy-filled feeling you can—whatever place or circumstance you can imagine—and then know that you have not come even a little bit close to beginning to fathom what this reward will be like, because every great pleasure we have in our experience is nothing but a small pointer to heaven.

The final words of C. S. Lewis's *Chronicles of Narnia* books capture this powerfully. After following the kids' adventures for seven novels, the series ends with a picture of heaven. Aslan, the great Lion and Christ figure of the stories, is ushering them into his world.

> As He spoke He no longer looked to them like a lion; but the things that began to happen after that were so great and beautiful that I cannot write them. And for us this is the end of all the stories, and we can most truly say that they all lived happily ever after. But for them it was only the beginning of the real story. All their life in this world and all their adventures in Narnia had only been the cover and the title page: now at last they were beginning Chapter One of the Great Story which no one on earth has read: which goes on forever: in which every chapter is better than the one before.[27]

Do you know the best part of all this? That God offers us this glorious reality not as a result of us being good enough, climbing our way up to heaven like religion tells us to do; but he himself comes down in the person of Jesus to rescue us, to *search us out* to bring us home! He initiates, accomplishes, and does everything in his power to pave the way. As the old theologians used to say, he is the "Hound of Heaven," who searches us out because he loves us so much. Our role is to put our faith, trust, and devotion in him, in the work he did for us on the cross and in the resurrection. This is the good news of the gospel, the very best news of all.

And here is a further encouragement to you. All God's searching isn't something that happened only in the past, as if Jesus did all the work and is waiting in heaven with his arms crossed to see how we respond. No, he continues to hound us, to hunt for us, seeking to awaken us from our slumber in every way he can. And if you ever doubt that, just remember the story I am going to tell you now. It's 100 percent true. Every last word of it.

And it will be the last word for this book as well.

The End. Based on a True Story.

Let's end where we began. Back with Sarah, the lady I told you about in the introduction. If you don't remember, I had wrongly informed her that her husband was dead. Turns out, I had the wrong guy.

But that wasn't the end of the story. Something happened a couple weeks later that I will never forget.

I was at work, sitting at my desk, when one of my fellow pastors walked into my office. He had a weird look on his face. "I was just praying as I drove in today," he said. "And I got the strangest impression that you are supposed to go and visit Sarah. Like, at her house."

I looked up from my desk and stared into his face. "Not in a million years," I thought. "I am the last person she wants to see. I am the reason she passed out in shock and grief, thinking she had lost the love of her life, only to find out it was all a mistake—my mistake."

"I am . . . not sure I'm the best person for this," I said and looked back to my computer. He didn't leave and instead doubled down. "No, I am serious. I don't want to be super spiritual with you, but I really felt like God was telling me this as I drove here. Like, as clear as day."

I looked back at him, just hoping this conversation would end. "Well, okay. I'm a little busy today, but I will go tomorrow." Honestly, I dreaded having to look that innocent lady in the face again. I figured I'd have to grovel and apologize and admit how incompetent I was.

"You are supposed to go today. As soon as possible," he said.

His voice had an intensity that was hard to ignore. I thought about it a moment more and stood up from my desk. "All right. I'll go." What was I going to do, *argue with God?*

I flipped open the church directory and looked up her address and drove to her house. I knocked on the door. No one answered. A car was in the driveway, so I assumed someone was home and kept knocking. Five minutes went by until finally I saw a figure through the glass. The door opened, and in front of me stood Sarah. In her pajamas. This took me by surprise because it was one o'clock in the afternoon.

"What do *you* want?" she said. The tone of her voice was cold to say the least.

"I just wanted to come by and check up on you, say hi, and you know—uh . . . Can I come in?" She looked a little confused, but I thought I caught the slightest twinkle in her eye. I brushed it off. It seemed I had woken her up from a deep sleep. She motioned for me to come in and take a seat on her couch in the living room. She went into the kitchen and a moment or two later appeared with a hot pot of tea. Pouring a couple of cups, she sat back in her chair. "Here I am," she said. The room was quiet.

"Uh, yeah, so I just wanted to come by as one of the pastors and make sure you were doing well, and, uh, well, I guess to apologize for everything that happened . . . Look, *I am sorry.* I can't believe I made that mistake. I have been turning it over in my head for weeks and am just sick about it."

Her face relaxed a little, and she even mustered up a bit of a smile. It was probably a pity smile, the young pastor doing his best and all that. We ended up talking for a while about our favorite theologians, had some laughs, and told lots of stories. She even broke out some old pictures of her and David in their younger years: their wedding photos and travel pictures. Before I knew it three or more hours had gone by. I told her I had overstayed my welcome. "Oh, nonsense!" she said. "I don't get many visitors, so this was a blessing."

She hesitated a moment and said, "Do you know why I am still wearing my pajamas at this hour?"

"I just figured you had a late night or got up late maybe?" I said.

She smiled and looked at the floor. "No." Silence lived between us for a moment. I wanted so badly to slice into it, but I hesitated, almost like something was holding me back.

She then said something I will never forget. "What happened that day, what you did, was so disturbing to me, so mixed up and messed up, it sent me into a very dark place. My emotions have gotten the best of me, and I feel I will never be the same." She started to cry.

"This morning I woke up in a dire state," she said through the tears. "I walked downstairs from my bedroom, into the kitchen, and said to God, 'Today I am going to kill myself.'"

It felt like my heart had stopped. The words took a moment to register in my mind. How could my mistaken actions, my stupidity, lead someone to feel so dark and lost that they would consider *ending their life*? She continued to stare at the floor. Shame and guilt flooded her face. My mind started racing. I was about to talk, but again I stopped myself.

She continued. "I told God I was going to take my life because all of this just wasn't fair, and my heart is just . . . done. I told him he and I were done too. How could he have allowed this? I was done with him and the pain and with my life. Unless . . ." At this she stopped and took a breath.

"Unless what?" I asked.

"I told him just a few hours ago: 'I will take my life unless you send someone to my door today, out of the blue, to encourage me.' That would be a sign *to let me know he still cares*." She looked up at me. "I told God that and then sat down on the chair in my living room and fell asleep and then woke up to the sound of you knocking at my door."

I couldn't talk. I had no words. How could I?

It was quiet but for the sound of her wiping tears from her eyes and clearing her throat. "I asked God to send someone to remind me he exists," she said, "and that he loves me, and I guess . . . I guess that person is you."

At that, her face lit up and she walked over to me. I stood up and wrapped my arms around her, reminding her that God indeed loved her deeply and that he *had* sent me so she would never think about harming herself again, that tomorrow would be a new day. After a while I asked if I could pray for her. We prayed and cried, and I walked out to my car a different person from the one who had arrived a few hours earlier.

Even as I write these words, I catch another glimpse of what God was doing. Like Jesus asking Peter if he loved him three times on the beach that day to reverse the three times he had denied and failed him, God wasn't just healing Sarah, he was healing me as well. That's why it had to be *me* who went over there—and no one else. I had lost all confidence in my calling as a pastor and preacher that day I made the mistake. I had begun to doubt that God had a place for me in ministry, or as a leader in any capacity. And this was his way not only to come out from behind the veil for *her*, to tell her that he loves her and has an amazing plan for her life no matter what pains and challenges she encounters, but to say all that to me as well.

He was saying to me, "You made a mistake, and it won't be your last, but I am going to use you. Not because *you* are perfect but because *I* am."

In that moment, I was forever healed of believing a million voices that would try to overtake my calling and misdirect my steps because of fear or doubt.

As we have seen many times over the course of this book, there are moments in life when something gets through. Someone reaches through and touches us, and this was one of those moments for me. I mean, I rarely question whether God is real, but like many of us, I don't always *feel* he is. But that day, there was no doubt.

Soulish things.

They are everything.

For you, I think that story says a couple of things. First, how can you hear a story like that and *not* believe in God? What are the statistical odds that such a thing would ever occur in the universe? Out of nowhere someone gets an impression and tells someone else who acts on it on exactly the right day, at exactly the right time, or else a person *dies*.

Doubt all you want, but God is still alive and active and moving! Hunting and haunting us. That's how good he is.

Second, this story is a reminder that not only does God exist, but he is *for you* and *he loves you*. Sometimes we forget that. God is not only real but also good and worth giving your life to and living for. Christ's heart is not drained by us coming to him but is filled up. He doesn't reluctantly forgive us but does so passionately. After all, *it's why he came*. It is what he loves to do. He wants you to find yourself by finding him. He is the only one who will guide us in the tension of the fact that while paradise is in our hearts, we aren't there yet. We instead live in the *in-between place*, "the barren but crowded place between two worlds, between the lost and found, the old and the new."[28]

And sometimes we forget how powerful this realization is—that God exists and we should live under him—for people who haven't had it as the undercurrent of their life. Who, like me, weren't born into families that lived this out. But when I discovered it at seventeen years old, nothing could make me turn back. For it was the discovery of one who had tried everything under the sun to find true joy, and having come up short, I finally surrendered to God instead of the alternatives offered by the world. And when I did, my joy was a delight "in having touched *firmness*; like the pedestrian's delight in feeling the hard road beneath his feet after a false short cut has long entangled him in muddy fields."[29]

Notes

INTRODUCTION

1. Leo Tolstoy, *A Confession*, trans. Aylmer Maude (Oxford University Press, 1911), 34.

2. This is not a direct quote but is the summation of ideas in Richard Dawkins, *The Selfish Gene* (Oxford University Press, 1976).

3. Elizabeth Barrett Browning, *Aurora Leigh* (Worthington Co., 1890).

4. C. S. Lewis, *The Weight of Glory* (HarperOne, 1949), 3–4.

5. John Calvin, *The* Institutes of the Christian Religion (Hendrickson, 2014), I.1.4.

6. Eugene Peterson, *Reversed Thunder: The Revelation of John and the Praying Imagination* (HarperOne, 1988), 65.

7. John Piper, *God Is the Gospel: Meditations on God's Love as the Gift of Himself* (Crossway, 2005), 47.

8. Paul Tillich, *Theology of Culture* (Oxford University Press, 1959), 10.

9. N. T. Wright, *Simply Christian: Why Christianity Makes Sense* (HarperOne, 2006), 4.

10. Micheal O'Siadhail, "Leisure," in *The Gossamer Wall: Poems in Witness to the Holocaust*. Also see Micheal O'Siadhail, *The Five Quintets* (Baylor University Press, 2019), 38.

11. Ron Dart, *Myth and Meaning in Jordan Peterson: A Christian Perspective* (Lexham, 2020), 16, emphasis added.

CHAPTER 1: LISTEN TO THE OLD ACHE INSIDE YOU

1. Yuval Noah Harari, *Sapiens: A Brief History of Humankind* (Penguin Random House, 2014), 233–34.

2. C. S. Lewis, *The Weight of Glory* (HarperOne, 1949), 3–4.

3. Zara Abrams, "Student Mental Health Is in Crisis. Campuses Are Rethinking Their Approach," American Psychological Association, October 12, 2022, https://www.apa.org/monitor/2022/10/mental-health -campus-care; Tracy Brower, MD, "Burnout Is a Worldwide Problem: 5 Ways Work Must Change," *Forbes*, July 24, 2022, https://www.forbes

.com/sites/tracybrower/2022/07/24/burnout-is-a-worldwide-problem-5
-ways-work-must-change/; Catherine K. Ettman et al., "Prevalence of
Depression Symptoms in US Adults Before and During the COVID-19
Pandemic," *JAMA Network Open* 3, no. 9 (2020): e2019686, https://www
.doi.org/10.1001/jamanetworkopen.2020.19686; "Anxiety Disorders—Facts
and Statistics," Anxiety and Depression Association of America, accessed
June 7, 2024, https://adaa.org/understanding-anxiety/facts-statistics; see also
Steven D. Levitt and Stephen J. Dubner, *Think like a Freak: The Authors of
Freakonomics Offer to Retrain Your Brain* (William Morrow, 2014), 32.

4. Dietrich Bonhoeffer, *Letters and Papers from Prison* (SCM Press, 1953), 31.

5. Donald Bloesch, *Theological Notebook: Spiritual Journals of Donald G.
   Bloesch* (Helmers & Howard, 1989), 183.

6. Sue Monk Kidd, *When the Heart Waits: Spiritual Direction for Life's Sacred
   Questions* (HarperOne, 1990), 89.

7. Quoted in Ron Dart, *The Myth and Meaning: An Inquiry into the Role of
   Symbolism in Human Experience* (Northshore Publishing, 1989), 17.

8. Quoted in Dart, *Myth and Meaning*, 17.

9. Eugene Peterson, *Reversed Thunder: The Revelation of John and the Praying
   Imagination* (HarperOne, 1988), 78.

10. Peterson, *Reversed Thunder*, 78.

11. Peterson, *Reversed Thunder*, 78.

12. John Piper, *Desiring God: Meditations of a Christian Hedonist*
    (Multnomah, 1996), 9.

13. Augustine, *Confessions* (Oxford University Press, 1991), 3.

14. Peter Kreeft, *I Burned for Your Peace: Augustine's* Confessions
    Unpacked (Ignatius Press, 2016), 21–23.

15. Jordan Peterson, *Beyond Order: 12 More Rules for Life* (Penguin Random
    House, 2021), 133.

16. Levitt and Dubner, *Think like a Freak*, 32.

17. Rodney Stark, *America's Blessings: How Religion Benefits Everyone,
    Including Atheists* (Templeton, 2013).

18. Quoted in Timothy Keller, "The Righteousness of God: The Attributes of
    God," November 1992 (Timothy Keller Sermon Archive, Logos).

19. A thought inspired by Rankin Wilbourne.

20. Peterson, *Reversed Thunder*, 37.

21. Peterson, *Reversed Thunder*, 37.

22. Russell Moore, *The Storm-Tossed Family: How the Cross Reshapes the Home* (B&H, 2018), 7–8.

23. G. K. Chesterton, *Orthodoxy* (John Lane Company, 1908).

CHAPTER 2: FIND OUT WHERE YOU CAME FROM

1. Herbert Spencer, *First Principles: A System of Synthetic Philosophy*, 4th ed. (D. Appleton and Company, 1882).

2. Christian Smith, *What Is a Person? Rethinking Humanity, Social Life, and the Moral Good from the Person Up* (University of Chicago Press, 2010), 7.

3. See Gen. 1:21–22, 24, 28–30; 2:7. See also Christopher Watkin, *Biblical Critical Theory: How the Bible's Unfolding Story Makes Sense of Modern Life and Culture* (Zondervan Academic, 2022), 84.

4. Timothy Keller, *King's Cross: The Story of the World in the Life of Jesus* (Penguin, 2011), 104.

5. Marilyn Schlitz, *Death Makes Life Possible: Revolutionary Insights on Living, Dying, and the Continuation of Consciousness* (Sounds True, 2015), 29, 66. See also Lee Strobel, *The Case for a Creator: A Journalist Investigates Scientific Evidence That Points Toward God* (Zondervan, 2004), 252.

6. Strobel, *Case for a Creator*, 269.

7. Klaus Dose, "The Origin of Life: More Questions than Answers," *Interdisciplinary Science Reviews* 13, no. 4 (1988): 348, https://doi.org/10.1179/isr.1988.13.4.348.

8. Francis Crick, *Life Itself: Its Origin and Nature* (Simon & Schuster, 1981), 88.

9. Anthony Flew, *There Is a God: How the World's Most Notorious Atheist Changed His Mind* (HarperOne, 2007), 75.

10. John C. Lennox, *2084: Artificial Intelligence and the Future of Humanity* (Zondervan Reflective, 2020), 37.

11. David Briggs, "Science, Religion Are Discovering Commonality in Big Bang Theory," *Los Angeles Times* (May 2, 1992), B6–B7.

12. James Houston, *In Pursuit of Happiness: Finding Genuine Fulfillment in Life* (NavPress, 1996), 61; see also Smith, *What Is a Person?*, 78.

13. Dominic Done, *Your Longing Has a Name: Come Alive to the Story You Were Made For* (Thomas Nelson, 2022), 27.

14. John Stott, *Authentic Christianity*, ed. Timothy Dudley-Smith (InterVarsity Press, 1996), 142.

15. Alister McGrath, *The Twilight of Atheism: The Rise and Fall of Disbelief in the Modern World* (Doubleday, 2004), 86–87.

16. G. K. Chesterton, *The Collected Works of G. K. Chesterton*, vol. 1. *Heretics, Orthodoxy, the Blatchford Controversies*, ed. David Dooley (Ignatius, 1986), 245.

17. Stott, *Authentic Christianity*, 137.

18. Stott, *Authentic Christianity*, 137.

19. Luc Ferry, *A Brief History of Thought: A Philosophical Guide to Living* (Harper Perennial, 2011), 72.

20. Ferry, *A Brief History of Thought*, 72.

21. John Gray, quoted in Nancy Pearcey, *Total Truth: Liberating Christianity from Its Cultural Captivity* (Crossway, 2004), 320.

22. Charles Darwin, *The Descent of Man, and Selection in Relation to Sex* (John Murray, 1871), ch. 21–General Summary and Conclusion.

23. Bruce Waltke, *Genesis: A Commentary* (Zondervan, 2001), 65–66.

24. Timothy Keller, *Center Church: Doing Balanced, Gospel-Centered Ministry in Your City* (Zondervan, 2012), 141.

25. Quoted in R. Paul Stevens, *Down-to-Earth Spirituality: Encountering God in the Ordinary, Boring Stuff of Life* (InterVarsity Press, 2010), 131.

26. C. S. Lewis, *The Weight of Glory* (HarperOne, 1949), 46.

27. J. R. R. Tolkien, *The Return of the King* (Houghton Mifflin, 1955), 1030.

28. Yuval Noah Harari, *Sapiens: A Brief History of Humankind* (Penguin Random House, 2014), 5.

CHAPTER 3: DON'T TRY TO BE GOD

1. Quoted in Adam Grant, *Originals: How Non-Conformists Move the World* (Viking, 2016), 29–30.

2. Bruce Waltke, *Genesis: A Commentary* (Zondervan, 2001), 68.

3. John Mark Comer, *Live No Lies: Recognize and Resist the Three Enemies That Sabotage Your Peace* (Waterbrook, 2021), 61.

4. Comer, *Live No Lies*, 64.

5. Fernando Pessoa, *The Book of Disquiet* (Penguin Classics, 2002), 384.

6. Quoted in John C. Lennox, *2084: Artificial Intelligence and the Future of Humanity* (Zondervan Reflective, 2020), 27.

7. Quoted in Paul Ratner, "Here's When Machines Will Take Your Job, as Predicted by A.I. Gurus," *Big Think*, June 4, 2017, https://bigthink.com/the-future/heres-when-machines-will-take-your-job-predict-ai-gurus/.

8. Quoted in William Gavin, "Elon Musk's Neuralink Showed Its First Human Patient Playing Chess," *Quartz*, March 21, 2024, https://qz.com/elon-musk-neuralink-first-human-patient-chess-1851354848.

9. Yuval Noah Harari, *Sapiens: A Brief History of Humankind* (Penguin Random House, 2014), 403.

10. Jonathan Haidt, "The Joe Rogan Experience #2121," PowerfulJRE, March 19, 2024, YouTube video, 2:01:40, https://www.youtube.com/watch?v=jOC-RyoBcbQ.

11. Francis Fukuyama, "The World's Most Dangerous Idea," *Foreign Policy* 144 (September–October, 2004), 42–43.

12. Paula Boddington, "Myth and the EU Study on Civil Law Rules in Robotics," *Ethics for Artificial Intelligence*, January 12, 2017.

13. Quoted in Lennox, *2084*, 143.

14. Quoted in Lennox, *2084*, 90.

15. For more on this, see Dr. Debra Soh, *The End of Gender: Debunking the Myths about Sex and Identity in Our Society* (Threshold Editions, 2020), 28.

16. Soh, *The End of Gender*, 17.

17. Carl R. Trueman, *The Rise and Triumph of the Modern Self: Cultural Amnesia, Expressive Individualism, and the Road to Sexual Revolution* (Crossway, 2020), 50.

18. Soh, *The End of Gender*, 9.

19. Soh, *The End of Gender*, 9.

20. Soh, *The End of Gender*, 17–18, emphasis added.

21. Dr. Louann Brizendine, *The Female Brain* (Harmony, 2006), 1, 21.

22. Carl R. Trueman, *Strange New World: How Thinkers and Activists Redefined Identity and Sparked the Sexual Revolution* (Crossway, 2022), 132.

23. Richard Dawkins, "Trans: When Ideology Meets Reality," July 29, 2023, in *The Poetry of Reality with Richard Dawkins*, https://richarddawkins.substack.com/p/trans-when-ideology-meets-reality.

24. Quoted in Jason McIntyre, "Serena Williams to David Letterman in 2013:

'Andy Murray Would Beat Me 6–0, 6–0 in Five Minutes,'" *The Big Lead*, June 28, 2017, https://www.thebiglead.com/posts/serena-williams-to-david -letterman-in-2013-andy-murray-would-beat-me-6-0-6-0-in-five-minutes -0ldkxwgrztpj.

25. Paula Johnson, "His and Hers . . . Health Care," TEDTalk, December 2013, https://www.ted.com/talks/paula_johnson_his_and_hers_health_care.

26. Nancy Pearcey, *Love Thy Body: Answering Hard Questions about Life and Sexuality* (Baker, 2018), 196.

27. Marni Sommer, Virginia Kamowa, and Therese Mahon, "Opinion: Creating a More Equal Post-COVID-19 World for People Who Menstruate," Devex, May 28, 2020, https://www.devex.com/news/sponsored/opinion -creating-a-more-equal-post-covid-19-world-for-people-who-menstruate -97312.

28. J. K. Rowling (@jk_rowling), "If sex isn't real," Twitter, June 6, 2020, 6:02 p.m., https://x.com/jk_rowling/status/1269389298664701952.

29. Katja Gutschke, Aglaja Stirn, and Erich Kasten, "An Overwhelming Desire to Be Blind: Similarities and Differences between Body Integrity Identity Disorder and the Wish for Blindness," *Case Reports Ophthalmology* 8, no. 1 (Jan.–Apr. 2017): 124–36, https://doi.org/10.1159/000456709; see also Chiara Fiorillo, "Woman Blinded Herself with Drain Cleaner to Fulfil 'Dream of Being Disabled,'" *The Mirror*, September 17, 2023, https://www.mirror.co.uk /news/us-news/woman-blinded-herself-drain-cleaner-30934249.

30. Dart, *The Myth and Meaning*, 107.

CHAPTER 4: LOOK UP, NOT IN

1. Mark Sayers, *The Disappearing Church: From Cultural Relevance to Gospel Resilience* (Moody, 2016), 11.

2. John Stott, *Issues Facing Christians Today* (Zondervan, 2006), ch. 15.

3. Stott, *Issues Facing Christians Today*, ch. 15.

4. Carl R. Trueman, *The Rise and Triumph of the Modern Self: Cultural Amnesia, Expressive Individualism, and the Road to Sexual Revolution* (Crossway, 2020), 97.

5. Trueman, *The Rise and Triumph of the Modern Self*, 97.

6. Quoted in Trueman, *The Rise and Triumph of the Modern Self*, 76–77.

7. Timothy Keller, "God Is with Us," December 1991 (Timothy Keller Sermon Archive, Logos).

8. Andrew Wilson, *Remaking the World: How 1776 Created the Post-Christian West* (Crossway, 2023), 7.

9. James K. A. Smith, *On the Road with Saint Augustine: A Real-World Spirituality for Restless Hearts* (Brazos, 2019), 11.

10. Augustine, *Confessions*, 3.7, 43.

11. Christian Smith, *What Is a Person? Rethinking Humanity, Social Life, and the Moral Good from the Person Up* (University of Chicago Press, 2010), 22.

12. Kirsten Birkett, "Naturalism in a Biblical Worldview," Henry Center, August 15, 2009, https://henrycenter.tiu.edu/wp-content/uploads/2013/11 /Birkett-Naturalism.pdf.

13. Kirsten Birkett, "Naturalism in a Biblical Worldview."

14. Sayers, *The Disappearing Church*.

15. See V. Thakur and A. Jain, "COVID 2019-Suicides: A Global Psychological Pandemic," *Brain, Behavior, and Immunity* 88 (2020): 952–53, https://doi .org/10.1016/j.bbi.2020.04.062; see also https://www.cdc.gov/nchs/products /databriefs. The total age-adjusted suicide rate increased from 10.7 deaths per 100,000 standard population in 2001 to a recent peak of 14.1 in 2021.

16. Craig Gay, *The Way of the (Modern) World: Or, Why It's Tempting to Live As If God Doesn't Exist* (Eerdmans, 1998), 1.

17. Gay, *Way of the (Modern) World*, 1.

18. Timothy Keller, *Making Sense of God: Making Sense of God: An Invitation to the Skeptical* (Viking, 2016), 100–102, emphasis added.

19. Keller, *Making Sense of God*, 142.

20. C. S. Lewis, *The Complete C. S. Lewis Signature Classics: Mere Christianity* (HarperOne, 2002), 177.

21. Peter Berger, *Pyramids of Sacrifice: Political Ethics and Social Change* (Anchor, 1976), 20.

22. Gay, *Way of the (Modern) World*, 74.

23. Timothy Keller, *Counterfeit Gods: The Empty Promises of Money, Sex, and Power, and the Only Hope That Matters* (Penguin, 2011).

24. Thomas Chalmers, "The Expulsive Power of a New Affection," https://www .monergism.com/thethreshold/sdg/Chalmers,%20Thomas%20-%20The%20 Exlpulsive%20Power%20of%20a%20New%20Af.pdf.

25. Iain Provan, *Ecclesiastes/Song of Songs*, NIV Application Commentary (Zondervan, 2001), 63.

26. Quoted in John Stackhouse, *Making the Best of It: Following Christ in the Real World* (Oxford University Press, 2008), 63–66.

CHAPTER 5: LIVE AS A VICTOR, NOT A VICTIM

1. Christian Smith, *To Flourish or Destruct: A Personalist Theory of Human Goods, Motivations, Failure, and Evil* (University of Chicago Press, 2015), 4.

2. Timothy Keller and Kathy Keller, *God's Wisdom for Navigating Life: A Year of Daily Devotions in the Book of Proverbs* (Penguin, 2017), 56.

3. Keller and Keller, *God's Wisdom for Navigating Life*, 56.

4. J. I. Packer, *Knowing God* (InterVarsity Press, 2021), 19.

5. Richard Lovelace, *Dynamics of Spiritual Life: An Evangelical Theology of Renewal* (InterVarsity Press, 2020), 212.

6. Greg Lukianoff and Jonathan Haidt, *The Coddling of the American Mind: How Good Intentions and Bad Ideas Are Setting Up a Generation for Failure* (Penguin, 2018), 6.

7. Lukianoff and Haidt, *The Coddling of the American Mind*, 27.

8. Adam Grant, *Think Again: The Power of Knowing What You Don't Know* (Viking, 2021), 3–18.

9. It is actually an adaptation of Tolkien's original poem from *The Fellowship of the Ring*, but in the Amazon TV show *The Rings of Power: The Lord of the Rings*. Season 1, Episode 6, "The Battle of Dagorlad."

10. United States Golf Association (USGA), "U.S. Open Epics: Tiger and Rocco," July 18, 2018, https://www.youtube.com/watch?v=zodrcuCHh3Q.

11. Rudyard Kipling, "If," https://www.poetryfoundation.org/poems/46473/if---.

12. Brennan Manning, *The Ragamuffin Gospel: Good News for the Bedraggled, Beat-Up, and Burnt Out* (Multnomah Books, 2005), 14.

13. Quoted in Malcolm Gladwell, *David and Goliath: Underdogs, Misfits, and the Art of Battling Giants* (Little, Brown and Company, 2013), 106.

14. Gladwell, *David and Goliath*, 140–43.

PART III: THE PROBLEM OF PAIN

1. Gabor Maté, *The Myth of Normal: Trauma, Illness, Healing in a Toxic Culture* (Penguin, 2022), 363.

2. William Shakespeare, *Romeo and Juliet*, prologue.

CHAPTER 6: LOOK PAIN AND SUFFERING SQUARE IN THE FACE

1. Ernest Becker, *The Denial of Death* (Free Press, 1973), 283–84.

2. Christian Smith, *To Flourish or Destruct: A Personalist Theory of Human Goods, Motivations, Failure, and Evil* (University of Chicago Press, 2015), 223.

3. William Shakespeare, *Macbeth*, act 4, scene 3.

4. Peter van Inwagen, *Christian Faith and the Problem of Evil* (Eerdmans, 2004), xii.

5. Sam Harris, *Letter to a Christian Nation* (Knopf, 2006), 55–56.

6. Alvin Plantinga, *Warranted Christian Belief* (Oxford University Press, 2000), 212.

7. Bertrand Russell, "A Free Man's Worship," in *The Basic Writings of Bertrand Russell*, ed. R. E. Egner and L. E. Dononn (Routledge, 1992), 67.

8. George Orwell, "Notes on the Way," in *A Patriot After All*, ed. Peter Davidson (Random House, 2000), 124.

9. Quoted in Timothy Keller, *Walking with God through Pain and Suffering* (Dutton, 2013), 99.

10. Walter Brueggemann, *Genesis*, Interpretation: A Bible Commentary for Teaching and Preaching (John Knox Press, 1982), 50.

11. Quoted in C. J. Mahaney and Robin Boisvert, *How Can I Change? Victory in the Struggle against Sin* (Sovereign Grace Ministries, 1996), 41.

12. C. S. Lewis, *The Problem of Pain* (Macmillan, 1962), 55, 57.

13. Thomas Aquinas, *Summa Theologica* (Benziger Brothers, 1915), 444.

14. Christopher Watkin, *Biblical Critical Theory: How the Bible's Unfolding Story Makes Sense of Modern Life and Culture* (Zondervan Academic, 2022), 156.

15. Quoted in Gary M. Burge, *John*, NIV Application Commentary (Zondervan, 2000), 126, italics original.

16. C. S. Lewis, *Surprised by Joy* (HarperCollins, 2002), 23. See also Alister McGrath, *C. S. Lewis: A Life: Eccentric Genius, Reluctant Prophet* (Tyndale, 2013), 23–34.

17. C. S. Lewis, *A Grief Observed* (HarperOne, 1961), 15.

18. C. S. Lewis, *Mere Christianity* (Broadman & Holman, 1999), 153.

19. Ernest Becker, *The Denial of Death* (Free Press, 1973), 68.

20. Kelly M. Kapic, *Embodied Hope: A Theological Meditation on Pain and Suffering* (IVP Academic, 2017), 61.

21. C. S. Lewis, *God in the Dock* (Eerdmans, 1970), 53.

22. Millard J. Erickson, *Systematic Theology*, 3rd ed. (Baker Academic, 2013), 581.

23. Erickson, *Systematic Theology*, 581.

24. Jurgen Moltmann, quoted in Philip Yancey, *The Jesus I Never Knew* (Zondervan, 1995), 183.

25. Plato, *Meno*, trans. W. K. C. Guthrie (Cambridge University Press, 1976). The theory of anamnesis (recollection) is discussed primarily in sections 81a to 86c.

26. N. T. Wright, *Simply Christian* (HarperOne, 2006), 3.

27. Francis Spufford, *Unapologetic: Why, Despite Everything, Christianity Can Still Make Surprising Emotional Sense* (Faber & Faber, 2012), 15–16.

28. Jordan Peterson, *Beyond Order: 12 More Rules for Life* (Penguin Random House, 2021), xxii.

29. J. R. R. Tolkien, *The Fellowship of the Ring* (Houghton Mifflin Harcourt, 2004), 394.

30. Jordan Peterson, *Beyond Order*, 133–34.

31. Daniel L. Migliore, *Faith Seeking Understanding: An Introduction to Christian Theology*, 2nd ed. (Eerdmans, 2004), 139.

32. Viktor E. Frankl, *Man's Search for Meaning* (Rider, 2011), xi.

33. Frankl, *Man's Search for Meaning*, xii.

34. Fyodor Dostoevsky, *The Brothers Karamazov*, bk. 4, ch. 2. Various publishers; originally published in 1880.

CHAPTER 7: TRANSFORM STRUGGLES INTO STRENGTHS

1. Craig Gay, *The Way of the (Modern) World: Or, Why It's Tempting to Live As If God Doesn't Exist* (Eerdmans, 1998), 185.

2. Carl R. Trueman, *The Rise and Triumph of the Modern Self: Cultural Amnesia, Expressive Individualism, and the Road to Sexual Revolution* (Crossway, 2020), 44–45.

3. Trueman, *The Rise and Triumph*, 164.

4. Ernest Becker, *The Denial of Death* (Free Press, 1973), 198.

5. Becker, *The Denial of Death*, 193.

6. Quoted in Timothy Keller, *Walking with God Through Pain and Suffering* (Dutton, 2013), 14.

7. Becker, *The Denial of Death*, 193.

8. Viktor E. Frankl, *Man's Search for Meaning* (Beacon, 2006), 117.

9. Philip Rieff, *The Triumph of the Therapeutic: Uses of Faith After Freud* (Chatto & Windus, 1966), 24–25.

10. Becker, *The Denial of Death*, 284.

11. Gay, *The Way of the (Modern) World*, 230.

12. Gay, *The Way of the (Modern) World*, 54.

13. Henri de Lubac, quoted in Gay, *The Way of the (Modern) World*, 15.

14. Timothy Keller, *Walking with God Through Pain and Suffering*, 16, italics original.

15. Keller, *Walking with God Through Pain and Suffering*, 16.

16. "The Lord of the Rings: The Fellowship of the Ring Appendices (Part 1)," Everything in Middle Earth, November 10, 2019, YouTube video, 40:48, https://www.youtube.com/watch?v=HPmb3Al25pM.

17. Frederick Buechner, *Wishful Thinking* (Harper & Row, 1973), 46.

18. John Stott, *The Cross of Christ* (InterVarsity Press, 1986), 160.

19. Keller, *Walking with God Through Pain and Suffering*, 10.

20. Keller, *Walking with God Through Pain and Suffering*, 121.

21. Dorothy Sayers, *Christian Letters to a Post-Christian World* (Eerdmans, 1969), 14.

22. Cited in Philip Yancey, *Where Is God When It Hurts?* (Zondervan, 1990), 181.

23. Tim Elmore, *A New Kind of Diversity: Making the Different Generations on Your Team a Competitive Advantage* (Maxwell Leadership, 2022), 38–42.

24. Dan G. McCartney, *Why Does It Have to Hurt? The Meaning of Christian Suffering* (P&R, 1998), 56.

25. Justin Taylor, "An Analysis of One of the Greatest Sentences Ever Written," *The Gospel Coalition* (blog), October 30, 2017, https://www.thegospelcoalition.org/blogs/justin-taylor/an-analysis-of-one-of-the-greatest-sentences-ever-written/.

26. Blaise Pascal, *Pensées*, trans. W. F. Trotter, 1910. Project Gutenberg, 2006, Fragment 507.

27. Martha Snell Nicholson, "The Thorn: A Poem." Quoted in John Piper, *Providence* (Crossway, 2021), 381.

28. Martin Luther King Jr., *Strength to Love* (Harper & Row, 1963), 22.

29. Carrie Fisher, *Wishful Drinking* (Simon & Schuster, 2008), 105, emphasis added.

30. Fisher, *Wishful Drinking*, 153.

31. *The Howard Stern Show*, aired December 14, 2021.

32. J. R. R. Tolkien, *The Lord of the Rings* (HarperCollins, 2005), bk. 6, ch. 3.

33. Charles H. Spurgeon, *The Treasury of David*, various publishers; originally published by Passmore & Alabaster, 1869.

34. C. S. Lewis, *The Problem of Pain* (1940, repr., HarperOne, 2014), 91.

35. Quoted in Keller, *Walking with God*, 188–89.

36. Quoted in Keller, *Walking with God*, 188–89.

37. Chaim Potok, *The Chosen* (Fawcett Crest, 1987), 233.

38. Potok, *The Chosen*, 251.

39. Quoted in Yancey, *Where Is God When It Hurts?* (Zondervan, 1977), 242–43.

40. Charles Spurgeon, *Lectures to My Students* (Passmore & Alabaster, 1875), 34.

PART IV: THE PROBLEM OF PURPOSE

1. S. D. Gordon, *Quiet Talks with World Winners*, quoted in John MacArthur, *The Macarthur New Testament Commentary: Matthew 24–28* (Moody, 1989), 334.

2. C. S. Lewis, *The Weight of Glory and Other Addresses* (1941; repr., HarperCollins, 2001), 26.

CHAPTER 8: LIVE OUT WHAT YOU WERE MADE FOR, NOT SOMEONE ELSE

1. James Loder, *The Logic of the Spirit: Human Development in Theological Perspective* (Jossey-Bass, 1998), 3–4.

2. John G. Stackhouse Jr., *Why You're Here: Ethics for the Real World* (Oxford University Press, 2017), 18.

3. Nancy Guthrie, *Even Better than Eden: Nine Ways the Bible's Story Changes Everything about Your Story* (Crossway, 2018), 63.

4. Peter L. Berger, *The Sacred Canopy: Elements of a Sociological Theory of Religion* (Doubleday, 2010), 4.

5. Dallas Willard, *The Divine Conspiracy: Rediscovering Our Hidden Life in God* (Harper, 1998), 398.

6. Willard, *The Divine Conspiracy*, 398.

7. Willard, *The Divine Conspiracy*, 378.

8. Willard, *The Divine Conspiracy*, 395.

9. Christopher Watkin, *Biblical Critical Theory: How the Bible's Unfolding Story Makes Sense of Modern Life and Culture* (Zondervan Academic, 2022), 99.

10. C. S. Lewis, *The Four Loves* (HarperCollins, 1960), 89.

11. "75: Jordan Peterson—Carry That Weight," *The Warrior Priest Podcast*, December 20, 2020, https://thewarriorpriestpodcast.wordpress.com/2020/12/20/75-jordan-peterson-carry-that-weight/.

12. "75: Jordan Peterson—Carry That Weight."

13. Jordan Peterson, *Beyond Order: 12 More Rules for Life* (Penguin Random House, 2021), 134–37.

14. Martin Luther, "An Open Letter to the Christian Nobility," in *Three Treatises* (Fortress, 1960), 14–17.

15. R. Paul Stevens, *Down-to-Earth Spirituality: Encountering God in the Ordinary, Boring Stuff of Life* (InterVarsity Press, 2010), 13.

16. Quoted in John Piper, *Don't Waste Your Life* (Crossway, 2013), 141.

17. Quoted in Mike Foster, *People of the Second Chance* (Waterbrook, 2017), 27–28.

18. John Ortberg, *You Have a Soul: It Weighs Nothing but Means Everything* (Tyndale Momentum, 2014), 138.

19. Dane Ortlund, *Gentle and Lowly: The Heart of Christ for Sinners and Sufferers* (Crossway, 2020), 215.

20. Thomas Goodwin, *The Heart of Christ in Heaven Towards Sinners on Earth* (London: James Nichol, 1862), originally published 1651.

CHAPTER 9: BECOME THE BEST IN THE WORLD AT THE FOLLOWING THREE THINGS . . .

1. Jonathan Haidt, *The Happiness Hypothesis: Finding Modern Truth in Ancient Wisdom* (Basic, 2006), 82.

2. Christian Smith, *What Is a Person? Rethinking Humanity, Social Life, and the Moral Good from the Person Up* (University of Chicago Press, 2010), 7.

3. N. T. Wright, *The Challenge of Jesus: Rediscovering Who Jesus Was and Is* (InterVarsity Press, 1999), 154.

4. Sue Johnston, *Hold Me Tight: Seven Conversations for a Lifetime of Love* (Little, Brown and Company, 2008), 7.

5. C. S. Lewis, *The Collected Letters of C. S. Lewis, Volume 1: Family Letters 1905–1931*, ed. Walter Hooper (HarperCollins, 2004), 914.

6. Blaise Pascal, *Pascal's Pensees* (1958), 113.

7. Pascal, *Pascal's Pensees*, 113.

8. Saint Augustine, *Confessions*, trans. R. S. Pine-Coffin (Barnes & Noble, 1992), 1:20.

9. Peter Kreeft, *Heaven: The Heart's Deepest Longing*, expanded ed. (Ignatius Press, 1989), 20–21.

10. Roger Scruton, *The Soul of the World* (Princeton University Press, 2014), 37.

11. Scruton, *The Soul of the World*, 37, emphasis added.

12. Yuval Noah Harari, *Sapiens: A Brief History of Humankind* (Penguin Random House, 2014), 491.

13. John Lennox, 2084: *Artificial Intelligence and the Future of Humanity* (Zondervan Reflective, 2020), 128.

14. Andy Crouch, *Culture Making: Recovering Our Creative Calling* (InterVarsity Press, 2008), 23.

15. Crouch, *Culture Making*, 24.

16. See "Shaped to Make a Difference Complete Audio Series," PastorRick.com, https://store.pastorrick.com/shaped-to-make-a-difference--complete-audio-series.html.

17. Christopher Booker, *The Seven Basic Plots: Why We Tell Stories* (Continuum, 2005), 33.

18. Crouch, *Culture Making*, 67.

19. Walsh, *Subversive Christianity*, 91.

20. Huston Smith, *The Soul of Christianity: Restoring the Great Tradition*, repr. ed. (HarperOne, 2016), xvii.

21. Quoted in Smith, *The Soul of Christianity*, 21.

PART V: THE PROBLEM OF DEATH

1. J. R. R. Tolkien, *The Return of the King* (Houghton Mifflin, 1955), 973.

2. Dallas Willard, *The Divine Conspiracy: Rediscovering Our Hidden Life in God* (Harper, 1998), 390.

CHAPTER 10: YOU ONLY LIVE TWICE, NOW LIVE LIKE IT

1. John Bunyan, *The Pilgrim's Progress* (Penguin Classics, 2008), 181.

2. Bunyan, *The Pilgrim's Progress*, 199.

3. This whole paragraph is a reworking of the opening words of Timothy Keller's book *On Death* (Penguin, 2020), 1–4.

4. Ernest Becker, *The Denial of Death* (Free Press, 1973), 26.

5. Viktor E. Frankl, *Man's Search for Meaning* (Rider, 2011), xiii.

6. Erma Bombeck, *Eat Less Cottage Cheese and More Ice Cream: Thoughts on Life from Erma Bombeck* (Andrews McMeel, 2003), 27.

7. J. I. Packer, *18 Words: The Most Important Words You Will Ever Know* (Christian Focus Publishing, 2008), 202.

8. Packer, *18 Words*, 395.

9. N. T. Wright, *The Resurrection of the Son of God* (Fortress, 2003), 90.

10. 2 Cor. 5:8 KJ21; Phil. 1:21–23; see also Dan. 12:1–3; Eccl. 12:7; Luke 16:19–31; 23:43.

11. Lisa Miller, "On the New Science of Heaven," in *Time* magazine: *Heaven and the Afterlife* (December 15, 2023), 64.

12. Keller, *On Death*, 42.

13. C. S. Lewis, *Mere Christianity* (Broadman & Holman, 1999), 137.

14. C. S. Lewis, *Reflections on the Psalms* (A Harvest Book/Harcourt, Inc., 1958), 94–95.

15. Randy Alcorn, *Heaven* (Tyndale, 2004), 79.

16. John Piper, *Future Grace: The Purifying Power of the Promises of God* (Multnomah, 1995), 398.

17. Alcorn, *Heaven*, 45.

18. Eugene Peterson, quoted in Darrell Johnson, *Discipleship on the Edge: An Expository Journey through the Book of Revelation* (Regent College, 2004), 360.

19. Alcorn, *Heaven*, 7, 78.

20. Alcorn, *Heaven*, 78.

21. J. I. Packer, *Concise Theology* (Crossway, 1993), 259; 275.

22. Bob Goudzwaard, quoted in Johnson, *Discipleship on the Edge*, 386.

23. N. T. Wright, *Surprised by Hope* (HarperOne, 2008), 161.

24. For example, Luke 19:17–19; Rom. 5:17; 1 Cor. 6:2; 2 Tim. 2:12; Rev. 1:6; 5:10; 20:4; 22:5.

25. Dallas Willard, *The Divine Conspiracy*: Rediscovering Our Hidden Life in God (Harper, 1998), 398.

26. Victor Hugo, "The Future Life," quoted in Alcorn, *Heaven*, 440.

27. C. S. Lewis, *The Last Battle* (Collier, 1956), 168–71.

CHAPTER 11: PREPARE YOURSELF FOR DEATH

1. Calvin Miller, quoted in Randy Alcorn, *Heaven* (Tyndale, 2004), 461.

2. Cited in Keller, *On Death* (Penguin, 2020), 33.

3. Cited in Alcorn, *Heaven*, 446.

4. Aaron Earls, "Jonathan Evans Delivers Viral Eulogy of His Mother Lois Evans," Lifeway Research, January 3, 2021, https://research.lifeway.com/2020/01/08/jonathan-evans-delivers-viral-eulogy-of-his-mother-lois-evans/.

5. Richard Baxter, *The Saints' Everlasting Rest* (New York: Robert Carter, 1846), originally published 1650.

6. James K. A. Smith, *How to Inhabit Time: Understanding the Past, Facing the Future, Living Faithfully Now* (Brazos, 2022), 174.

7. C. S. Lewis, *Mere Christianity*, 137.

8. Quoted in Keller, *On Death*, 88.

9. J. I. Packer foreword to David Watson, *Fear No Evil* (Shaw, 1984), 7.

10. Charles Spurgeon, *Morning and Evening* (London, 1870), February 7.

11. John Piper, *Future Grace*: The Purifying Power of the Promises of God (Multnomah, 1995), 354.

12. Piper, *Future Grace*, 354–56.

13. J. I. Packer, *18 Words: The Most Important Words You Will Ever Know* (Christian Focus Publishing, 2008), 205.

14. A collection of quotes by Charles Spurgeon on death: https://www.spurgeon.org/resource-library/blog-entries/10-spurgeon-quotes-on-dying-well/.

15. C. S. Lewis, *The Screwtape Letters*, in *The Complete C. S. Lewis Signature Classics* (HarperOne, 2022), 155.

16. Viktor E. Frankl, *Man's Search for Meaning* (Beacon, 2006), 91.

17. J. I. Packer, *Concise Theology* (Crossway, 1993), 271.

18. C. S. Lewis, "Hell," in *Readings in Christian Theology*, vol. 3, *The New Life*, ed. Millard Erickson (Wipf and Stock, 1999), 500. For more on hell, see my book *The Problem of God* (Zondervan, 2017), ch. 6.

19. Lewis, "Hell," 500.

20. Lewis, "Hell."

21. Lewis, "Hell."

22. Darrell Johnson, *Discipleship on the Edge*: An Expository Journey through the Book of Revelation (Regent College, 2004), 357, emphasis added.

23. Piper, *Future Grace*, xii–xiii.

24. Quoted in Keller, *On Death*, 27.

25. C. S. Lewis, *The Screwtape Letters*, 205.

26. J. R. R. Tolkien, *The Return of the King* (HarperCollins, 2005), 1030.

27. C. S. Lewis, *The Last Battle* (HarperCollins, 1956), 228.

28. Mark Buchanan, *Your God Is Too Safe* (Multnomah, 2001), 14.

29. C. S. Lewis, *Reflections on the Psalms* (Harcourt, 1958), 58.

The Problem of God

Answering a Skeptic's Challenges to Christianity

Mark Clark

WITH FOREWORD BY LARRY OSBORNE

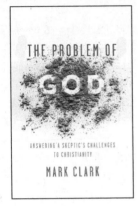

9780310535225
(Softcover Book)

A skeptic who became a Christian and then a pastor, author Mark Clark grew up in an atheistic home. After his father's death, he began a skeptical search for truth through the fields of science, philosophy, and history, eventually finding answers in the last place he expected: Christianity.

In a winsome, persuasive, and humble voice, *The Problem of God* responds to the top ten interrogations people bring against God, and Christianity, including:

- Does God even exist in the first place?
- What do we do with Christianity's violent history?
- Is Jesus just another myth?
- Can the Bible be trusted?
- Why should we believe in hell anymore today?

Each chapter answers the specific challenge using a mix of theology, philosophy, and science. Filled with compelling stories and anecdotes, *The Problem of God* presents an organized and easy-to-understand range of apologetics, focused on both convincing the skeptic and informing the Christian.

025986108397
(Video Study)

9780310108436
(Study Guide)

The book concluding with Christianity's most audacious assertion: how should we respond to Jesus's claim that he is God and the only way to salvation.

ZONDERVAN®
.com

The Problem of Jesus

Answering a Skeptic's Challenges to the Scandal of Jesus

Mark Clark

WITH FOREWORD BY RAY JOHNSTON

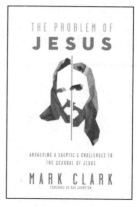

9780310108306
(Softcover Book)

Here is a portrait of Jesus that in some ways will affirm what traditional Christianity has always understood about him . . . and, in other ways, upend it altogether.

Award-winning author Mark Clark delves into the person and work of Jesus of Nazareth: his parables and miracles, his controversial challenge of discipleship and obedience, his seemingly insane claim to be God, and what his death and resurrection (if they did happen) actually mean.

Mark is unafraid to tackle questions such as:

- What would first-century Jews have immediately recognized about Jesus that modern Christians often miss?
- What do the Gospels accomplish, and can we trust them?
- Is there a problem with science and Jesus's miracles?
- What are the barriers stopping people from following him?
- And what *is* Christianity in light of an accurate portrayal of the object of its faith?

The Problem of Jesus engages with ideas from all realms of study: from Malcolm Gladwell and Jordan Peterson to historians, scientists, and philosophers; from N. T. Wright to C. S. Lewis; from *Star Wars* to *Pretty Woman*—all unite to form a breathtaking and accurate portrait of Jesus, the man, the message, and the mission, who forever altered the course of human history.

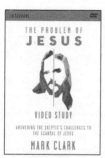

025986108335
(Video Study)

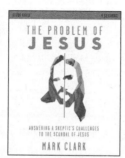

9780310108375
(Study Guide)

.com